# BRAZILIAN JIVE

The Reverb series looks at the connections between music, artists and performers, musical cultures and places. It explores how our cultural and historical understanding of times and places may help us to appreciate a wide variety of music, and vice versa.

reverb-series.co.uk
Series editor: John Scanlan

*Already published*

**The Beatles in Hamburg**
Ian Inglis

**Van Halen: Exuberant California, Zen Rock'n'roll**
John Scanlan

**Brazilian Jive: From Samba to Bossa and Rap**
David Treece

**Tango: Sex and Rhythm of the City**
Mike Gonzales and Marianella Yanes

# BRAZILIAN JIVE

## FROM SAMBA TO BOSSA AND RAP

DAVID TREECE

REAKTION BOOKS

*For my father, Ted Treece, 1926–2011*

Published by Reaktion Books Ltd
33 Great Sutton Street
London EC1V ODX, UK
www.reaktionbooks.co.uk

First published 2013

Printed and bound in Great Britain
by Bell & Bain, Glasgow

A catalogue record for this book is available from the British Library
ISBN 9 781 78023 085 6

# CONTENTS

1 BRAZILIAN JIVE TALK: MUSIC, LANGUAGE, COMMUNITY  7

2 THE BOSSA NOVA REVOLUTION  56

3 THREE MASTERS, THREE MASTERPIECES: JOBIM, MORAES, GILBERTO  97

4 GUNS AND ROSES: BRAZIL'S MUSIC OF POPULAR PROTEST, 1958–68  113

5 ORPHEUS IN BABYLON: MUSIC IN THE FILMS OF RIO DE JANEIRO  159

6 RAP, RACE AND LANGUAGE: THE AESTHETICS AND POLITICS OF BLACK MUSIC-MAKING  177

Chronology  207
References  210
Glossary of Terms  221
Select Bibliography  225
Discography and Filmography  226
Acknowledgements and Photo Acknowledgements  227
Copyright Acknowledgements  228
Index  229

Song transcriptions comprise some examples which, in the interests of accessibility, dispense with traditional musical notation in favour of an alternative method, requiring no prior specialist knowledge on the part of the reader to be comprehensible. Lyrics are set out on a vertical axis, each space in this vertical field corresponding to the narrowest interval in the Western melodic scale, the semitone. Consecutive syllables of the song lyric appear at the appropriate pitch level in relation to their neighbours, giving an accurate visual impression of the song's melodic profile (rhythmic features of melody are not accounted for but, when particularly significant, these are explained separately).

All translations from texts in Portuguese are by the author. In the case of the song-texts, chapters Two and Three include versions intended to be suitable for singing: 'Desafinado', 'Chega de saudade', 'É preciso perdoar', 'Garota de Ipanema' and 'A Felicidade'.

The Glossary of Terms (pages 221–4) explains relevant musicological terms and Portuguese words and phrases most commonly used when discussing Brazil's music, culture and history.

# 1 BRAZILIAN JIVE TALK: MUSIC, LANGUAGE, COMMUNITY

Little by little one could begin to pick out the modulations of a song, rather strange if truth be told. Who could dare to perform it in such a place as that? I sharpened my eyes and ears, and could make out Paulo Pinto down below beginning a samba. He was standing there and gesticulating, pretending to shake a non-existent rattle; slowly he came forward, bent down and passed beneath the ends of the hammocks. At first it was heard as a grumble, a confused mumbling; prudence and fear for sure; the passengers and soldiers mustn't think that some disorder or misbehaviour was breaking out in the hold. These precautions disappeared, the notes began to rise, still hesitant, and became clearer, the lament seemed to turn into a stubborn demand. . . . They had lain in utter indifference, in a cowardly, apathetic resignation; the discipline of the incarcerated, implicit and cold had imposed its order, one of hushed conversations, vague gestures, discreetly taken steps, respect for invisible figures of authority, the irascible general or the uncouth black soldier. In minutes this had disappeared. Stooped backs straightened up; the coughing and clearing of throats had ceased: oppressed lungs were uttering hoarse cries, enlivening the monotonous chanting of the chorus. These were no longer a few scattered contributions: dozens of human wrecks were rising up, marching, their arms held

high, a forest of naked, thin, filthy limbs, and the song
reverberated like a profound threat.

Graciliano Ramos, *Memórias do Cárcere* (Prison Memoirs, 1953)[1]

## FINDING A VOICE: MUSIC AND LANGUAGE, MUSIC VERSUS LANGUAGE?

Why do we study, read and write about popular music? If
we are interested in the relations between culture and society
as a whole, then we doubtless share a fascination with how
music has intervened in, commented on and made sense of
the experience of individuals and communities across history.
We wish to understand the role played by music in popular and
official celebrations, religious worship and other rituals, the
relations between music and other artistic forms such as cinema,
literature and theatre, between music and ideology, music and
politics, music and the evolution of local, regional, ethnic, national
and global cultural identities.

But there is surely something more to how music commands
our attention, how it intrigues and even impassions us. The distinctiveness of musical experience, its capacity to make meaning
like no other art form, cannot be reduced to those relationships
it sustains with phenomena beyond itself, relationships it in any
case shares with literature, the visual arts or theatre, for example.
The unique impact that music has on people's lives is not to be
understood by examining the sociology or economy of record
sales, by subjecting song lyrics to discourse analysis or even by
reconstructing the biographies of musicians, however useful
these matters may be to comprehending the larger world that
music inhabits.

No, our intuitive sense of the special power of music to signify
derives from something else which we recognize (when we are
not just talking about it) in the immediacy of its effect on us, as

organized sound: I have in mind the concrete, *material*, as well as symbolic character of music as patterns of vibration that, before and after their interpretation by our brains, are produced from, and mediated through, the human body. By making us actually 'live' complex processes of temporal and spatial awareness through our bodies as well as our minds, music has a powerful capacity to evoke associations, memories and even visualizations with an especially vivid sense of immediacy and intensity.

But unlike language, music does not primarily represent, speak of or symbolize a world outside of itself, beyond the cuckoos, steam engines, or *Psycho*-stabbings of film or programme music – and even these examples are usually approximations, not to the object or event itself, but to the movements, gestures and emotions that are associated with them. Rather, by setting in motion complex sonic structures of pulse, pitch, texture and architecture that our brains' aural faculties interpret according to our awareness of ourselves in time and space, music incorporates or embodies a different, alternative way of being in the world. Robert Jourdain puts it like this:

> Music mimics experience rather than symbolizes it, as language does. It carefully replicates the temporal patterns of interior feeling, surging in pitch or volume as they surge, ebbing as they ebb. It leads opposing forces into battle and then to reconciliation . . .
>
> It's important to recognize that music represents many kinds of interior feelings, not just overtly emotional ones . . . It can mimic not just the panther's fury, but also what the panther feels as it walks or jumps or climbs. This is accomplished by replicating the rhythms of such motions, by modulating harmony to imitate the body's stresses and releases, and by making melody follow the geometry of physical actions.[2]

In fact, I would argue that most music does not even mimic specific objects, beings or events in the world but rather dramatizes the processes of movement and change that animate our experience of time. In music we live out micro-dramas of physiological and psychological flux akin to those of our 'ordinary' existence, only intensified, concentrated and organized according to a conscious design and purpose: micro-dramas of gestural response, of quickening pulse, of weightless agility and leaden oppression; of excitement, anticipation, recognition and surprise; of tension, release, anticlimax and depression; of repetition, variation and transformation. And these micro-dramas of our individual, inner existential flux have their macro-counterpart at the level of the mythic, which music is equally capable of evoking, such as the processes of birth, growth, seasonal change and death. As Leonard Meyer put it, the very 'vagueness' of music's referential meanings, its flexibility of connotation, is a virtue, for 'it enables music to express what might be called the disembodied essence of myth, the essence of experiences which are central to and vital in human existence.'[3] And here Meyer cites philosopher Susanne Langer:

> The human mind has an uncanny power of reorganizing symbolic forms; and most readily, of course, will it seize upon those which are presented again and again without aberration. The eternal regularities of nature, the heavenly motions, the alternation of night and day on earth, the tides of the ocean, are the most insistent repetitious forms outside our own behavior patterns . . . They are the most obvious metaphors to convey the dawning concepts of life-functions – birth, growth, decadence, and death.[4]

This restructuring or intensification of our self-awareness as sentient beings to which Meyer and Langer are referring is something we experience musically as an extraordinary and transient mode of living in space-time, both 'real' and virtual, to which we sometimes attach the terms transcendence or ecstasy ('standing outside ourselves'). This, surely, is what makes music feel significant, what enables it to intervene so powerfully in the wider world. Because of its capacity to incorporate or embody afresh, in real time, the remembered and transformed patterns of sonic pulse, texture and structure that have been felt and heard by past and present generations, the sensation of the musical experience as something shared, historically and socially, is not just projected or contemplated in our collective imagination, but is lived as authentically, viscerally ours in the here and now.

As John Shepherd and Peter Wicke point out in their book *Music and Cultural Theory*, most writing on music is concerned, not with this primary level of musical signification, but with two other, secondary realms: on the one hand, we have the musicological analysis of those formal, abstract relational structures set up by melody, harmony and tonality; on the other, there is the domain of the semantic, those connotative meanings we attach to specific styles, melodic phrases, harmonic and timbral colouring, or rhythmic patterns, whose cultural and social resonances are the result of specific moments and acts of association in historical time and place – this, the connotative approach to musical analysis, is what generally occupies the students of popular music and ethnomusicology.[5] Either, then, the music is treated as if it were no more than an abstract set of internal, structural relations divorced from the socio-cultural experience of playing and listening; or it is reduced entirely *to* that environment of social and cultural forces within which it resonates. The sonic and aural character of music-making, the very quality that makes it so distinctive and compelling, is somehow lost between these two opposing perspectives.

My contention is therefore that we ought to take more seriously than we do the primary signifying power of the musics we listen to, and that the study of music, if it is to be anything more than just another branch of aesthetics or of cultural studies, should seek to match the uniqueness of its subject by striving to address and relate both its aesthetic and its social dimensions; that it should try to do justice to the special capacity of music, as Shepherd and Wicke put it, to 'gather up and reveal to us the structures of the internal and external social worlds and the relations obtaining between them' by taking us into, rather than away from, the materiality of its own sonic medium and the other reality it constructs.[6]

In its capacity to mobilize and realize human identities, to overcome the experience of alienation between self and world, and to construct, or reconstruct, a powerfully felt sense of community, music would seem to share something with language; yet we should treat with some scepticism the familiar assumption that language and music are necessarily kindred modes of expression, at least for the reasons usually cited. If, as argued above, music is not primarily a symbolic or figurative medium of communication, nor is it the 'universal language' it is sometimes romantically claimed to be (we only have to think of the violent clashes over musical taste between different generations, or the prejudice and mutual incomprehension that arise over musical traditions that are variously perceived by different listeners as civilized, transcendent or mere 'primitive jungle drums').

To take the distinctiveness of musicality seriously, as a symbolic practice that is materially mediated, performed and experienced, should encourage us to reclaim a more central and exemplary place for it in our intellectual and educational practices, alongside rather than subordinate to language and textuality. What would it mean for us if, as musicologists Shepherd and Wicke have hypothesized, music were granted the same primacy that language currently enjoys, as a model for so much of our theorizing and analysis of culture?[7] It is an intriguing and challenging suggestion, which calls for a radical leap of the imagination; but a necessary one, if we are to fully understand cultures such as Brazil's. As Paul Gilroy, the author of *The Black Atlantic: Modernity and Double Consciousness*, argues, one of the consequences of elevating the linguistic and the textual to the privileged status of authority they enjoy in Western academic life, as models for all other forms of cognitive exchange and social interaction, has often been to negate the sense of human agency that lies at the heart of cultural expressions such as those of the Black Diaspora, and their history of resistance:

> Urged on by the post-structuralist critiques of the metaphysics of presence, contemporary debates have moved beyond citing language as the fundamental analogy for comprehending all signifying practices to a position where textuality (especially when wrenched open through the concept of difference) expands and merges with totality. Paying careful attention to the structures of feeling which underpin black expressive cultures can show how this critique is incomplete. It gets blocked by this invocation of all-encompassing textuality. Textuality becomes a means to evacuate the problem of human agency, a means to specify the death (by fragmentation) of the subject and, in the same manoeuvre, to enthrone the literary critic as mistress or master of the domain of creative human communication.[8]

We can certainly learn something from a society such as Brazil's, where music-making appears to figure so centrally, where musicality, as a multi-faceted and integrated mode of activity and expression rooted in Afro-Americans' pluralistic conceptions of the world, really does seem to vie with textuality for primacy in people's lives. What can Brazilian culture teach us, not only about music's power as an alternative source of meaning and agency, but about its interaction *with* the realm of language?

Let us look, then, at the idea of Brazil as a quintessentially 'musical culture', as opposed to other supposedly more literate or literary civilizations. There is the obvious, self-evident fact of the country's extraordinary richness and diversity of musical traditions, a bewildering and ever-proliferating range of genres and sub-genres, from the array of carnival music (not only samba) to songwriting traditions such as *modinha, samba-canção*, bossa nova and MPB, dance-forms such as *forró, frevo, coco* and *samba-rock*, competitive and improvised forms of singing such as *embolada, samba de partido alto*, northeastern *repente* and rap, homegrown versions of international styles like rock, punk, soul, electronica and drum'n'bass, and the musics associated with Brazil's huge heritage of religious practices, regional festivals and celebrations, not to mention the rich veins of baroque, modernist, post-tonal and improvisational avant-garde experimentation, and so on, and so on. To attempt a proper explanation for this volume and diversity of musical practices would require a different kind of book,[9] but there are two key arguments that I shall comment on here.

The first of these is fairly uncontroversial: Brazil's geographical and ethnic profile, which combines enormous regional diversity with a history of interaction between indigenous Amerindian, African and European cultural traditions, continually fuelled and renewed by migration (both internal and external) and more recently by the power of the mass media. In a late industrializing postcolonial society like Brazil, the traditional wellsprings of ritual, religious and community-based culture not only coexist with modern post-industrial, commercial forces of cultural production but dialogue and interact with them with a dynamism rarely encountered elsewhere. In the last century Brazil has experienced most dramatically that process of combined and uneven development of which Trotsky spoke, of vertiginous development alongside deep stagnation and backwardness, which means that in Brazil the traditional and the modern are lived and felt as different temporalities simultaneously; and if, as I would argue, music is essentially how we dramatize our experience of time, then it is well suited to articulating that polymetric, multi-temporal experience of the postcolonial world.

But there is another, more contentious argument: a widespread assumption that Brazil's strong musical culture is somehow a counterpart to, a way of compensating for, the relative poverty or weakness of its linguistic culture, that the performative medium of music 'fills in' for low levels of literacy and language competence. This idea is akin to those attempts to account for the high profile of music and dance in the cultures of the African diaspora in terms of their intrinsic 'orality' and 'corporeality', either because of the suppression of African linguistic traditions under colonial slavery or, in more explicitly racist terms, because the essence of Africanness is imagined to reside in the body, by contrast to the innately cerebral, rational and logocentric character of European civilization. This is one of the great fallacies about African and diasporic cultural expression, for in reality language (whether in religious liturgical texts, narratives, song or improvised verse) is central rather than peripheral to these musical traditions.[10] Brazilian musicality, with Afro-Brazilian musicality at its centre, has thrived precisely because of its interaction with a rich vein of linguistic inventiveness in the realms both of popular and erudite expression: whether the rhyming, riddling and improvising of the *repentistas*, *jongueiros* and *emboladores*, the social chronicling of the *sambistas* and rappers, or the lyricism of the *modinha* composers and the bossa nova and MPB songsmiths.

In fact, the ancient phenomenon of song, what the Brazilian academic and composer-musician Luiz Tatit has characterized as the intonational transition between melody and speech,[11] is a reminder that, even if they do represent radically distinct faculties and domains of human experience, music and language would also seem to be profoundly, if obscurely, connected to each other.

It was once believed that while the linguistic functions of the brain are processed predominantly in the left hemisphere, and the musical functions in the right, as Anthony Storr put it,

> It is probably the case that as a listener to music becomes more sophisticated and therefore more critical, musical perception becomes partly transferred to the left hemisphere. However, when words and music are closely associated, as in the words of songs, it seems that both are lodged together in the right hemisphere as part of a single Gestalt.[12]

More recent research on brain activity and musical experience suggests that the organization of linguistic and musical functions is even more complicated than this and that, to say the least, there is plenty of overlap in the lateralization of given activities, like the identification of melodic patterns, speech or non-speech sounds.[13]

Some would say that human beings have *evolved* for music, that our brains are especially wired for music, just as they are for language; certainly, that moment when we literally 'burst into song', either on stage, in the screen musical or in the privacy of our bathroom, and realize the transition from spoken to musical intonation remains a dramatic reminder of where our expressive faculties have their deepest, earliest origins: in the power of the human voice both as a sonic and a symbolic medium of communication. Luiz Tatit's approach to understanding the uniqueness of the song-form as a whole, and of its individual practitioners and compositions, takes as its starting-point this core relationship between speech and melody,[14] and the analogous ways in which they are structured: sonically, as a successive alternation between continuity and segmentation (vowels and consonants, extended tones and their interruption); and spatially, as more or less systematic and significant patterns of pitch variation (intonation or prosody in the case of speech, and melodic contour in the case of music). Just how each song, singer or composer negotiates that threshold where speech becomes intoned as song, where the dynamic features of language and melody seem naturally to over-lap, coincide or elide with each other, is what determines in Tatit's analysis the unique 'diction' of the songwriter or her composition.

Nevertheless, as we can all recognize, our awareness of how rooted language is in the material, somatic origins of the speech act often seems tenuous because of the tendency of language towards abstraction. Language is such a constant, ongoing functional neces-sity in our everyday lives that we literally take it for granted, above all when we speak our native language so automatically that it often loses any special, intrinsic connectedness to our sense of being and authenticity.

When we sing, by contrast – which demands an unusual, conscious effort of concentration and focus in order to organize the unstable variables of speech into the consistent patterns of melody – something profoundly self-affirming takes place. The process of setting the entire body into vibration and projecting those vibrations beyond oneself into an ever-expanding acoustic space seems to *position* us in the world, in time and space – and therefore to realize us – in a unique way. We gain our sense of place and identity in the world not just through the abstract, symbolic relations that language articulates (the 'grammatical' relations of person, tense, mood and so on) but in terms of the material, physiological and emotional processes of movement and change that music animates and that reveal and affirm us as living inhabitants of the world, rooted in our biological being but extending ourselves beyond it.

It is this that makes so moving and profound that moment when someone 'finds her voice', as the character Ruth does in the u.s. tv series *Six Feet Under* at a critical moment of existential disorientation after finding herself widowed and redundant since her children have begun to make their own independent lives.

We witness a quiet, intimate moment of self-discovery as, in the
stark solitude of her kitchen, she listens to one of the female folk-
singers of her youth on the radio, and then begins to sing along,
tentatively at first but soon growing in strength and confidence.
Luiz Tatit comes close to what is at stake when talking about the
miracle of song:

> The voice which speaks . . . foreshadows the living body,
> the breathing body, the body which is there, at the moment
> of singing. Out of the speaking voice emanates the most
> ordinary oral gesture, that closest to human imperfection.
> It is when the artist seems to be a person. It is when the
> listener also feels himself to be something of an artist.[15]

But if that dimension often seems to be missing when we use
*spoken* language, there are moments when our exercise of our
linguistic faculties does share a similar vitality, the sense that we
are accessing something profoundly authentic about ourselves. The
most obvious example, of course, is in dramatic performance, in
theatre. Something very comparable (and equally moving) happens
when we master a foreign language; and by this I mean much more
than the competent manipulation of a repertoire of linguistic
rules and codes, the 'skills acquisition' that is emphasized so
much in contemporary policies around language education. No,
something more radical happens when, as learners of a second
language, we somehow break through the barriers of inhibition
and mechanical effort and get beyond that laborious process
of inner simultaneous translation to a point where we start to
mobilize our entire being (like the singer) so as to project ourselves beyond ourselves, to enter as a performer in the midst
of that foreign cultural universe we have chosen to explore.

## SAMBA IN THE RING: MAKING SPACE FOR AFRO-BRAZILIAN IDENTITY AFTER SLAVERY

So perhaps the separation or opposition between language and music is an artificial one – it is by no means universal, and is a relatively modern idea. Certainly it would not make much sense in most traditional cultures and earlier civilizations, such as those of West Africa or classical antiquity, where the term *mousike* signified a unity of cultural practices, integrating dance, melody, poetry and elementary education, while the word *melos* referred to musically determined verse, or music and poetry in one.[16] One of the things that happened to the West African cultures which reached Portuguese America as a result of the slave trade was that their integrated, holistic attitude to the cultural-artistic event or ensemble (as simultaneously dance, drumming, song, lyrical invention and religious worship) clashed with a modern Western European attitude of specialization. Indeed, once manual work became synonymous with slavery, the idea of a wider-reaching division of labour between the black body and the European mind became entrenched in postcolonial discourse, setting up a whole series of racialized dichotomies which still persist today, as encapsulated in the 'Samba da Bênção' (Samba of Blessing) by Vinicius de Moraes and Baden Powell: 'Se hoje ele é branco na poesia / Ele é negro demais no coração' (If today [samba] is white in its poetry, it is black, so black in its heart); as if there were a natural separation of functions between the supposedly white domain of intelligence, language and artistic sophistication, and the mindless, pulsating energy of the black body, made only to move us and to move for us.

But, in reality, the character of Afro-Brazilian cultural life has always confounded rigid dichotomies and stereotypes such as this; indeed, the very plurality and unity of meanings that the term samba simultaneously denotes is symbolic of that principle of integrated multidisciplinary practice. If, today, samba can still signify a distinctive set of rhythmic patterns, a dance step, a variety of song-forms and a party where all these elements may be performed, its etymological history is even richer than this. Musicologist Kazadi wa Mukuna, who made one of the first serious studies of African contributions to Brazilian music, notes that something called samba was in vogue in urban Rio de Janeiro as early as 1878, when an advertisement in the *Gazeta de Notícias* for the pantomime *Aladdin and the Magic Lamp* invited people to join 'O Samba'.[17] But it is unclear exactly what was being referred to here, especially given the ambivalence of the term even as late as the 1920s.

In many colonial and nineteenth-century accounts of slave dances such as *batuque* and *lundu*, samba is associated with a gesture that may or may not be erotic in meaning – the *umbigada* – in which a thrust of the navel (*umbigo* in Portuguese) brings two dancers together.[18] In the languages of present-day Angola, which supplied a large proportion of the Portuguese slave-trade to Brazil, samba or *semba* refers to a pelvic movement often perceived as obscene by outsiders. In Quicongo, *sàmba* is a dance characterized by a bump of one dancer's chest against the other's, while in the Quimbundo version, the *semba*, the bump occasionally separates the two dancers.[19] In the eastern hinterland of Luanda, it refers to the dance tradition of the belly bounce: 'motional emphasis on the pelvis, buttocks, etc., especially pelvis thrusts or circular pelvis movements described in United States jazz dance history as "Congo grind" are always suspect of a Congo/Angola background.'[20]

But elsewhere, samba seems to denote a more general expression of physical *jouissance*:

The word *Samba* is likely to be of Angolan origin, though it occurs as a verb in many Bantu languages I know and is often associated with specific types of body movement. In the large Ngangela group of dialects in inner Angola *kusamba* (v.) means: to skip, gambol, expressing an overwhelming feeling of joy. It is possible that Angolans in Brazil originally used this verb

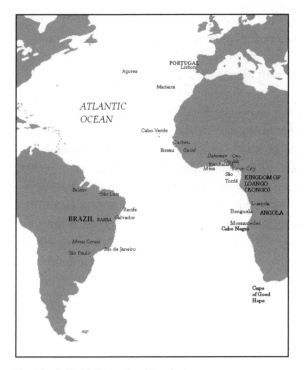

The Atlantic World: Portugal and its colonies.

during the *batuques* (generic name for dances of Angolan origin) in the *imperative*. In moments of heightened physical and psychical states some people perhaps shouted to the solo dancer: 'Samba! Samba!' (Skip! Gambol!) As time passed the word could have become a new label for the dance itself.[21]

In Bernardo Maria Cannecattim's *Collection of Grammatical Observations on the Bunda or Angolan Language and Abbreviated Dictionary of the Conguesa Language* (1859) 'samba' is found with the meanings 'devotion, prayer, pray'. Although by the end of the nineteenth century it had come to signify a kind of popular dance, this earlier religious dimension is preserved in the cult of the 'samba de caboclo', which is characterized by a union of ludic and religious meanings. According to Barboza da Silva, it could also refer to a woman having the sacred functions of a Yoruba *ekedi* or ritual assistant, that is, as 'holy dancer, initiate (*iaô*), orisha priestess'.[22]

And, finally, samba can denote a kind of rhythmic-melodic improvisation, something particularly associated with the variant of the song-form known as *samba de partido alto* ('broken high samba'), often regarded reverentially as the foundational, 'roots' source of the urban tradition. Taking the form of a challenge involving two or more contenders, a choral refrain and an impro- vised solo, *samba de partido alto* probably has its origins in the *jongo* parties still practised in the rural interior of Rio de Janeiro, and both can be traced back to the Congolese *batuque* gatherings that became central to slave culture. The following description is from Alfredo de Sarmento's *Os sertões d'África* (The Hinterlands of Africa, 1880):

The lyrics of the heathen songs are always improvised in the moment, and they generally consist of narratives of amorous episodes, witchcraft or military deeds. There are blacks who gain a reputation as great improvisers, and they are listened to in silence most religiously and applauded with frantic enthusiasm. The chant is always the same and the refrain they all sing in a chorus is unchanging, as they clap their hands in time and occasionally utter shrill cries.[23]

Such accounts are remarkably widespread across Brazil's post- colonial cultural history and geography. In the southeastern state of Rio de Janeiro, the phenomenon known as *jongo*, an important antecedent of modern urban samba brought by Bantu-speaking slaves from the Ndongo and Kongo kingdoms of central West Africa, and still practised today, enacts a comparable process of linguistic-melodic invention integrating religious, musical and choreographic elements:

> With the fire lit in the clearing and the drums set in place, nearly always facing the church or chapel, the pounding of the *tambu* and the *candongueiro* [percussion instruments] can be heard and the honking of the *puíta* [a friction-drum] resounds far and wide. The dancers approach. The *jongo* is about to begin. 10 o'clock at night, usually.
>
> Close to the group of instrumentalists a post is fixed in the ground with one or two lamps. The *jongueiros* [*jongo* players] arrange themselves in a ring, men and women alternating, numbers permitting. The row of instrumentalists intersects the circle like a secant. The dance begins. The ring turns in an anti-clockwise direction and the dancers, with a swinging motion, shift two or three paces to the right or left. They do not embrace, but merely make as if to do so, and at the end of their steps, they exchange bows.
>
> The *jongueiro* who opens the dance places himself beside the *tambu* and casts the first *ponto*. The *ponto* is the *jongueiro's* utterance or chant . . .
>
> The atmosphere, which had been serious and ritualistic in character, now changes. Someone casts an unusual, challenging *ponto*, and everyone repeats the ending, now accompanied by the drums and by the *puíta*, while the rattling of the *guaiás* is also heard. The dancers move about excitedly and joyfully and the sing-song becomes an ensemble of different overlapping vocal parts forming unexpected harmonies.[24]

Afro-Brazilian musicianship has continued to insist on this integration of functions, bringing an equal knowledge of complex rhythmic patterns, melodic improvisation and lyrical eloquence and inventiveness to the magical, ritual, creative space of the

ring or *roda*, whether a clearing on the edge of the plantation,
a spit-and-sawdust bar, the *botequim*, or in the *fundo de quintal*, the
backyard. Take the following account, from the early 1930s, of
the process of collective, improvised composition found in the
rural samba of São Paulo state:

> With the instrumentalists lined up, the bass-drum in the
> centre, they all group around the latter, usually leaning
> forward, as if listening in a secretly held consultation . . .
> It is, then, the collectivity which decides the text-melody
> with which it is going to samba.
> In the consulting group, an individual proposes a text-
> melody. There is no special rite to this proposal. The soloist
> sings, and usually sings rather uncertainly, improvising. His
> song, in the overwhelming majority of cases, is a quatrain or
> distich [four, or two, lines of verse, respectively]. The chorus
> responds. The soloist sings again. The chorus again responds.
> And so, little by little, in this dialogue, one or other text-
> melody is established. The bass-drum is quite attentive.
> When he realizes that it has caught on and the group, easily
> memorizing what the soloist has proposed to it, responds
> unanimously and enthusiastically, he makes a strong beat and
> joins the rhythm in which they are singing. Immediately, to
> the commanding beat of the bass-drum, the other instruments
> begin playing as well, and the dance begins. When it happens
> that the *sambistas* cannot respond or memorize properly, or for
> some reason do not like what the soloist has proposed to them,
> the thing gradually dies away. I have never seen a formal collec-
> tive rejection. Sometimes it is the same soloist who, realizing
> his proposal is not very viable, proposes a new text-melody,
> interrupting the state of indecision in which they find them-
> selves. Sometimes another soloist emerges. In this way they
> continue until a proposal catches on and gets the samba going.

As soon as the instrumentalists have begun to play, they move forward in a line. The rows of dancers facing them retreat. Then it is the latter who advance as the instrumentalists retreat. The vision one has is of a human ball more or less organized in rows, and which, tightly pressed together, in a brusque bending and straightening movement of the torso, advances and retreats in a few steps.[25]

The ring-dance or ring-shout, of which the *batuque* was one variant,[26] along with the *samba de roda* and the *jongo*, has been defined as *the* distinctive cultural ritual of Afro-descendants across the Americas, fusing music and dance, the sacred and the secular, and providing both a space for the convergence of diverse musical practices, and for the symbolic performance of notions of community, solidarity, affirmation and catharsis. The ring (*roda* in Portuguese) gathers within itself

calls, cries, and hollers; call-and-response devices; additive rhythms and polyrhythms; heterophony, pendular thirds, blue notes, bent notes, and elisions; hums, moans, grunts, vocables, and other rhythmic-oral declamations, interjections, and punctuations; off-beat melodic phrasings and parallel intervals and chords; constant repetition of rhythmic and melodic figures and phrases (from which riffs and vamps would be derived); timbral distortions of various kinds; musical individuality within collectivity; game rivalry; hand clapping, foot patting, and approximations thereof; apart-playing, and the metronomic pulse that underlies all African-American music.[27]

The ring therefore constitutes a virtual space within which the slaves and their descendants could move freely in temporary defiance of the slave regime, where the black body was treated as a labouring machine in the grip of the plantation economy's chronometric logic. Here, instead, they could affirm the ritual, cyclical and polymetric temporalities of their traditional philosophies of life, and their conceptions of dialogue between individual and community, between traditional structures and creative improvisation. The magical, transformative force that was believed to be activated in the space of the *roda* or *terreiro* was *axé* – a word which, in Brazil today, has become a marketing slogan associated with a variety of Bahian Afro-pop (*Axé Music*). But in its traditional meaning within Yoruba religious culture, the transmission of *axé* implies an instance of communication with the cosmos in which, interestingly, not only music and dance, but the spoken word, too, is a vital mobilizing agent, 'because it presupposes that the one uttering it has breath – and therefore life and a history'.[28] In this transmission of energy between the human and cosmic realms, the *tongue*'s verbal utterances, like shouts, gestures and dances, act not so much through their linguistic, semantic meaning as in their power to connect individual and world via their shared origin in the body.

Furthermore, the *roda* represents an act of reappropriation, not only of the slave body, but of the territories from which it was severed and deprived through the violence of the slave trade and the Middle Crossing. Muniz Sodré considers the *terreiro*, the cleared ground or yard beyond the plantation fields or at the edge of urban settlements which became synonymous from the early nineteenth century with the temple of *candomblé* or Afro-Brazilian religion, to be the *egbé*, the foundational structure for the liturgical community through which exiled and dispossessed Africans could reclaim their symbolic patrimony in Brazil, as elsewhere in the Americas:

> The symbolic heritage of the black Brazilian (the cultural memory of Africa) was affirmed here as a political-mythic-religious territory, for the purpose of its transmission and

preservation. Having lost the former dimension of military power, what remained for the members of a civilization deprived of territory was the possibility of reterritorializing themselves in the Diaspora through a symbolic patrimony embodied in knowledge linked to the cult of many deities, to the institutionalization of ceremonies, danced dramatizations and musical forms.[29]

As an early example of this process of reterritorialization, the first modern *candomblé* temple of the northeastern state capital, Salvador da Bahia, was the Casa Branca or Engenho Velho (Axé Ilê Iya Nassô Oká in *Yoruba*), founded by free Africans:

An original synthesis came about within it: the bringing together of cults to orishas [divinities] which, in Africa, would have been carried out separately, whether in temples or in cities; the condensing of African geographical space itself into the morpho-symbolic devices of the 'roça' ['clearing'] (*oka*), another word for *terreiro* and which connotes liturgical communities situated in the bush, outside the urban context . . . Each of the temple-houses (*ilê-orixá*) is consecrated to a specific divinity of the Nago pantheon, thus concentrating within a small space the representations that are dispersed across vast regions in Africa . . . The (quantitative) smallness of the topographical space of the *terreiro* matters little, for it is there that is organized, in focal points of intensity, the symbology of a Cosmos. A 'qualitative' Africa is made present, condensed, reterritorialized.[30]

The turn of the twentieth century saw a new moment in this struggle for reterritorialization, which now shifted southwards to the city of Rio de Janeiro, preparing the ground for what we recognize today as the culture of modern, urban samba. The thousands of Afro-Brazilians who had migrated from Bahia and other regions into the capital in the years preceding and immediately following the abolition of slavery in 1888 initially settled in the Saúde district (the site of the infamous Valongo slave market), in a quarter near the harbour known as Pedra do Sal (present-day Morro da Conceição), where accommodation was cheapest and the men sought work as stevedores. But Saúde was one of the neighbourhoods affected by an urban reform programme under the modernizing agenda of Mayor Pereira Passos (1902–6), which brought about the levelling and clearance of large concentrations of popular tenements considered 'prejudicial to public health', a process described by one historian as the effective 'de-Africanization' of the city centre.[31] The slum clearance programme known as the Bota-Abaixo (literally 'pulling-down') demolished 700 working-class constructions alone, just to create the Avenida Central, and a further 600 communal dwellings and 70 houses housing 14,000 people, predominantly Afro-Brazilians.[32]

The evictions led to a migration of black residents or *baianos* ('the ones from Bahia') westwards towards the Campo de Santana and beyond up to the Cidade Nova (New Town), where they became concentrated around the Ruas Visconde Itaúna, Senador Eusébio, Santana and Marquês de Pombal, converging on the Praça Onze de Junho (June 11), a square that had escaped the Bota-Abaixo. Here they reinvented their sense of communitarian identity in what was later to become mythologized as the 'Little Africa' of Rio de Janeiro, drawing towards them the poorest populations from the surrounding hillside communities or *morros* of Mangueira, Estácio and Favela (which gave its placename to the generic Brazilian 'shanty-town'). The Praça Onze became immortalized as a centre of popular carnival and samba, as a meeting place for workers, musicians, composers, dancers, hustlers (*malandros*), practitioners of *candomblé* and of the combat game of *capoeira*, and Muslims and other immigrant communities such as Portuguese,

ZONA NORTE
Port
CENTRE
Cidade Nova
Saúde
Mangueria
Praça Onze
Av. Rio Branco
Vila Isabel
RIO DE JANEIRO
ZONA SUL
Botafogo
Urca
Morro da Babilonia
Leme
Copacabana
Ipanema

Rio de Janeiro, its coastline and districts.

Italians and Spanish.[33] But on the Rua General Caldwell side of the square there was also an opening towards the more affluent residents of the city centre, who were beginning to take a curious interest in the exotic ways of life of their lower-class neighbours.[34]

'The similarities with Congo Square, in New Orleans, are glaringly obvious', suggests Muniz Sodré, and we might think of these squares and the surrounding neighbourhoods intersecting at their corners precisely as an extension or recreation of the ring, writ large, in which different individuals could meet and engage, localizing themselves physically and symbolically. Sometimes an entire neighbourhood could take on the characteristics of a 'square', an instance of this being Lapa – the cradle of bohemian

Rio, on the edge of Santa Teresa and the Centre – which for decades operated as a kind of cultural intersection between the North Side and the South Side of the city.[35]

In the Cidade Nova, Muniz Sodré identifies three principal *terreiros* of the Gêge-Nagô cultural complex (meaning they were linked to the Ewe and Yoruba peoples, respectively, of present-day Nigeria and Benin): the *terreiros* were now actually houses belonging to *candomblé* priests João Alabá (in the Rua Barão de São Félix), Cipriano Abedé (in the Rua João Caetano) and Felisberto (in the Rua Marquês de Sapucaí). In their newly urbanized character, these centres of religious life would shape the emergent, syncretized cults known as *macumba* and *umbanda*, and despite the decline in their patrimonial character, they retained an important socializing role in congregating uprooted populations together and incorporating village structures into the city.[36] But the most celebrated of the guardians of Afro-Brazilian religious and cultural tradition, the epitome of the matriarchal *Baianas*, was Hilária Batista de Almeida or Tia ('auntie') Ciata, a *candomblé* priestess and confectioner whose varied social connections and hospitality made of her home, on the Rua Visconde de Itaúna side of the square, a venue for diverse and heterogeneous cultural gatherings.

One such gathering, bringing together musicians Ernesto dos Santos 'Donga', Mauro de Almeida 'Peru' and Bahiano, among others, led to a landmark recording of 1917 – not, as often erroneously claimed, the first samba, but one of the first major carnival hits to be recorded: 'Pelo Telefone' (On the Phone). In the manner of its composition, the circumstances and character of its recording, and its hybrid musical and lyrical structures, 'Pelo Telefone' is very expressive of this transitional moment in the social and cultural life of the 'Little Africa' of Cidade Nova. For one thing, the dispute concerning its authorship – it was officially registered under Donga's name, while its composition was wholly or partly a multilateral effort – points to a tension between the traditionally

Praça Onze in Rio.

collective spirit of samba improvisation as a communitarian act of creation, and the commercial pressures of the emergent music industry, which tended to impose an individualized economic and legal identity on the artist. That improvisational character also remained alive, in all its fluidity, in a certain proliferation of different variants of the lyrics that circulated around the time of the song's popular success in 1916, but this plurality would eventually have to give way to the 'textual' authority that became fixed in the studio recording of 1917.

The song's melodic and lyrical themes are heterogeneous in character, and probably have different origins, bringing together the ritual, erotic and ludic dimensions of the Afro-Brazilian cultural matrix and the contemporary realities of urban modernity, in particular the friction between popular street-life and state authority. The opening verses, across all their variants, seem to reference a recent episode in the ongoing struggle of the police authorities to control the illegal gambling activities that were rife in the city; they also point, through that modern medium of the telephone-call, to a certain ambiguity, a possible collusion or margin of tolerance between the forces of law and order and those of popular entertainment:

| | |
|---|---|
| *O chefe da folia* | The leader of the revelry |
| *Pelo telefone* | Let me know |
| *Manda me avisar* | On the phone |
| *Que com alegria* | That, no messing, |
| *Não se questione* | There should be fun |
| *Para se brincar* | And games |

OR:

| | |
|---|---|
| *O chefe da polícia* | The chief of police |
| *Pelo telefone* | Let me know |
| *Manda me avisar* | On the phone |
| *Que na Carioca* | That in Carioca Square |
| *Tem uma roleta* | There's a roulette wheel |
| *Para se brincar* | For us to play on |

OR:

| | |
|---|---|
| *O Dr Chefe da Polícia* | Mister Chief of Police |
| *Mandou me chamar* | Had me called in |
| *Só pra me dizer* | Just to tell me that |
| *Que já se pode sambar* | The samba party's now allowed |

The song's second melodic theme turns away from this topical realm to celebrate the euphoric, pleasure-filled space of carnival:

| | |
|---|---|
| *Ai, ai, ai* | Ah, ah, ah |
| *É deixar mágoas para trás* | You've got to leave your pain |
| *Ó rapaz* | Behind you, oh boy |
| *Ai, ai, ai* | Ah, ah, ah |
| *Fica triste se és capaz* | Just you try and be sad if you can |
| *E verás* | And you'll see |
| | |
| *Ai, ai, ai* | Ah, ah, ah |
| *Aí está o canto ideal,* | There's the ideal, |
| *Triunfal* | Triumphant song |
| *Ai, ai, ai* | Ah, ah, ah |
| *Viva o nosso carnaval* | Long live our unrivalled |
| *Sem rival* | Carnival |

Like the first theme and those that follow, all of them melodically distinct, these themes share a common, rather relaxed rhythmic character, based on a cell of 8 pulses organized into 5 stresses – 1+2+1:2+2 (heard in English jingles such as 'we are the champions!/bring out the Branston!'). This pattern, now widely disseminated across Brazilian popular music and known as the *brasileirinho*, has been identified by Mukuna and others as one of the Bantu *time-lines* used to orientate the complex polymetric fabric of West African percussive music.[37] Its relaxed swing is more characteristic of the first phase of urban samba (barely distinguishable rhythmically from the *maxixe* or *tango brasileiro*), and from the end of the 1920s it would give way to the more extended and densely complex rhythms we associate with carnival samba, once the percussion battalions or *baterias* become a compulsory feature of the *escolas de samba* and their parades.[38]

Finally, the fourth theme of 'Pelo Telefone', based on a traditional folkloric motif, uses that most characteristic structure of Afro-Brazilian musical performance, call-and-response, to invoke the erotic ecstasy of the dance as a feminized and naturalized experience:

| | |
|---|---|
| *Ai, ai, rolinha* | Ah, ah, little dove |
| *Sinhô, sinhô* | Sinhô, sinhô ['massa'] |
| *Se embaraçou* | She got all in a tizz |
| *Sinhô, sinhô* | Sinhô, sinhô |
| *É que a avezinha* | This little bird |
| *Sinhô, sinhô* | Sinhô, sinhô |
| *Nunca sambou* | Never danced the samba |
| *Sinhô, sinhô* | Sinhô, sinhô |
| *Porque este samba* | 'Cos this samba |
| *Sinhô, sinhô* | Sinhô, sinhô |
| *De arrepiar* | That makes you tingle |
| *Sinhô, sinhô* | Sinhô, sinhô |
| *Põe perna bamba* | Makes your legs turn to jelly |
| *Sinhô, sinhô* | Sinhô, sinhô |
| *Mas faz gozar* | But it gives you a thrill |

## SYNCOPATION, JIVE TALK AND THE ART OF RESISTANCE

'Pelo Telefone' therefore dramatizes the insertion of the Afro-Brazilian cultural matrix into the urban landscape of the Cidade Nova, artfully negotiating a place for its ritual conceptions of time and space, defying the strict order of the modern state and economy with its ethos of playful, mischievous inventiveness in a language of quick-wittedness and charming eloquence, and celebrating the erotic agility of a body that yearns to move freely across its squares and streets.

These are all values and qualities that we will encounter elsewhere within the Afro-Brazilian cultural universe: for example, in the context of the combat game of *capoeira*, with its preference for dodging, ducking and diving, for graceful evasion rather than

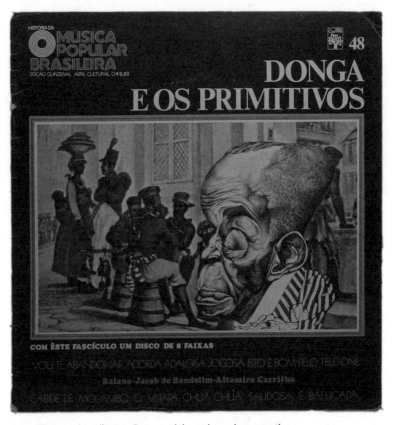

An LP album paying tribute to Donga and the early samba generation.

confrontation, for ambivalence; and both can be seen as musical and choreographic expressions, respectively, of an entire ethos that has pervaded urban black culture and popular culture in twentieth-century Brazil, the art of *malandragem*, which I shall translate as 'hustling' or 'jive'. It is now well known that the social and cultural figure of the *malandro*, or hustler, has played a central role in the history of samba,[39] but in two ways: as a thematic *subject* for samba compositions, the *malandro* has been a heroic (or anti-heroic) icon of popular social and cultural life, particularly

*Capoeira* in Salvador, Bahia, *c.* 1941.

of the 1930s and '40s, expressing dissent from the official values of family, work and deference to authority, and representing a countercultural ethos of playfulness, the circumvention of social rules, a defiance of discipline, matched by verbal wit and dexterity.

But as we shall see, there is no clear boundary between the *malandro* as this mythical, dramatic protagonist of samba discourse, and the *malandro* as performer-artist, since many sambistas have themselves cultivated the persona of the *malandro*, such as Geraldo Pereira, Bezerra da Silva and Wilson Batista, who made his career in the 1930s and '40s. Batista certainly walked the walk, talked the talk and lived the life, one of partying, womanizing, flirtation with petty crime and bare economic survival from the precarious royalties he got from his songwriting; he died literally without a penny to his name. His classic portrait of the *malandro*, 'Lenço no Pescoço' (A Scarf around my Neck), is self-assuredly cheeky, defiant, proudly work-shy and, in the classic 1933 recording by Silvio Caldas, irresistibly charming and seductive:

| | |
|---|---|
| *Meu chapéu do lado* | With my hat askew |
| *Tamanco arrastando* | Dragging my clogs |
| *Lenço no pescoço* | A scarf around my neck |
| *Navalha no bolso* | A razor in my pocket |
| *Eu passo gingando* | I saunter along |
| *Provoco e desafio* | I provoke and challenge |
| *Eu tenho orgulho* | I'm proud |
| *De ser tão vadio* | I'm such a loafer |
| | |
| *Sei que eles falam* | I know they're always talking |
| *deste meu proceder* | about this way that I go on |
| *Eu vejo quem trabalha* | I see people working |
| *andar no miserê* | and living in misery |
| *eu sou vadio* | if I'm a loafer |
| *porque tive inclinação* | it's because that's the way I felt |
| *eu me lembro, era criança* | I remember when I was a kid |
| *tirava samba-canção* | I used to make up samba songs |
| | |
| *Comigo não* | Don't mess with me |
| *Eu quero ver quem tem razão* | I wanna see who's right or wrong |
| *Meu chapéu do lado . . .* | With my hat askew . . . |
| *E eles tocam* | And they play |
| *e você canta* | and you sing |
| *eu não dou* | and I don't care |

What this suggests is that, for black Brazilians especially, *malandragem* posed the option of 'performing' a certain kind of marginalized social identity as art, of aestheticizing that identity, of transforming it into style, and that this very probably represented an alternative way of negotiating a place in, and against, the modern, post-Abolition social and economic order. The Republic had never addressed the challenge of how to transform its Afro-Brazilian population from slaves into citizens following Abolition in 1888; all it offered was the prospect of limited social mobility for a handful of individuals and immiseration for the massive majority, and it meanwhile remained violently hostile to the persistence or emergence of any kind of autonomous collective black political identity. In these circumstances, as Cláudia Matos puts it, 'To turn the struggle for life into art implies a performative talent that is simultaneously about playing games and playing for real, manipulating a language that is at once ludic and functional.'[40]

The *malandro*'s swinging lateral stride or *ginga* (the antithesis of the urgent, forward march of the obedient office-worker) enacts, like the *capoeira* player's evasive movements, a taking possession of the urban space while somehow remaining invisible, simultaneously present and absent. Indeed, in its constant shifting of weight from side to side, the *ginga* is a key principle in *capoeira*, a dialectical state of ambivalent vacillation (echoed musically in the two-tone figure of the tuned bow, the *berimbau*, which accompanies it) between suspended, dynamic preparation and movement, between the *esquiva* (dodge) and the *ataque* (lunge): 'You are always leaving it or returning to it.'[41] This still point of waiting or expectation, out of which the *capoeira* endlessly moves or to which she returns, recalls the condition of 'bodily silence' which, according to Sodré, is the black body's condition of preparedness, surviving slavery as an alternative repository of wisdom and discourse. Rather than a mere forgetting of the body by the conscious subject, this is a distancing of the body from discourse,

from speech, when the latter is perceived to be inadequate
communicatively; and a condition of readiness, a zero-state of
silent irreducibility ('situated before and after the word') that is
the pre-condition, the point of departure, for all real speech,
music and the construction of meaning.[42]

Musically we could say that this corresponds to the phenomenon of syncopation, the sensation whereby, instead of falling
'on the beat', a voice or instrument anticipates or lags behind
the regular pulse, provoking a corresponding or compensatory
response in the body, a swing. The *syncope* (in medical parlance
a brief heart failure or missing beat, which sometimes leads to a
loss of consciousness) 'could be the *missing-link* that explains the
mobilizing power of black music in the Americas'. In inviting
the listener to fill in the rhythmic gap, the 'empty time', with a
beat produced by the body, for example by clapping, swinging
or dancing, it invokes and concretizes the missing body of the
black man repressed by slavery but which, as seen in the ring-
dance of the batuque, the slaves insisted on mobilizing.[43] Ralph
Ellison captured this relationship between musical movement
and the black man's ambiguous spatial location in the American
city in his *Invisible Man*:

> Invisibility, let me explain, gives one a slightly different sense of
> time, you're never quite on the beat. Sometimes you're ahead
> and sometimes behind. Instead of the swift and imperceptible
> flowing of time, you are aware of its nodes, those points where
> time stands still or from which it leaps ahead. And you slip into
> the breaks and look around. That's what you hear vaguely in
> Louis' [Armstrong] music.[44]

At the same time, as well as posing an immediate, creative
response to the conditions of the present, playfully imagining
and even living an alternative lifestyle to the one on offer, the

*malandro* aesthetic also expresses a continuity with a set of values, a philosophy of music and of life, that is felt to be ancestral, inherited, connecting the black experience to some older African heritage and history. To understand this dimension, we need to know that the *malandro* is a close relative of a divinity from the West African, Yoruba and Afro-American religious pantheon: Exu. In the transition from the religious to the secular world, from the temple to the street, Exu's reincarnation as the *malandro* is clearly visible in the eclectic twentieth-century urban cult of Umbanda, where the figure of Zé Pelintra is closely associated, if not directly identified, with Exu.

Also known in the Americas as Esu-Elegbara, Echu-Elegua, Papa Legba or Papa La Bas, Exu is one of many different incarnations of the trickster figure, whose special prominence in the New World relative to the other divinities or orishas, it has been suggested, has to do with his essential ambiguity or indeterminacy, the possibility he holds out of an escape from fate, from the apparent inevitability of a destiny circumscribed by slavery, for example.[45] Exu is the 'ultimate master of potentiality' with the force to make all things happen and multiply,[46] and that potentiality includes sexual potency and the resource of language, of which he is also the interpreter and guardian. Henry Louis Gates Jr gives us a wonderful account of these multiple, interrelated functions in his book *The Signifying Monkey*:

Each version of Esu is the sole messenger of the gods
. . . he who interprets the will of the gods to man: he who carries the desires of man to the gods. Esu is the guardian of the crossroads, master of style and of stylus, the phallic god of generation and fecundity, master of that elusive, mystical barrier that separates the divine world from the profane. Frequently characterized as an inveterate copulator possessed by his enormous penis, linguistically Esu is the ultimate copula,

connecting truth with understanding, the sacred with the profane, text with interpretation . . . In Yoruba mythology, Esu is said to limp as he walks precisely because of his mediating function: his legs are of different lengths because he keeps one anchored in the realm of the gods while the other rests in this, our human world.[47]

So, the *malandro* inherits from Exu his creative, interpretative capacity for mischief, for ambivalence and trickery, in which music and language are complementary resources and forms of mediation. The closest we might get in English to this holistic, integrated concept of *malandro* speech-as-music-as-play-as-trickery is the North American term 'jive', which has those same multiple meanings of musical style (the style of jazz played by big bands in the 1930s); 'to jive' is to play, or dance to, jive music, while the noun also refers to the jargon or slang of jazz musicians and enthusiasts; by extension, it also means a kind of deceptive, nonsensical or glib chatter; 'to jive' is to talk nonsense, to kid someone, to cajole or mislead. At the heart of both jive and *malandragem* is the ludic instinct, as a strategy for survival as well as an existential alternative to the alienated world of capitalist labour: 'Wager, bluff, subterfuge, blarney, it's all part of a kind of *game*', says Matos, 'which constitutes one of the chief dimensions of the *malandro* diction and attitude. This game is a vital posture and activity in a world where the hero is constantly under threat, "snookered" . . . , and needs skill and luck to confront adversity.'[48]

In the so-called *samba-de-breque* ('break' samba) that emerged in the late 1930s, the proximity between music and speech becomes an explicit, foregrounded feature of the performance, where the melodic-rhythmic continuity is momentarily suspended, or even completely interrupted, to give way, as Cláudia Matos puts it, to 'pura falação, conversa de malandro' (pure patter, jive talk): 'It is a moment when the performer takes the opportunity to exercise fully his linguistic artistry, displaying inventiveness and poetic mastery, the "gift of the gab" . . . The syncopated swing of the voice, cultivating the idea of imprecision and instability, reiterates in performance the ambiguity that characterizes the *malandro* character, world-view and discourse. The boundaries between speech and song are constantly shifted, as are the boundaries between good and evil, reality and imagination, history and fiction.'[49]

But this *malandro* spirit of playfulness, subversion and independence has always had to contend with its repressive antithesis. The reactionary counter-tradition to *malandragem* within Brazil's history is the voice of authoritarian populism and dictatorship, in which notions of community and popular agency have been appropriated by a centralized state apparatus in the relentless pursuit of its interests. Here, language has become an oppressive force, the vulgar sloganeering of state propaganda, the debased rhetoric of official ideology (such as Family, Work, Nation, or 'Brazil, love it or leave it!'). Under President Getúlio Vargas's Estado Novo (New State) of 1937–45, for example, the mobilizing, transformative power of music was harnessed to the project of state- and nation-building to convert the spontaneous and potentially riotous disorder of popular street carnival into the disciplined, competitive civic spectacle of the avenue, with its patriotic themes, its samba schools and its business ethos. Samba itself was now enlisted to move an entire people, the corporate body politic of the nation, in the same direction, and to the same beat. This was a form of public mass mobilization, as orchestrated by the state, that was, of course, becoming familiar across the fascist states of pre-War Europe to which the Brazilian president was openly sympathetic. In 1937, having already suppressed the incipient anti-fascist popular front movement, the National Liberation Alliance, Vargas closed off all avenues of dissent, outlawed independent political and labour organization, and installed the so-called New State, which replaced any semblance of democracy with a fully fledged dictatorship. In

Samba in a Brazilian bar or *botequim* shown on an LP cover.

the music industry, the state's intervention consisted of a two-pronged policy of censorship and incentives in an attempt to tame and co-opt the *malandro* figure, turning him into a regenerated paragon of hardworking patriotic virtue and family values.

And yet, even at the height of the regime, the grassroots tradition of *samba* was still able to imagine and even to mobilize other forms of collective identity directly opposed to the Vargas state and its folklorized image of a racially and socially harmonious nation. We can find a remarkable account of the spirit of resistance this musical tradition inspired in the memoirs of one of the leading novelists of the time, Graciliano Ramos, an extract of which appears at the start of this chapter. Graciliano Ramos is one of the inimitable literary voices from the first half of the twentieth century whose severely honest, critical style of naturalism produced a disturbing psycho-linguistic study of class hatred and cruelty, patriarchal repression and social exclusion.

Writing in his autobiographical *Prison Memoirs* of his harrowing experiences as a political prisoner in the clampdown that preceded the Estado Novo dictatorship in 1937, Graciliano movingly recalled a brief but inspiring respite in the nightmarish ordeal of the detainees crowded into the hold of a prison-ship, the *Manaus*. Several aspects of his account of the incident are striking: first, there is the central, compelling spectacle itself, a demonstration of the power of music to galvanize the seemingly broken, defeated and cowed victims of totalitarianism, and to restore to them a sense of dignity and revolt; then there is Graciliano's observation, as a writer, that the prime moving force is not the linguistic, semantic content of the song-text, but the sonic energy of the music. This is all the more telling as it comes from a writer who elsewhere confessed his indifference to music:

However hard I tried, I could not make out the words to the song, and this enhanced its value. Doubtless the words were unimportant and full of mistakes. Unable to distinguish them, I was interested only in the uproar that was rising out of the darkness. A few voices joined that of the sambista, forming a strident ensemble, and the torrent of sound swelled, overflowed, fresh tributaries joining it, and shifting its course. Nothing had been pre-arranged. A plaintive murmuring, then the rumbling of a muffled anger, and now unexpected new voices joining in, bodies rising from the hammocks, annihilated figures emerging from the darkness, spectres taking on flesh and blood, their feet resolutely pounding the floor . . .[50]

Brazil's most important twentieth-century poet, Carlos
Drummond de Andrade, also faced the challenge of what to
do as a writer in the face of the manipulation and distortion of
language by populism, dictatorship and censorship. In his struggle
to reclaim the possibility of an authentic sense of community,
and of communication, in the shadow of international fascism
and of Vargas's New State, Drummond's search for an alternative
artistic model led him, if not quite to music, then at least to
something very close to it. In his 'Song to the Man of the People
Charlie Chaplin' published in the volume *A Rosa do Povo* (1945), he
saw in Chaplin, the star of silent cinema, a master of the balletic
movement, of the mischievous, magical, subversive and wordless
gesture, conjuring out of the apparently inert detritus of the
world an armoury of creative weapons, more eloquent than
words themselves:

> And the flowers that you love so when they're trampled,
>     they speak,
> the pieces of candle that you eat in extreme penury,
>     they speak,
> the table, the buttons, the tools of your trade and the
>     thousand seemingly closed things, speak,
> each bit and piece, each object from the attic, the more
>     obscure the more they speak.[51]

In Drummond's vision of Chaplin, the corrupted, debased
language of totalitarianism is exchanged for the truth of gesture,
action, performance. And, I would suggest, in the spirit of *malandragem*, Drummond sees in Chaplin – the universal, multifarious
'worker of the world' – the possibility, for all of us, of human
labour being redeemed from its alienated, oppressive condition and
transformed into creative, emancipatory performance, into art:

There is labour in you, but capricious, but benign,
and out of it spring non-bourgeois skills,
products of air and tears, garments
that give us wings or petals, and trains
and ships without any steel,
where friends in a ring travel through time,
books come to life, pictures talk to each other,
and everything freed is resolved
in an effusion of priceless love, and laughter, and sun.

## MPB: REINVENTING THE SONGWRITER'S CRAFT

In the late 1950s, in the years following Getúlio Vargas's second
administration and his suicide, a revolution in song, the bossa nova
revolution, opened up, once again, the possibility for that tradition
of dialogue in Brazilian culture between language and music to
construct a new, more authentic sense of community. For all that
the reputation of bossa nova has suffered in the past through its
associations with notions of lightweight 'easy listening' or muzak
(something due in part to its intrinsic, deceptively subtle minimalism), it is remarkable that this music continues to attract and
fascinate new generations of listeners half a century on. I am
convinced that this fascination derives from the fact that bossa
nova is a profoundly hybrid approach to making and performing
songs, combining the two major civilizational dimensions of
Brazil's historical formation: on the one hand, ancient African-
derived traditions of music-making (involving circular, reiterative,
'modal' themes, interlocking and overlapping patterns of rhythmic
and verbal duration); and, on the other, the 'modern' European
concepts of harmonic and tonal progression and modulation.

Another way of putting this is to say that bossa nova brings
together two conceptions of time: the cyclical, ritualistic pre-
industrial world of repetition, of the eternal return, and the

forward-moving, progressive, accumulative temporality of our secular, modern age. In combining these two notions of musical time, it sustains a permanent, unresolved tension, a subtle dissonance, a groundless, disembodied state of 'suspended animation', where we lose our sense of tonal and temporal rootedness, where time is somehow slowed down or revealed in its process of becoming. And in that virtual moment of 'suspended animation, almost as if in a meditative trance, we can join our fellow listeners and performers in a magical state of communion or 'grace' (*graça* is a keyword in the lexicon of bossa nova lyrics).

It is tempting, then, given the undeniable richness, inventiveness and sophistication of songwriting in Brazil, both in the samba tradition that became consolidated in the first half of the twentieth century and in the post-bossa nova era known as MPB,[52] to speculate whether there is some essential affinity between this artform and the national consciousness or culture as a whole. Certainly Luiz Tatit's characterization of the singer/songwriter as a musical juggler, innately gifted with an 'anti-academic talent, a pragmatic skill uncommitted to any regular activity',[53] is suggestive of that icon of popular cultural identity we have already encountered, the *malandro* or trickster, famous for his intuitive expertise and agility, his opportunism and passion, his lyricism and charm. Cultural historian José Miguel Wisnik (also, like Tatit, a songwriter and performer) goes further when he argues that Brazilian popular song constitutes a modern form of *gai saber*, the culture of the Provençal troubadors celebrated by Nietzsche in *The Gay Science* as 'that unity of *singer, knight* and *free spirit* which distinguishes the wonderful early culture of the Provençals from all equivocal cultures'.[54] For Nietzsche, the term expressed the anti-German, anti-professorial, anti-academic spirit of the philosophical ideal, where intellectual seriousness and discipline are tempered by the life-affirming bodily experience of art in a fusion of the Apollonian and Dionysian principles:

Let us dance in myriad manners,
freedom write on *our* art's banners
our science shall be gay!

Let us break from every flower
one fine blossom for our power
and two leaves to wind a wreath!
Let us dance like troubadours
between holy men and whores,
between god and world beneath!
('To the Mistral, A Dancing Song'[55])

This is translated by Wisnik into the contemporary Brazilian
context as the notion of a 'poetic-musical wisdom', by which the
intellectual acumen of literary culture has been able to acquire new
life through the 'innocence of joy' that resides in more elemental
forms of music and poetry, in the culture of carnival. Brazilian
popular song of the last half-century expresses this 'mode of
thinking' to the extent that it has offered a rich terrain of dialogue between composers and public, difference and confluence,
erudite and popular cultures.[56]

What, then, is the significance of this extraordinarily intense
exchange between literature and music, the extreme permeability
between bourgeois and popular cultures in Brazilian songwriting
since the 1960s, as illuminated by Wisnik? The examples he
chooses to characterize this period – the poets Torquato Neto,
Haroldo and Augusto de Campos, singer / songwriters Gilberto
Gil, Milton Nascimento and Caetano Veloso – correspond very
closely to that select community of artist-intellectuals related
by affinities of avant-garde experimentalism and literariness to
the idea of a Brazilian Modernist 'tradition'. The aspiration to
reconcile avant-garde aesthetic and intellectual concerns with
popular cultural expressions and traditions was arguably the

central project of this post-1960s generation of middle-class artists, not least its musician members, following the critiques of bossa nova by the left-wing popular culture movement and the revolutionary explosion of eclecticism unleashed by Tropicália in 1967–8. But it is a remarkable fact that the current of songwriting that emerged out of the legacy of that project acquired a kind of hegemony within the national and international perception of the country's musical life, arguably at the expense of other, less prestigious but more 'commercially' popular currents and artists – a hegemony expressed in the confusing acronym MPB (Música Popular Brasileira).[57]

The rise of MPB coincides with a period when the relationship between singer/songwriter and audience was being radically redefined, as the mass media and culture industry drastically widened the gap between artist and community, pulverizing the organic ties that had once united them, yet simultaneously drew the artist and the individualized spectator together in a new and different kind of proximity via the television screen, the hi-fi speaker or stereo headphones. The shift away from traditional practices of collective musical composition, as exemplified in *samba de partido alto*, to the individualized creative experience of the post-MPB singer/songwriter in the era of the recording studio and MTV video, condensed into 50 years or less the many centuries which separate and unite our contemporary musical culture and the ancient culture of *mousike*. Yet precisely because of this paradox of Brazil's late and highly uneven development, through which ancient traditions survive alongside the modern sometimes only as memory, sometimes as living practice, the contemporary, university-educated songwriter has an especially acute awareness both of how removed he is from the collective sources of his art and, at once, how inescapably immediate they are. Conscious of its marginality in the midst of a society whose forms of self-expression continue to be chiefly oral, Brazil's literary-intellectual culture has continually sought a melody for its texts in popular music. Only in this way can it strive to restore an imagined wholeness to a contradictory, divided world, to seek to reunite with tones that which words have broken up.

The 'tragic optimism' of bossa nova and the 'gay pessimism' of tropicalismo which, for Wisnik, constitute the two complementary faces of a national musical culture, symbolically projecting a utopian destiny for the country in the harmonization of literature and song, textuality and orality, elite intellect and popular spontaneity, should therefore be more properly defined as the particular ideological expression of the MPB generation of post-1960s artists. For them, at least, the democratization of Brazil's cultural resources has been a privilege within reach. Since the 1990s, in the era of hip-hop, new generations of Brazilian musicians and audiences have been exploring what that permeability between popular and literary culture, between orality and textuality, might mean for the lives of a still under-educated, disenfranchised majority.

In this introductory discussion of Brazil's musical culture, I have drawn attention first to the special capacity of music in this country, as elsewhere, to make its practitioners realize what it can feel like to be complete, integrated human beings; by setting our bodies and our surroundings into simultaneous vibration so as to incorporate the world and its rhythms and tones into ourselves and at the same time amplify our own presence in this life, as far as our singing and playing are able to reverberate across the air.

Second, and following from this, I have described how music has been able to sustain and reinvigorate the identities of individuals and communities, even against the worst of odds, such as through the traumatic experience of slavery. The power of musical memory, recall and transmission was crucial in enabling individual and collective psyches to resist the shattering effects of enslavement and the Middle Passage; while the creative transformation of those remembered traditions has been able to enact a utopian alternative to the suffering and oppression of the here and now, to make it possible literally to feel in one's bones the dream of moving freely and creatively in another time and space.

And, third, I celebrate music's ability to overcome the separation and estrangement we commonly experience between ourselves and our fellow human beings, between ourselves and that world in which, and upon which, we work – the separation we have come to recognize as *alienation*. When we perform or hear music – that is to say, when we enact or experience afresh, through the interplay between mind and body, the remembered and transformed patterns of sonic pulse, texture and structure that have been felt and heard by past and present generations – we do not just project or contemplate the sensation of shared musical experience in our collective imagination, but *live* it as authentically, viscerally *ours* in the here and now. The musician is therefore the epitome of Karl Marx's characterization of man as the 'self-mediating being of nature'; and musicality suggests to us a model for that positive, self-sustaining form of life-activity which, Marx argued, must replace alienated labour in the process of human development, in that realization of the 'human essence', of 'humanness', of the 'universality and freedom of man'.[58]

The Austrian musicologist Victor Zuckerkandl, writing over half a century ago, offered some of the most insightful reflections on this relationship between music and the world, and on what makes music and language essentially different forms of expression. For Zuckerkandl, whereas words turn people toward each other, making the speaker address her companions as 'others', musical tones turn them all in the same direction, transmuting individuality into community. At the same time, the musical intonation of speech allows the singer to reintegrate the world into herself, to 'live' that which has been projected or objectified in language:

> Words divide, tones unite. The unity of existence that the word constantly breaks up, dividing thing from thing, subject from object, is constantly restored in the tone. Music prevents the world from being entirely transformed into language, from becoming nothing but object, and prevents man from becoming nothing but subject.[59]

So, we need the communicative power, sophistication and complexity of language, but on its own it has a tendency to objectify and alienate us. As a counterbalance, music can restore us to ourselves and to our sense of community. If that dual function of language and music is arguably a universal human necessity, in Brazil, as we have seen, the relationship between these two modes of expression has a particularly rich and compelling history. It is surely significant, therefore, that in the work of one of Brazil's most consummate and innovative literary artists we should find a celebration of the musical experience just as I have outlined above, and especially in its potential to 'take over' at the point where words quite literally fail us, where language reaches the limits of its ability to explain, to console or unite people at times where their very existence is in question.

João Guimarães Rosa is the great figure of Brazilian prose fiction from the middle of the twentieth century, known for his radical reinvention of the literary Portuguese language and of the mythical world of the frontier lands or *sertão*. Guimarães Rosa's enduring theme is a world in a state of flux, and in the moving short story 'Soroco, his Mother, his Daughter' he confronts us with the tragedy of a family shattered by the trauma of bereavement. Years after the loss of his wife, the long-suffering widower Soroco can cope no longer with a mother and daughter driven mad by their grief, and reluctantly sends them off to be cared for in a distant town.

As their train pulls away from the remote village, Soroco, lost for words, finds himself compelled to intone the strange, wailing song with which the two women have been consoling themselves. Soon, irresistibly, the entire village takes up the melody in a collective expression of sorrow for the loss, dispersal and disorientation suffered by human beings in a world beset by change. And in this instinctive, ritual act of communion, Soroco, whose sense of self had been shattered by his burden of guilt and solitude, now discovers that he is not, after all, alone but has been restored to some more transcendent place of belonging. What ordinary language alone could make no sense of has been transformed by the poetry of song, reconstituting the structures of social and individual identity that the volatility of experience appeared to have destroyed:

> Suddenly the old lady left Soroco's arm, and went and sat at the foot of the steps up to the railway carriage. – '*She won't do anything, Mister Station-master . . .*' – said Soroco softly: – '*She doesn't even answer when you call her . . .*' At that the young woman took up her singing again, turned towards the people, towards the empty space above them, her face a picture of stunned repose, it wasn't that she wanted to make a show of herself, she was just acting out the impossible, grand old days of yesteryear. But they saw the old lady give her a magical look, as of some age-old presentiment – of unbounded love. And, beginning quietly, but then with her voice gathering strength, she, too, took up the other woman's selfsame song, that no one could understand, following her example. Now they were singing together, singing without end . . .

And now indeed, all that could be heard was the heartening sound of their carolling, that evocative reel testifying to the manifold changes of this life that could inflict their grief on you, passing sentence with no due regard, none at all, for the whys and wherefores, only for what had been, what was to come.

Soroco.

If only it would all be over and done with. The train pulling in, the engine manoeuvring separately to pick up the carriage. The train whistled and went on its way, leaving forever.

Soroco didn't wait for everything to disappear off into the distance. He didn't even look. He just stood there, hat in hand, more square-jawed and unhearing than ever – which made him somehow all the more amazing. There the sad fellow stood, irrevocably, the few words he might have said, stifled. Suffering this way things had of being, in the boundless emptiness, beneath his burden, uncomplaining, an example to everyone. And they told him: – 'That's the way of the world . . .' Everyone was misty-eyed, awe-struck with respect for him. All of a sudden they all felt a great fondness for Soroco.

He shook himself, as if breaking free from something that had never happened, and turned to go. He was going home, as if he were going somewhere far away, beyond all reckoning.

But then he stopped. Such a strangeness came over him, he seemed to be about to lose his very self, and cease to be. In an excess of spirit, as it were, beyond all meaning. And what happened was something no one could have anticipated: who could have made sense of it? All of a sudden – he burst into song, full-throated, loud, but just to himself – and it was the very same, crazy song the two women had been singing all that time. He sang and sang without end.

A chill, a sinking feeling passed over the crowd of people – just momentarily. The people . . . And there was nothing prearranged about it, no one had any notion of what was going on: everyone, all at once, out of sorrow for Soroco, began to join in, too, with that aimless singing. And with their voices raised so high! Everyone walking with him, with Soroco, and singing, how they sang, as they walked behind him, those furthest back almost running, no one was to be left out of the singing. It was something you would never, ever be able to forget. There wasn't an event to compare to it.

Now the people were really taking Soroco home. They were going, along with him, wherever that song was going.[60]

# 2 THE BOSSA NOVA REVOLUTION

## FROM SONG TO STYLE: BOSSA NOVA IN BRAZIL AND IN THE WORLD

When Brazilian songwriter and performer Antônio Carlos (Tom) Jobim died in December 1994, twentieth-century Western music lost one of its most important popular artists.[1] While that claim can be justified on the strength of Jobim's achievements as a songwriter alone, it is indisputable if we consider his role as a co-founder, together with singer-guitarist João Gilberto and lyricist Vinicius de Moraes, of Latin America's most successful musical export, bossa nova.

Of all the continent's styles and traditions, bossa nova is arguably the one which has enjoyed the greatest consistent commercial popularity outside the region over the half-century after its emergence in the late 1950s, and with the boom in 'World Music' since the 1990s it has gained a new lease of life. Since the first performance of the Jobim/Moraes composition 'Garota de Ipanema' (The Girl from Ipanema) in August 1962, and over 40 individual recordings in Brazil and the u.s., by 1990 it had become the fifth most frequently played song of all time worldwide, clocking up over 3 million performances. A further six of Tom Jobim's compositions have been performed over 1 million times, second only to the record established by the Lennon and McCartney partnership.[2] Today, a catalogue of bossa nova titles such as 'Desafinado', 'Águas de Março' and 'Insensatez'

Tom Jobim in Rio de Janeiro, 1991.

remain firm standards within the repertoires of international vocalists and jazz musicians. In Brazil itself, an alliance of established bossa nova artists and a new generation of interpreters revitalized the tradition from the late 1990s onward, followed by a wave of fusions involving more recent forms such as electronica and drum 'n' bass. Take, for example, Marcos Valle's *Nova Bossa Nova* (1997), Bebel Gilberto's *Tanto Tempo* (2000), which sold over 1 million copies worldwide, and DJ Marky and DJ Patife's remix, with Fernanda Porto, of Tom Jobim's 'Só Tinha Que Ser Com Você' (2002).[3]

Paradoxically, as we shall see in chapter Four, the very success enjoyed internationally by bossa nova soon raised questions inside

A bossa nova guide for guitar.

Brazil as to its *popular* status, understood in terms of the word's social, ideological and political meanings. How could a style devised primarily by and for the white, middle-class intelligentsia of Rio de Janeiro's affluent South Side (*Zona Sul*) be related to the central, mainstream tradition of Brazilian popular music – samba – whose driving force has been its capacity to express the emergent identity of poor, urbanized blacks following the abolition of slavery? Did the dissonant harmonies and chromatic melodies of bossa nova not have more to do with the imported 'high art' traditions of European modernism or with North American West Coast jazz than with local musical experiences rooted in popular religion, dance and celebration? And was the introspective, coolly complacent sophistication of bossa nova, with its innocuous language of 'love, smile and flowers', not inherently alien to the ideas of resistance and protest that popular music might be expected to express in a country as socially and economically divided as Brazil?

Meanwhile, that same commercial ubiquitousness abroad has inevitably been associated, for many, with banality and dubious artistic value. Bossa nova is probably the single style which most immediately calls to mind the phenomenon of muzak, the epitome of 'easy listening', 'elevator' or 'piped' music supplied to businesses, shopping malls, department stores, airports and waiting-rooms for the purpose of instilling a mood of compliant passivity and receptiveness in the consumer. In that sense, it would seem to typify Frankfurt critic and sociologist Theodor Adorno's gloomy vision of popular music as social cement, a grey background filling in the silent spaces between alienated individuals in the age of mass culture, as capitalism binds commercially produced art and the desires of its consumers together in 'totalitarian' circles of manipulation. In his famous essay 'On the Fetish Character in Music and the Regression of Listening' (1932), Adorno argued that the reification of popular song, the demands upon it to conform to the pressures of mass saleability as one more, infinitely repeatable commodity in the marketplace, would tend to standardize and degrade its internal structures, emptying them of critical force and autonomy and condemning them to reproduce and reinforce the forms and values of the existing order:

> it seems to complement the reduction of people to silence, the dying out of speech as expression, the inability to communicate at all. It inhabits the pockets of silence that develop between people moulded by anxiety, work and undemanding docility. Everywhere it takes over, unnoticed, the deadly sad role that fell to it in the time and the specific situation of the silent films. It is perceived purely as background. If nobody can any longer speak, then certainly nobody can any longer listen.[4]

As we shall see, *repetition* is, indeed, a key structural principle of bossa nova composition and performance, as well as being somehow emblematic of its supposed vulgarization and debasement as an over-exposed, endlessly reproduced style. Superficially the music's formal and performative characteristics seem to render it self-evidently susceptible to those tendencies towards standardization and blandness. Melodies often consist of a single, simple motif reiterated in different registers – the familiar opening and middle themes of 'Garota de Ipanema' are obvious instances, but a glance at a range of song transcriptions from the repertoire will reveal many other examples, such as 'O barquinho' (The little boat), 'Discussão' (Argument) and 'Insensatez' (Foolishness). On occasions this tendency is taken to deliberate extremes by the repetition of single note, as in João Donato's and Caetano Veloso's 'A rã' (The frog) or the Jobim and Mendonça composition 'Samba de uma nota só' (One-note samba).

The characteristic harmonic colouring of the style arises from an avoidance of the simple triad (notes i-iii-v of the scale) found in traditional samba in favour of chords built up on the seventh

element of the scale, with added diminished fifths, sixths, major
sevenths and so on, one of whose effects is to blunt the emotional
contrast between major and minor keys, and to blur or obscure
the location of the harmonic root, the sense of a tonal centre
and of cadence, and thus the movement towards closure and
completion. The diffuse, nebulous quality of this harmonic texture,
influenced in part by late Romantic and modernist European
composers such as Chopin, Debussy and Ravel, marked a radical
innovation in Brazilian popular music, but like its counterparts in
the international art-music world or in the visual arts, the aesthetic
has lent itself to the proliferation of bland reproductions in the
mass culture industry.

Meanwhile, the 'cool' minimalist vocal delivery typified by
João Gilberto, and internationalized by Astrud Gilberto in the
English-language collaboration of 'The Girl from Ipanema'
with Stan Getz, established a seemingly untutored approach to
performance that is devoid of any marks of individual expression or
character such as vibrato and dynamic contrast, almost appearing
to dispense with technique altogether. Instead it blends seamlessly
into an instrumental texture which, dominated by acoustic stringed
instruments, the guitar and piano, and by light percussion, seems
to sacrifice clarity of impact, sustainability and intensity in favour
of an attenuated, dissipated sound. The typical thematic material
and vocabulary of bossa nova lyrics, at least in its first phase up
to about 1962 – 'sand, sea and sun', or 'love, smiles and flowers',
in the words of Jobim and Mendonça's 'Meditação' (Meditation)
– apparently supports the general perception of this music
abroad as complacent, lightweight and devoid of emotional
intensity or depth.

And yet there is a huge gap between the (especially non-
Brazilian) perception of bossa nova abroad in the above terms,
as uncritical, anodyne and symptomatic of an atrophied musical
culture, and its reputation and force inside Brazil as a benchmark of

craftsmanship, an almost 'classical' model within the contemporary popular songwriting tradition, and one that continues to inspire and produce new creative work. To understand that disparity, we will certainly need to examine bossa nova's significance as an intervention in the musical culture of mid-twentieth-century Brazil. First, though, it is worth considering the particular processes by which this revolutionary approach to Brazilian songwriting and performance entered the wider musical culture of North America and Europe as a style and ethos.

Following its initial exposure to U.S. and European audiences via the Franco-Brazilian film *Black Orpheus* (dir. Marcel Camus, 1959), where it figured for the first time in a cinematic soundtrack, it is reasonable to suppose that the bossa nova boom abroad had much to do with the sheer weight of the U.S. music industry's promotional machinery, after it was embraced by the jazz fraternity following a watershed (although somewhat shambolic) concert in New York's Carnegie Hall in November 1962. It is true that the first major bossa nova success in the U.S., Stan Getz and Charlie Byrd's *Jazz Samba*, made the number one position in the Billboard pop chart in the same year with recordings of 'Desafinado' and 'Samba de uma nota so', among others, achieving unprecedented sales in the hundreds of thousands.

But like Getz's second hit, *Big Band Bossa Nova*, this should more accurately be described, as McGowan and Pessanha note, as a jazz-bossa fusion, and it was Getz rather than the Brazilian composers who received the Grammy award for the album.[5] Apart from collaborations such as the *Getz/Gilberto* record of 1964 (which also received Grammys for best album, jazz performance and engineering), most of the successes of the boom featured Brazilian names, not as principal artists, but as composers or supporting musicians under the direction of American bandleaders, as indicated by titles such as *Do the Bossa Nova with Herbie Mann* and *Cannonball's Bossa Nova*.[6]

Apart from the politics of the u.s.-Brazilian collaborations, relegating the Brazilians to this subordinate status, the major musical consequence of mediating bossa nova's international dissemination through American jazz was to transform what was and is preeminently a *song-form* into an instrumental style, merely one of a range of textural colourings within the jazz palette. Its rhythmic component even became foregrounded to the extent that it acquired an independent life as a category within competitive ballroom dancing – a delicious irony, given the failed attempts of u.s. choreographer Lennie Dale to create a dance for bossa nova during his visit to Brazil in 1962.[7] The complex, integral relationship between melodic and harmonic structure, rhythmic movement, the lyrical, discursive argument and its vocalization – which, as we shall see, was and remains vital to the music's quiet intensity – was thus effectively dismembered. This arguably helped to prepare bossa nova for the emasculation and homogenization to which, in Mary Yelanjian's description, all styles are inexorably subjected when repackaged by the Muzak corporation and shorn of their vocal and lyrical content.[8]

As an early symptom of this process, in the editing of the version of 'Garota de Ipanema' for the *Getz/Gilberto* album produced by Creed Taylor, João Gilberto's solo vocal introduction in Portuguese was removed in order to make it more packageable for radio broadcasting.[9] Attempts at translation have not prevented the breakdown of that integral dialogue between lyric and melody which is so crucial to the character of bossa nova, not to mention all song. Ruy Castro has noted the erroneous tendency to pigeonhole the members of bossa nova songwriting partnerships as either lyricists or composers; in the cases of 'Desafinado' and 'Samba de uma nota só', for instance, it is assumed that Tom Jobim was responsible exclusively for the musical component and Newton Mendonça for the lyrics, whereas a much more integrated collaboration is likely to have been the reality.[10]

Indeed, if we are to account for the enduring power of the
bossa nova aesthetic within Brazil across half a century, beyond
its initial impact on the contemporary musical landscape of the
mid-1950s, we need to take seriously its distinctive character as
*song*. Here we can be helped by the insights of Luiz Tatit and José
Miguel Wisnik, in their general commentaries on the songwriter's
art. For Tatit, as we saw previously, the songwriter's skill consists
of organizing and reconciling two tendencies inherently shared
by speech and sung melody: the melodic continuity of resonating
tones and vowels, and the segmentation and articulation of those
tones by means of consonantal breaks. In order to render these
tendencies compatible rather than mutually antagonistic, the songwriter draws on the resources used in day-to-day speech, which itself
combines the musicality of vocal intonation with the segmentation
of verbal discourse in order to arrive at a single integrated *diction*:

> To compose a song is to seek out a convincing diction. It means
> eliminating the frontier between speaking and singing. It means
> making out of continuity and articulation a single project of
> meaning. To compose is, moreover, to decompose and compose
> at the same time. The songwriter decomposes the melody with
> the text, but recomposes the text through its intonation. He cuts
> out and immediately smoothes over again. He renders contrary
> tendencies compatible through his oral mode of delivery.[11]

Far from seeking a melodic form for a pre-existing textual content,
then, the art of the songwriter is to uncover and organize what Tatit
calls the various forms of 'speech camouflaged in melodic tensions',
to regulate and order melodically and rhythmically the essentially
unstable expressive variables of pure speech, transferring these
meaningful zones of tension *to the text*, where they can acquire
thematic form as amorous separation, the mobilization of a character into action, or colloquial argument. However, what is so often

mistakenly assumed to be a hierarchy of melody and text, the subordination of 'form' to 'content', is provocatively overturned by Wisnik: 'the music is not a *prop* for truths which are to be told by the lyrics, like a passive screen onto which a figurative image is projected; perhaps the contrary is actually more often the case, where the lyrics appear as a vehicle which bears the music.'[12] He thus anticipates Tatit's opening statement of the phenomenon in *O Cancionista*, where he says: 'In the world of the songwriters it is not so much what is said that matters but the manner in which it is said, and the manner is essentially melodic. On this basis, what is said is often transformed into something magnificent.'[13] As we shall see, the bossa nova repertoire offers an extraordinary example of this level of artistic achievement within the realm of songwriting.

On the other hand, if we are to explain the longevity of bossa nova's appeal to successive generations *outside* Brazil, both at the level of the musical idiom in general and of individual compositions, then I believe we must also return to those ideas of primary musical signification that were raised in the last chapter; in particular, those ways in which music is able to embody and dramatize the processes of movement and change which animate our experience of time. In its magical capacity to hold together two distinct conceptions of time and movement, and therefore two civilizational temporalities, bossa nova was, and remains, a profoundly utopian as well as critical response to the experience of modernity; it is this that arguably explains its continuing appeal both to Brazilians and non-Brazilians over half a century on.

## AN ECOLOGICAL RATIONALITY: TENSION, HARMONIZATION AND THE NEW SENSIBILITY

My starting-point is to remember that all sound consists of movement and change – pulses, or cyclical waves of energetic flux and

Vinicius De Moraes.

reflux, transmitted via the medium of air and registered as physiological alterations in the anatomy of our ears. As these changes
are translated into electrical impulses, firing off neurons in the
brain stem and the auditory cortex, they trigger complex networks
of memory, connection and alteration which we perceive as trans-
formations in our acoustic environment, and to which we can
react in turn, physiologically, emotionally and mentally.[14] If sound
is to be understood in this way, as the process by which the effects
of movement and change in the external environment are intern-
alized and incorporated by the conscious human body, then music
structures and organizes this phenomenon in such a way as to
dramatize (to make us undergo in a heightened, concentrated and
intensified way) the experience of transformation, of movement
from one state of being to another.

In that sense, as José Miguel Wisnik reminds us in *O Som e o
Sentido* (Sound and Meaning), what we perceive distinctly as rhythm,

melody, harmony and timbre are simply different manifestations of the same phenomenon. The regular energetic pulse that, up to 10 hertz or cycles per second, we still perceive only as a beat, begins to be heard as a 'note' from that threshold onwards, as the acceleration of a pulse's frequency turns quantitative into qualitative change, translating the temporally perceived vibration into a spatially perceived vibration; what is really a variation in time, the acceleration of a pulse, is heard as a vertical relation of pitch, the up and down of melody, as the rising frequency of the sound wave is experienced as an ascent away from the gravitational inertia of the earth.[15] These spatio-temporal variations, which are then heard 'horizontally' as successive notes in a melody, can of course be sounded simultaneously, in the vertical structures we call harmony, while the unique combination of additional, natural overtones or harmonics, which each musical instrument produces when it sounds a single tone, accounts for the distinctive timbres or textures of musical colour. And these basic elements of musical creativity, all of them different expressions of the fundamental phenomenon of movement – the pulse – can then, in their turn, set in motion ever more complex dramas of change and transformation, of harmonic modulation and tonal development.

If all music is structured, meaningful sonic movement and change, then, we could ask: what specific kinds of movement animate the distinctive musical universe of bossa nova? The concept I propose here to characterize the bossa nova aesthetic – *suspended animation* – is intended to encapsulate a certain paradox of dynamic equilibrium, a delicately sustained integration of contrapuntal forces shifting endlessly between tension and resolution. Furthermore, this dynamic equilibrium, which to my ears is the source of bossa nova's almost hypnotic, incantatory fascination, cannot be abstracted from the act of performance because it resides precisely in the effort to incorporate and sustain, in real time, that live interaction and tension between the vocal articulation of melody, the rhythmic and harmonic sequences played by the guitar, and the lyrical unfolding of the song's internal, structural logic. This internal cohesion integrating all its constituent elements – formal, performative and semantic – makes it problematic to isolate a separate 'bossa nova rhythm', to sing a lone, unsupported 'bossa nova melody', or even to perform bossa nova songs 'in translation' – the whole is so much more than the sum of its parts that, when heard alone, each constituent element can sound weak and unremarkable.

The sense that the bossa nova aesthetic posed a radical, if subtle and underestimated, challenge to traditional musical sensibilities was present from the beginning, and often self-consciously so, to the point of being incorporated thematically into the lyrical and musical content of certain songs. The Jobim/Mendonça composition 'Desafinado' (Off-key), first released by João Gilberto in 1958, can be viewed almost as a manifesto of the new wave – the formulation 'bossa nova', literally meaning 'new flair', being directly referenced during the course of the song. The opening phrases begin by adopting the idiom of an injured lover's protest that he is misunderstood, and at the same time manage to voice a witty defence of an original way of singing:

| | |
|---|---|
| *Se você disser que eu desafino, amor* | Darling, if you tell me that I sing off-key, |
| *Saiba que isto em mim provoca imensa dor* | Don't you know it's hurtful for a guy like me? |
| *Só privilegiados têm ouvido igual ao seu* | Acuter ears like yours belong to just a chosen few |
| *Eu possuo apenas o que Deus me deu.* | Mine are tuned the way that God designed them to. |

The point about an incompatibility of tastes or sensibilities is made musically as well as textually, as the sinuous opening theme leads twice to a dissonant clash, with awkward falling intervals on the words 'desafino' (I sing off-key) and 'imensa dor' (enormous pain).

Figure 1 'Desafinado' – the song's key melodic theme unsettlingly rises and falls, then drops steeply and dissonantly on the keywords 'desafino', 'imensa dor', 'classificar' and 'anti-musical', denoting a clash of musical tastes.

*-mu-*

*-ta-*

*in-*      *-ssi-*      *-por-*   *-men-*

*-cê*   *-sis-*      *com-*      *-to de -ti-*

*an-*    *-sical*

*vo-*     *-te cla-*    *Meu*

*em*   *-ficar*

*Se*

The 'off-key' mistake is reiterated twice more ('If you really must describe the way I play / as simply devoid of musicality') with an even steeper and more dissonant fall (a major 7th interval) on the Portuguese word "anti-musical" (see Fig. 1). But the clash now leads, via an unexpected modulation and a more relaxed, descending harmonic sequence, to the magical revelation that, literally, 'Whether right or wrong, I'm sorry, I'll just have to say / That this is bossa nova, it's the new reality' (literally 'it's really natural'). As well as defending the sophisticated, bluesy chromaticism of bossa nova – which, it turns out, isn't really off-key at all – the song ends by discreetly arguing for a different rhythmic sensibility, too, the subtle syncopation of the new *batida* or (heart-) beat:

| | |
|---|---|
| *Você com a sua música esqueceu* *o principal* | There's something you've forgotten, though you think your playing's smart |

| | |
|---|---|
| *Que no peito dos desafinados,* | For within those who sing |
| *no peito bate calado* | off-key, deep within them |
| | quietly beating |
| *Que no peito dos desafinados* | In the breast of those who |
| *também bate um coração.* | sing off-key there also |
| | beats a heart. |

The argument dramatized in 'Desafinado' was more than just a sophisticated musical joke, however. It was part and parcel of a deliberate and conscious struggle to establish the hegemony of the style as the voice of a 'modern' social and cultural identity for a new generation of listeners. André Midany, the 24-year old head of the international repertoire department of the Odeon record label, understood in 1957 that young Brazilians 'didn't have their own music'.[16] Bossa nova, which was intended to supply this need, was defined by composer Ronaldo Bôscoli at a concert in Rio de Janeiro's Naval School in November 1959 as 'everything that's modern, absolutely new and avant-garde about Brazilian music'. In the same spirit, the movement's name was appropriated by other sectors of society and culture: in the press, in football commentary, in the promotion of refrigerators, washing-machines and other locally produced consumer durables, and even in politics – for instance, the progressive, reformist camp of the otherwise right-wing, anti-populist União Democrática Nacional was described as the 'bossa nova' of the party.[17]

At first sight, at least, the new music symbolized the optimistic modern spirit of that self-confident, university-educated genera-tion of middle-class, overwhelmingly white Brazilians who were the beneficiaries of Brazil's post-war economic boom, particularly the so-called 'Golden Years' of Juscelino Kubitschek's presidency (1956–61). Promising 'fifty years' development in five', Kubitschek's programme of developmentalism, with its emphasis on manu-facturing-based import substitution, also had profound social consequences, not least in sharpening the stratification of the capital city, Rio de Janeiro, between the mainly working-class Zona Norte or North Side and the affluent Zona Sul of Copacabana and Ipanema, and between the hillside *favelas* and the beaches and apartment blocks down below. But as well as expressing something of this new sense of social identity, bossa nova voiced a determination to break with the ideological atmosphere of the previous two decades, particularly the twilight years of the political culture known as *getulismo*, the inward-looking, sentimental national-populism that had been identified with the administrations of Getúlio Vargas (1930–45 and 1951–4).

Bossa nova's picture-postcard image of Rio de Janeiro's Zona Sul as 'mountains, sun and sea' would have to be assertively constructed in the face of other, less flattering representations of contemporary urban life (it is an image which, incidentally, has had to compete since the crisis of the 1980s with the city's growing reputation for violence and insecurity). Journalist and songwriter Antônio Maria, for example, contemptuously described nocturnal Copacabana in the 1950s as a sordid assortment of 'loose women, paedophiles, lesbians, cannabis dealers, cocaine addicts and thugs of the worst order. . . . Men would calmly urinate in bar doorways and bullies would beat up defenceless people, a few yards away from policemen who, instead of intervening, would pick their teeth and laugh coarsely.' The windows of apartment blocks concealed illicit liaisons, adulterous affairs, marriage break-ups, shootings, murders, burglaries and suicides. And to top it all, there was a water shortage.[18] All this should be seen against the turbulent political background of the mid-1950s, in particular journalist Carlos Lacerda's war against the 'quagmire' of the Vargas administration, and the President's suicide on 24 August 1954.

What, then, was the musical correlative of this era immediately preceding bossa nova? The prevalent musical idioms of that period were the twin voices of heroism and tragedy, represented by the *samba-exaltação* (exaltation-samba) and the *samba-canção* (song-samba) respectively. The *samba-exaltação* was a carnival-esque hymn of patriotic celebration exemplified by Ary Barroso's 'Aquarela do Brasil' (Watercolour of Brazil, 1939), popularized internationally as 'Brazil': 'Brazil / My Brazilian Brazil / . . . / Brazil, samba that makes you / Swing, that makes you sway / Brazil of my love / Land of Our Lord / Brazil, Brazil / All mine, all mine.'[19] The *samba-canção*, meanwhile, was part of a long-standing tradition of romantic song that had by now become a vehicle for the divas of tragic-romantic drama, such as Dalva de Oliveira and Maysa. Either way, the instrumental sound of the period was brassy, flamboyant, emotionally full-on, and designed to project at top volume a larger-than-life vocal subject – the epic persona of the nation, or the persona of a suffering, lovelorn victim-heroine. For the new generation of composers, such as Roberto Menescal, Ronaldo Bôscoli and Tom Jobim, the sombre, melodramatic lyrics of the *samba-canção*, with its themes of suicide, solitude, abandonment, revenge and hatred, were best summed up in the epithet 'defeatest'.[20] Take Evaldo Gouveia and Jair Amorim's 'Só Deus' (Only God), recorded in 1959 by Maysa: 'Only God, who is heaven, / can tell the anguish that I feel / the hours that I've spent / in my despair without you here / just as well they told you nothing / all for the best no-one believed it / for God, who heard my cries, / for him too it was all too much.'[21]

Two of João Gilberto's first solo releases, 'Hô-bá-lá-lá' and 'Bim-bom', initially circulated via homemade recordings heard in the apartments of the Zona Sul in mid-1957, deliberately ridiculed with their nonsense language the melodramatic, florid exuberance of lyrics such as these.[22] Similarly, Bôscoli's pre-bossa samba 'Mamadeira atonal' (Atonal feeding-bottle), which, although never recorded, was familiar to all who frequented the local colleges and nocturnal gatherings in the neighbourhood, prefigured

'Desafinado' in its aggressive defence of the right to be atonal, off-key, 'unsquare' and modern: 'Go complain to daddy / If I was born modern like this / Go and ask your mummy / If dissonance is what I've got inside of me / I drank from the baby's bottle and my lullabies were atonal / And my dreams are rocked / By a mean rhythm.'[23]

It is not difficult to see how bossa nova cut through all the overblown, populist sentimentalism and vulgarity of the mid-1950s with its pared down, instrumental minimalism, its 'difficult', playfully dissonant melodies and harmonies, its tricky, off-centred rhythmic pulse, its clever, often ironic lyrics, and above all its discreet, eminently cool vocal subject: for the first time, the seamless, integrated fabric of musical structure, instrumentation and performance seemed designed to put at centre stage, not the personality of the singer-subject, who had now literally 'lowered' his or her voice to the point of quiet understatement, but the *song* itself. To listen to a bossa nova composition was no longer to be confronted, overwhelmed even, by the spectacle of national or personal drama, as declaimed in semi-operatic style by its protagonists, but to be engaged in intimate conversation, to join in an intelligent, elegant, playful, multi-layered and above all modern counterpoint.

Indeed, there was a conscious struggle to establish the re-strained singing style ('*cantar baixinho*') invented by João Gilberto, which ousted the prevailing fuller-throated delivery epitomized by stars such as Lúcio Alves. Ironically one of Gilberto's first professional engagements was his appointment in 1950 as a substitute for the existing 'crooner' of the vocal group Garotos da Lua, Jonas Silva, whose nasal, vibrato-less voice was judged incapable of competing with the demands of orchestral backing and audience alike.[24] It was only later that Gilberto developed and perfected his now familiar technique, during painstaking hours spent isolated in the ideal acoustic environment of his sister's

João Gilberto's 1961 LP (Odeon MOFB 3202).

bathroom in Diamantina, in the interior of Minas Gerais state. The asymmetrical *batida* rhythm of the guitarist's right hand, freeing the form from the tyranny of the traditional samba's regular binary pulse, required a controlled vocal instrument, without distracting effects or devices, capable of matching and countering precisely the subtle shifts, advances and retreats of the tempo punctuated by the guitar chords.[25] Only subsequently was this technique more widely disseminated through the informal *academias* or teaching sessions held in the apartments of Roberto Menescal and Carlos Lyra.

So, typified by the performing style of João Gilberto, and by the songwriting partnerships of Menescal, Lyra, Tom Jobim, Vinicius de Moraes, Newton Mendonça and Ronaldo Bôscoli, the initial, 'classic' phase of bossa nova, dating roughly from 1958 to 1962, achieved an extreme, finely crafted integration of all the above elements of musical form, textual structure and performative technique. Each of the songs' constituent features – reiterative, chromatic melodic phrasing (that is, using the steps found in traditional scales but all the narrower, less familiar intervals, too), enriched dissonant harmonies, extended polyrhythmic patterns, chamber-like percussive and acoustic instrumentation, and a 'cool', almost colourless voicing of conversational lyrics – carries equal importance, no one being foregrounded over the others. Across the song repertoire of this phase we find a remarkably insistent pattern unfolding within that seamless, integrated texture, both at the level of musical structure and lyrical narrative. The pattern can be summarized as a movement from tension, typically built on the interplay between rising or descending melodic figures and harmonic modulations, and verbalized thematically in terms of argument, pain or separation, towards a goal of reunion, reconciliation and resolution.

An initial example of this movement towards harmonization can be found in Tom Jobim and Vinicius de Moraes's 'Chega de saudade' (No more longing), whose 1958 version by João Gilberto is often seen as the inaugural recording of the new style. First, the song's opening statement of separation and longing appears in a sombre D minor key as an oblique, angular series of narrowly falling and leaping intervals pitched against a downward harmonic progression and bass figure:

| | |
|---|---|
| *Vai minha tristeza,* | Blues, you've got to tell her |
| *e diz a ela* | I can't ever |
| *que sem ela não pode ser,* | be without her, no way, no how, |

| | |
|---|---|
| *Diz-lhe, numa prece* | Pray for her returning, |
| *que ela regresse,* | my heart is burning, |
| *porque eu não posso mais sofrer.* | I need to end this pain, and now |
| *Chega de saudade* | Take this longing from me |
| *a realidade é que sem ela* | It's all wrong, and since she's gone |
| *não há paz, não há beleza* | there's no more beauty, no more gladness |
| *É só tristeza e a melancolia* | Only sadness, and this sorrowful feeling |
| *Que não sai de mim, não sai de mim, não sai* | That won't leave me be, won't ever leave me be. |

Then a transformation takes place: the tense, reiterated sequence of intervals in the minor mode gives way to its optimistic, major other, via a radical harmonic modulation (a process so often expressive, in Western tonal music, of a shift of consciousness, onto another plane or into another language). This bridge in the relaxed, 'bright' D major mode imagines the crazy dream of the lover's joyful return, opening up the original melodic theme into ever-more expansive, arabesque variations suggestive of ecstatic fantasy:

Figure 2 'Chega de saudade' – a tense, angular theme that falls and leaps through awkward intervals; transformed from minor to major, though, the same figure becomes an expansive dance of joy, a dream of amorous reunion.

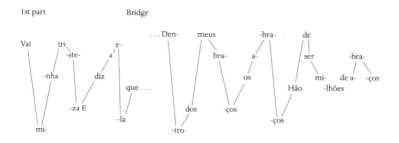

| | |
|---|---|
| *Dentro dos meus braços os abraços* | With my arms around you, love will |
| *hão de ser milhões de abraços* | surround you, and our kisses and caresses will be endless, |
| *Apertado assim, colado assim, calado assim* | Let me hold you near, come closer dear and whisper in your ear, |
| *Abraços e beijinhos, e carinhos sem ter fim* | There'll be no end to all our kisses, dear |

The paradigmatic example of this pattern of tension and reconciliation, the most extreme example, in fact, in the ironically explicit, self-conscious parallel between its musical and thematic strands, is the Tom Jobim / Newton Mendonça composition 'Samba de uma nota só' (One-note samba). The first four verses are heard at the same monotone pitch, which is then counterposed to another repeated note, an interval of a fourth above, dramatizing the amorous dialogue between a pair of lovers united in their difference but complementarity, distinct beings but bound together:

| | |
|---|---|
| *Eis aqui este sambinha* | Here's this little samba |
| *Feito numa nota só* | Made of just a single note |
| *Outras notas vão entrar* | Other notes are going to enter |
| *Mas a base é uma só* | But it's based on just one note |
| *Esta outra é consequência* | This other one is a consequence |
| *Do que acabo de dizer* | Of what I've just said to you |
| *Como eu sou a consequência* | Just like I'm the inevitable |
| *Inevitável de você* | Consequence of you |

The middle section takes us away from this statement of balanced complementarity, the exclusive coupling of two notes, to range 'promiscuously' up and down the entire scale, literally exhausting all the possibilities of adventure outside the original marriage of equals (Fig. 3): 'There are so many people around/ Who talk a lot and don't say anything/ Or hardly anything/ Now I've used up all the scale/ And in the end I'm left with nothing/ It's come to nothing.'

Figure 3 'Samba de uma nota só' – in the middle section the melody runs up and down the entire melodic range, using every single note in the scale.

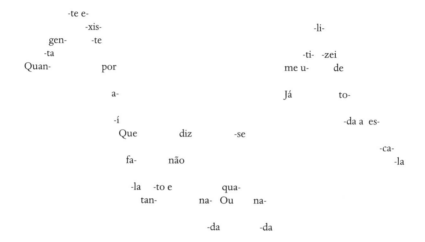

But, this time at least, the urge for variation, for 'a change', leads irresistibly back to the tried and tested first love – the final converging harmonic sequence and its resolution allow the two notes and their separate lives to be neatly reconciled with each other as one: 'And I've come back to my one note / Just like I come back to you/ I'm going to sing with my one note/ /The way that I love you/ And if you go after every note/ Re mi fa sol la si doh / You always end up with no note at all/ So just stay with a single note.'

So, the general pattern (of which this is almost a parody) is a dialectical one which typically moves from a state of conflict or discord towards one of resolution and harmonization. The state of conflict is often suggested by tightly pitched melodic themes revolving around closely adjacent, sometimes identical notes, as if in search of a stable settled centre; and it is expressed verbally as romantic separation, conflict, incomprehension or loss: 'I've seen the confusion,/ You want opinion/ To prevail over reason. . ./ Why exchange a yes for a no/ If the result is solitude instead of love?' ('Discussão' [Argument], Jobim/Mendonça); 'How can you explain these tears of pain/ Why so heartless, so uncaring?/ The fragile love you had, you made her sad/ Left her all alone to bear it' ('Insensatez' [Foolishness], Jobim/Moraes):

Figure 4 'Insensatez' – from beginning to end, in descending registers, the song reiterates a two-part theme: a sequence of oscillating, adjacent notes followed by a downward, sliding figure: the search for stability and 'sameness' seems to struggle against the forces of entropy and loss.

```
                      -ção
                      sem
    in-  -sa- Que -cê        mais
    A -sen- -tez  vo- fez -ra-    cuida-
                      Co-
               -do          por-   quem            nun-
                                                    -ca
                       Vai   -que    pe- per-          per-
                                 não -de -dão  é       -doa-
                                        Não
                                                        -do
```

Resolution is articulated in the language of reconciliation and consolation, the shift from argument to dialogue, from incomprehension to reason, and the completion of the self in the love and companionship of the other, as in 'Eu não existo sem você' (I don't exist without you, Jobim/Moraes) or 'Você e eu' (I am you plus me, Lyra/Moraes). And all this is performed musically in the tension between an insistently reiterated melodic theme and a bass figure or harmonic line that descends (or ascends) chromatically, that is to say, by narrow, sliding steps – it is almost as if the urge for *repetition*, for sameness, stability, familiarity, is anxiously straining against that proverbial 'sinking feeling', the relentless slide down the slippery slope of depression.

We could characterize the idiom arising out of this structural logic as an 'ecological rationality'; that is to say, the subjective and objective life of the individual, the flux of human experience from the projection of desire towards its satisfaction, and the musical unfolding of the song itself, all seem to be ordered by the same 'natural' cycles and relationships. Operating through a continual dialogue between lover and beloved, self and world, lyrical argument and musical form, the songs enact a kind of harmonization of time, space and consciousness in which the musical drama, its human actors and their natural settings converge towards an equilibrium of intimate communion and understanding, a magical state of 'grace'.

Tom Jobim's personal commitment to this idea of the song as a medium of integration between the self and the natural world was an explicit, consistent feature of his work. One of his finest compositions, 'Águas de março' (March rains), identifies 'the promise of life in your heart' with the eternal rhythms and cycles of a rural landscape in an endlessly circular melodic and harmonic structure. Indeed, Jobim's ecological perspective became an increasingly active political concern up to the end of his life, when he was a prominent supporter of the movement to defend the last areas of original forest on Brazil's Atlantic coast.

The cultural environment which the first generation of bossa nova artists inhabited in the Rio de Janeiro of the late 1950s, meanwhile, sheds further light on this philosophical dimension of their music. Prior to the rise of Marxist and left nationalist ideas, one of the chief intellectual influences on that generation was French existentialism. In literary circles, for example, the presence of this current of thinking could be keenly felt in the work of one of the period's most successful young writers, Clarice Lispector.[26] The idyllic, semi-rural tranquillity of Rio's southern beachside neighbourhoods in those years, safe as yet from the economic and social explosion that

Tom Jobim in Rio de Janeiro, 1969.

would soon transform the urban landscape, must have offered
an ideal objective correlative for the kind of inner spiritual
integrity, the grace-filled enlightenment of 'being in the world',
that Lispector's characters strive to discover. It is that striving for
wholeness, for completion of the self in the other, in the rhythms
of nature and in the rationality of musical form, which defines
the 'liturgical', magical quality of the classic phase of bossa nova
composition and performance.

So, in Jobim's 'Corcovado' (Quiet Nights), Rio de Janeiro's
mountain landscape forms a natural objective correlative for the

unity of self and world, viewed through a window of contemplation from within a domestic space of intimacy. A circular
structure beginning and concluding on the same unresolved
Am6 chord holds suspended together the principal melodic
theme and a series of complementary ideas – 'A little corner,
a guitar / This love, a song / To make happy the one you love' –
that have replaced the dying flame of a former sorrow with the
eternity of new companionship. Roberto Menescal and Ronaldo
Bôscoli, meanwhile, typically project the subjective gaze into
the rhythms of the seascape, in songs such as 'Nós e o mar'
(Us and the sea), 'Ah! Se eu pudesse' (Ah! If only I could) and
'O barquinho' (The little boat). Here the drifting vessel, along
with its corresponding melodic theme repeated in descending
registers, transports the solitary couple into an endless cycle of
tides and sunsets, suspended in the song's open-ended, circular
refrain, 'A tardinha cai / O barquinho vai' (The evening falls /
The little boat drifts on).

It is tempting to interpret the idiom and posture of this
classic phase of bossa nova, with its formal sophistication, its
dialogue of reconciliation and its ecological rationality, as an
expression of the affluent, bourgeois complacency of post-war
Rio de Janeiro's residential beachside neighbourhoods. The
typical settings for the music's live performance, the apartment,
nightclub or university students' union, physically enhanced
the sense of domestic intimacy and familiarity in an almost
whispered dialogue between the singers and their small audience
of peers. It is unarguably the case that the music's technical
sophistication and rationality in many ways reflected the self-
conscious modernism of a new technocracy. But it is equally
true, according to Roberto Menescal, that for the composers and
performers at least, the professionalization of music-making made
possible by bossa nova actually offered a viable alternative to more
utilitarian careers implicated in the construction of the new

capitalist economy, such as engineering, medicine or architecture.[27]
Johnny Alf, the singer-songwriter, pianist and precursor of bossa
nova, has also observed that, before the movement's assimilation
into the mainstream recording industry and the promotional
control this involved, some relative autonomy was available to
the artists to produce for reasons, and under conditions, of their
own choosing.[28]

The relative artistic autonomy afforded by bossa nova, and its
pursuit of a certain aesthetic harmonization of self and world, an
existential integrity in dialogue with one's immediate surroundings
and fellow human beings, suggests that the movement therefore
represented in some sense an attempt to articulate a more authentic kind of community, albeit one confined for the moment to the
middle-class intelligentsia of Rio's Zona Sul. If, on the one hand, it
offered an alternative to the sentimentalism and national-populist
rhetoric of the Vargas era, which had spectacularized the relationship between performance, artist and audience, the intimate
musical dialogue of bossa nova also suggested a certain critical
distance, an implicit resistance to the developmentalist rhetoric
of the Kubitschek era, with its ethos of mass consumerism.

With this notion of musical community in mind, we can
perhaps make sense of Carlos Lyra's rather surprising claim
about the movement which he helped to found: 'Bossa Nova
isn't some rich "little daddy's boy" thing. Quite the contrary, it is
the meeting of different socio-economic classes, races, political
and religious ideologies, which are united around a single objective.'[29] Lyra, who later became one of the leading left-wing critics
of the first bossa nova generation, was doubtless fully aware of
its obviously narrow social base among the white bourgeois youth
of Copacabana and Ipanema. Yet here he seems determined to
emphasize how, even before the ideological debates of the early
1960s, bossa nova's ethos of mutual understanding, harmonization
and existential integrity was capable of bringing together a relatively

heterogeneous gathering of individuals around a common, let us say utopian, vision of artistic community.

## MODAL AND TONAL: THE DUAL TEMPO OF BRAZILIAN MODERNITY

We shall now explore the utopian implications of the bossa nova aesthetic further, in terms of its performance of a very particular conception of movement and time; it is a hybrid conception that combines the two major civilizational dimensions and temporalities of Brazil's historical formation and sustains them both simultaneously, inviting the listener to enter that state of 'suspended animation' in which the forward-looking, transformative impulse of progressive time co-exists with the ritual time of repetition and the eternal return. The kind of movement we have identified in bossa nova song-structures so far – from a state of conflict based on melodic reiteration, harmonic tension and dissonance, via an act of transformation or modulation, to a mood of resolution and relaxation – is without doubt a key organizing principle which is implicitly and often explicitly reflected in the lyrical narrative of many songs.

Nevertheless, when summarized in musical terms, as above, this logic does not appear especially remarkable; after all, the dialectic between harmonic dissonance and its resolution, rising through increasing levels of complexity and duration, is arguably the prime moving force within the history of Western music. To that extent, my description would seem to place bossa nova firmly within Western – that is, European – traditions of tonal music, apparently supporting the rather common, nationalist view of bossa nova as an essentially imported, art-music addition to Brazilian culture, rather than originating primarily in local popular traditions.

In actual fact, however, I do not share that view, as tonality represents only one half of bossa nova's profoundly dualistic, ambivalent character. It is all too easy to over-emphasize this dimension because of its associations with a particular notion of musical sophistication and modernity, and the undoubted impact this has had on the harmonic texture and colour of Brazilian popular music. There is a tendency in song analysis, an effect of the value attached in Western art music to extended musical architectures, to think only in terms of narrative events and structures; in other words, to define the meaning of the song in terms of the outcome of its narrative logic, the endpoint or conclusion of its dramatic movement, rather than paying due attention, as we should, to the *ongoing* forms of movement and states of being that it evokes in the *unfolding present* of musical time. Indeed, while one or two bossa nova compositions appear to end, and actually stop, on a 'conclusive note' beyond which we cannot go (for example, 'Samba de uma nota só'), this is not typical, and is deceptive even in those exceptional cases; more often, implicitly or explicitly, there is a movement of 'eternal return' (as in jazz), a potentially endless recapitulation of the central structural pattern, or even simply of a single, off-centred pulse and chord – holding us forever suspended, rhythmically and harmonically. This effect, of a kind of musical suspended animation, is just as strong a force within bossa nova as the forward-moving narrative of tension and resolution, and it points us towards a wholly other cultural universe, one inhabited, amongst others, by African traditions of music-making.

In fact, bossa nova's unique complexity, intensity and appeal can only be understood as a function of the *two* world-historical musical civilizations or epochs that it brings together – the modal and the tonal. In that sense, bossa nova did not only represent a revolutionary historical watershed, a liberating break with the grandiloquent, sentimental legacy of national-populism. It was also *crucial* in another sense, on a deeper, transhistorical level, as a reassertion of the structural duality of Brazilian culture, a reaffirmation of its fundamental vectors: on the one hand, the village-centred, seasonally oriented, ritualistic world, of repetitive, cyclical, interlocking rhythms and melodies weaving an ever denser fabric around the stable, grounded focus of home, community and tradition – the *modal* system, which is shared by most pre-modern, traditional cultures worldwide; and, on the other hand, that peculiarly modern musical civilization that emerged out of the European Renaissance and Baroque: the decentred, restless, individualistic pursuit of change and development, the flight from repetition and familiarity, the deliberate postponement of satisfaction through ever longer and more complex sequences of relation and tension, progression and dissonance – in other words, the world of harmonic adventure, experiment and transformation, stretching from the seventeenth to the twentieth centuries, that we call the *tonal* system.[30]

Perhaps the most remarkable aspect of bossa nova is precisely the coexistence and dialogue within it between these two apparently antithetical systems, the modal and the tonal. There is a strikingly high incidence in the bossa nova repertoire of what I would call modal melodic themes: simple, reiterated patterns centred on the root note of the home key and revolving around a narrow pitch range. On the other hand, the extended harmonic sequences found in bossa nova, with their quality of surprise and originality, of a complex, unfolding musical and argumentative logic, bring most evidently to mind the modern tradition of tonality. After all, we know that some of the founding composers of bossa nova such as Tom Jobim were trained in the compositional techniques of Romantic and modernist tonal music, from Chopin through Debussy and Ravel to Villa-Lobos. And those traditions share with post-war jazz an enriched harmonic palette and an appetite for ever more daring forms of musical transformation and modulation. In fact, it is the so-called 'altered chord', the addition of ever more dissonant tones and intervals to the basic triad, that opens up potential relations with otherwise more remote, foreign-sounding chords, and that eventually makes possible the unexpected migration into another key.

But the altered chord also has another function in bossa nova which, contrary to the endless urge for harmonic modulation and tonal migration, actually seems to defer all forward movement in favour of a kind of groundless, disembodied state of suspension. Many compositions open and close with chords such as these, with added sixths, sevenths and ninths, whose effect seems to be to disorientate our sense of harmonic rootedness, so that we lose our grip on the so-called 'tonic', the fundamental tone upon which melodic scales are built and which gives us our sense of 'home'. These chords are a vertical, harmonic expression of the horizontal chromaticism (step-by-step movement through the entire succession of semi-tones, or narrowest intervals, of the scale) that, as was noted earlier, is a regular feature of both melodic and bass figures in bossa nova. Leonard Meyer's explanation of the disorienting effect of chromaticism in Western music is relevant to the discussion here:

> Chromaticism in Western music is not exclusively or even predominantly a melodic phenomenon; it is also a harmonic phenomenon. As such it is capable of arousing affective aesthetic experience, not only because it may delay or alter the expected diatonic progressions which are the norms of tonal harmony, but also because it tends to create ambiguity and uncertainty as to harmonic direction. Chromatic passages of considerable duration, passages which are often modulatory, appear to be ambiguous because they obscure the feeling of tonal center, because the ultimate end of the progression cannot be envisaged or because more than one tonal center is indicated. Such ambiguity creates suspense and uncertainty which, as we have seen, are powerful forces in the shaping of affective experience.[31]

So in 'Desafinado', for example, the idea of a modern musicality at odds with conservative, conventional ways of listening is not only suggested by the individual dissonant intervals in which the argument is articulated ('Darling, if you tell me that I sing off-key,/ Don't you know it's hurtful for a guy like me?/ Acuter ears like yours belong to just a chosen few/ Mine are tuned the way that God designed them to'). More than this, the entire opening statement and its reiteration are so obscure and adventurous in their harmonic-melodic progression that they challenge the listener to identify any tonal anchor or home, not to mention the ultimate destination towards which the argument is moving.

But besides the contribution of melodic and harmonic chromaticism to bossa nova's ambivalence, to the tension between forward, progressive movement and its suspension, there is another key element to consider, one we might expect to be central to any analysis of musical time and movement: rhythm. There is actually no single, uniform rhythmic pattern that is shared universally by all bossa nova compositions, but instead a series of variants of a certain approach to organizing time. These variants have two things in common: they seem to lack an easily predictable pulse that might fall and order the duration in equal parts, whether 'on' or 'off' the beat; in other words, these are not binary, ternary or quaternary rhythms (in 2, 3 or 4), and there is no strong accentuation on the second pulse, as in traditional samba. But it is not the case that there is *no* regularity or consistency; rather the regularity is an *asymmetrical* one (dividing the duration unequally), and the recurrence of these asymmetrical patterns is extended over a relatively long time period, forcing us to stretch our sense of the perceptual present beyond what we are used to.

Some observers have convincingly suggested that bossa nova rhythms do not so much mark a complete departure from traditional samba as foreground what would traditionally be heard as a less prominent, subordinate pattern within the texture of the *bateria* (percussion ensemble), such as the *tamborim* rather than the *surdo* (bass-drum) or the *repique* (snare-drum). Certainly, the *batida* or plucked pulse of the guitarist's right hand does seem to resemble the extended, asymmetrical patterns one associates with percussion instruments such as the cowbell (*agogô*), whose function, in the West African traditions that are the foundation of Afro-Brazilian music, was to provide a distinctive *timeline* around which interlocking polyrhythmic layers could be arranged and improvised. Walter Garcia, on the other hand, in a meticulous, close analysis of João Gilberto's right-hand technique, the *batida*,[32] has argued that these patterns are actually variants of one basic, recurring motif in samba and many other genres of Brazilian popular music, the *brasileirinho* (1-2-1 2-2).

Whatever their origin, I would argue that the really significant feature of these patterns is that of *extended asymmetry*. One of the effects of these asymmetrical rhythms is to disturb predictable patterns of melodic-linguistic accentuation, so that rather than significant verbal syllables and strongly accented beats always coinciding, as in most forms of song, they often miss each other, setting up a kind of maladjustment or asynchrony. This adds another layer of tension to those we have already seen, between harmonic root and melody, or between repetitive, modal figures and chromatically descending harmonies. This maladjustment, which we could call a kind of verbal syncopation or metric dissonance,[33] is a familiar phenomenon in jazz singing, where the vocalist delays or anticipates a phrase so that the separation between word/melody and chord/pulse is held in a state of suspension. João Gilberto is a master of this technique, which seems to intensify the impression of temporal elasticity, to stretch the duration of the present by emphasizing the tension between onward movement and circularity. Listen, for example, to his performance of 'Garota de Ipanema' on the *Live in Montreux* album (1987).[34]

The second effect of the extended assymetry of bossa nova rhythms is to disorient our sense of temporal location, rather like those enriched dissonant chords that, as we have seen, displace and confuse our sense of harmonic rootedness. There is no longer any clear, reliable beginning or end to the periodic cycles of musical time, no bar-lines, as in many traditions of West African music, where there is an endless fabric of interlocking patterns of varying duration with several possible points of entry. So the opening pulse of 'Desafinado' gives us little clue as to where and when the melody is going to start. This kind of time isn't exactly going anywhere; in fact, the point about 'Desafinado' is precisely to defend the possibility of a different order of tunefulness and a different temporal order, a different heartbeat, from those that are everyday and familiar to us: 'There's something you've forgotten, though you think your playing's smart/ For within those who sing off-key, deep within them quietly beating/ In the breast of those who sing off-key there also beats a heart.'

What we can see emerging, then, is a powerful homology, or structural correspondence, between the rhythmic and melodic-harmonic phenomenon of 'suspended animation' and a lyrical, thematic evocation of states of being where time is somehow suspended, slowed down or revealed in its process of becoming – the beating heart of the 'desafinado', or the still-life perfection of the window-side scene in 'Corcovado', with 'infinite time to dream': 'I want life always to be this way,/ With you close to me,/ Until that old flame goes out'. One of the most intense performances of this phenomenon, the experience of time in its becoming, is João Gilberto's recording of the Alcyvando Luz and Carlos Coquejo composition 'É preciso perdoar' (You must forgive), from his eponymous 1973 album.[35]

The song opens with a Cm7(9) chord heard as a lone, asymmetrical pulse, whose periodicity and harmonic identity are so ambivalent as to obscure its location in time and place. We are not

João Gilberto performing in 1966.

prepared for the entry of the voice, which, against this disembodied pulse, intones, prayer-like, the first, sustained note of a reiterative, modal theme, revolving around the root of the chord (see Fig. 5), before repeating more or less the same figure at the same and then a higher register; meanwhile, an inexorably descending bass figure leads the harmonic sequence chromatically down to a darkly dissonant Fm7(b5) chord, and then back to the initial statement of harmonic and rhythmic suspension:

| | |
|---|---|
| *A madrugada já rompeu* | Ah, morning light's just broken through |
| *você vai me abandonar* | soon you'll leave me all alone, |
| *eu sinto que o perdão* | I'm sorry it was so, |
| *você não mereceu* | there's no forgiving you |
| *eu quis a ilusão* | I wished the dream was true |
| *agora a dor sou eu* | now pain is all I know |

Figure 5 'É preciso perdoar' – an ostinato melodic pattern or loop, endlessly repeated in different registers, returns hypnotically to the 'root' or fundamental note of the scale, which sounds constantly throughout, like a drone, suspending the song in a state of imminence or eternity.

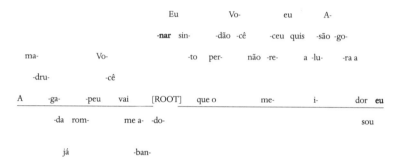

When this micro-drama of musical movement is combined with the song's beautifully concise lyrical argument – a lover's sorrowful regret for a tragic moment of loss – the effect is quietly electrifying: we begin the song at a hauntingly poignant moment, an infinitesimal threshold of imminence, between the evidence of time's inevitable passing, as dawn has just that second broken, and the plain certainty that abandonment must follow. That suspended moment of imminence gives way, at a suddenly higher pitch on the syllable 'abando-**nar**', to a concentrated cycle of emotions (anger, resentment, an admission of error, of self-deception) vocalized as a quietly desperate series of reiterated phrases, as control slips inexorably away beneath us in the downward harmonic slide. When we are returned to the initial disembodied, timeless, placeless chord, the sense that 'agora a dor sou eu' (literally 'now the pain is me'), is almost palpable; the self is not just overwhelmed by grief, but has been thrown into a limbo where there is nothing else but the pain, where it defines his being.

After this, another more lively modal theme is repeated in two registers, the second a tone lower than the first: this has its lyrical counterpart in a philosophical aphorism, of the kind commonly found in the Afro-sambas composed by Baden Powell, Vinicius de Moraes and Edu Lobo in the mid-1960s, and which here advocates a kind of selflessness in love, pitying the lover who has been unable to 'let go' and so find a deeper level of belonging:

| | |
|---|---|
| *Pobre de quem não entendeu* | None is so blind as can't see |
| *que a beleza de amar é se dar* | that, in love, you give and don't count the cost |
| *e só querendo pedir nunca soube* | Always asking for more, you can't know |
| *o que é perder pra encontrar* | how to find what you believed you had lost |

That brief interval of modulation and enlightenment leads back to the reprise of the first theme; but now the inescapable state of solitude and grief (the limbo of suspension) is tempered on the second hearing with a new emotional wisdom: the capacity for forgiveness, and the understanding that beyond tears and grief there lies a different kind of knowledge, a reconciliation with the world; the realm of timeless suspension, which had previously signified the endless horror of loss and solitude, is now the time-lessness of a transcendent eternity:

| | |
|---|---|
| *Eu sei que é preciso perdoar* | I know, forgiving's hard but we must try |

| | |
|---|---|
| *foi você quem me ensinou* | you're the one who taught me how, |
| *que um homem como eu* | for somebody like me, |
| *que tem por quem chorar* | whose lover made him cry, |
| *só sabe o que é sofrer* | the pain is only real |
| *se o pranto se acabar* | after the tears run dry |

## MUSICAL TIME, HISTORICAL TIME: IMMINENCE

So, the contrast between the modal and tonal systems is not only about the difference between a centred, stable, one-dimensional harmonic world and the endlessly shifting terrain of modulation; it is also an opposition between two conceptions of time: the cyclical, ritualistic world of repetition, of the eternal return, and the chronological, progressive, accumulative temporality of our secular, modern age. What does it mean when these two temporal models are brought together, as they are in bossa nova? What we have seen (or heard) is neither one thing nor the other – neither stillness, the halting of time, nor the forward consequential movement of historical development. In the tension *between* the two temporal models, between repetition and circularity, and the narrative, discursive thrust of tonality, what seems to be realized here is the impression of *actuality*, the continual unfolding of the present, the threshold of *becoming*, that endlessly renewed moment of suspended animation where the swing-boat reaches the turn, the peak of its cycle, and experiences a state of weightlessness, of imminence and potentiality.

We should be wary of attempting to 'interpret' this musical conception of movement and time – of actuality or becoming – too narrowly or reductively as a cultural and ideological intervention in mid-1950s Brazil. But we could venture the following: bossa nova gathers up and sets into mutual interaction two temporalities – the ritual-cyclical-repetitive and the chronological-progressive-historical – but allows primacy to neither of them.

In the mid-twentieth century, at a key moment in Brazil's contemporary development, when the prospect of overcoming the burden of its pre-modern, underdeveloped, rural legacy seemed most palpably within reach, and the slogan of 'fifty years' development in five' promised quite literally to accelerate historical time, bossa nova invited young Brazilians instead to 'stay cool', to resist the compulsion to join the headlong rush of progress and instead to live the moment, the actuality of 'now', in a spirit of relaxed but critical optimism.

Combining the modern rationality of formal refinement with a kind of secular spirituality, it affirmed, then as now, the two civilizational dimensions of Brazil's cultural identity without privileging either; in other words, it did not retreat nostalgically into the traditional world of non-Western musical culture, nor unequivocally embrace the futurist rhetoric of post-war developmentalism. Rather, and, I would argue, in a profoundly utopian spirit, it affirmed the possibility of sustaining both traditional and modern sensibilities and mentalities simultaneously in a state of creative, dynamic tension, of imminence. To that extent, but in a way not generally recognized, bossa nova implicitly offers us an independent version of that dialectical approach to Brazilian culture that is more often associated with 1920s modernist Oswald de Andrade's theory of cultural cannibalism, antropofagia, or with the Tropicália movement of the late 1960s.[36]

In 1956, just as bossa nova was transforming Brazil's soundscape, the pioneering musical theorist Victor Zuckerkandl was elaborating an eloquently descriptive model for characterizing the musical present; it is a description that perfectly captures the experience of time and movement in bossa nova as I have attempted to explain it, with the concept of suspended animation. For Zuckerkandl, consecutive musical tones follow one other, not with the arbitrary, mechanical inevitability of clock time, but as a necessary completion of each other; the beat 'two' follows 'one' as a future

that is already part of the 'now' of the first beat, which itself, though
past, goes on existing as the necessary object of that completion,
always proceeding towards 'two'. The present of musical time
continuously, endlessly brings into simultaneous 'virtual' existence
previous and future tones, not as remembered or anticipated, but
as 'stored' in an ever unfolding 'now':

> the present of musical experience is not the dividing point
> that eternally separates past and future; it is the stage upon
> which, for every ear, the drama of the being of time is played
> – that ceaseless storing of itself and anticipating itself which
> is never repeated, which is every instant anew.[37]

# 3 THREE MASTERS, THREE MASTERPIECES: JOBIM, MORAES, GILBERTO

As we have seen, the first bossa nova generation was characterized less by its individualism or cult of artistic personality than by its devotion to a collective utopian project and its spirit of community, which embraced a considerable number of composers and performers. Nevertheless, the combined contribution of three figures, in particular – Tom Jobim, Vinicius de Moraes and João Gilberto – remains a formidable one, accounting for a disproportionate share of the artistic achievement and reputation of the movement.

The majority of the compositions taken as exemplary of the bossa nova aesthetic in the previous chapter are single- or co-authored by Tom Jobim. And while far from all of Jobim's oeuvre should be classified as bossa nova, it is remarkable that, from Almir Chediak's five-volume collection of bossa nova songbooks,[1] something approaching a quarter of the songs anthologized are Jobim's. Equally remarkably, while Jobim co-composed with many partners, his collaborations with Vinicius de Moraes, dating from 1956, produced over 70 songs, compared to no more than twenty from each of the next most prolific partnerships, with Aloysio de Oliveira, Billy Blanco, Chico Buarque and Newton Mendonça.

Similarly, many of the musical examples that inform the preceding analysis are drawn from the repertoire of compositions recorded by João Gilberto on his first three domestically produced albums (*Chega de saudade*, 1959; *O Amor, o Sorriso e a Flor*, 1960, and *João Gilberto*, 1961), and on the 1973 album that also bears his name, known in Brazil as his 'white album'.[2] It may be argued that Gilberto's style of interpretation is unique, perhaps, as some have suggested, a bossa nova sub-style of its own, and that it should be viewed as representative of a 'traditional' historical path, as distinct from the more 'international', cool-jazz version represented by Tom Jobim.[3] But while this may be borne in mind as a qualifier to any generalizations about bossa nova as a whole, I would nevertheless insist that João Gilberto's performing style is *both* inimitable *and* profoundly characteristic of the spirit of this musical aesthetic, just as the Jobim/Moraes songwriting repertoire embodies the core, defining features of its interpretation of the tempo of Brazilian modernity: its drama of imminence, its tension between the mythic, ritual time of the eternal return, and the quotidian time of the contemporary city. And in their interpretation of this, the central ethos of the movement, Jobim, Moraes and Gilberto converge as a single, integrated and compelling voice.

After all, although it has produced a huge repertoire, bossa nova is nevertheless not easily reducible to a body of compositions or even to a set of structural formulae. Instead, as a living tradition, it should best be defined literally and non-programmatically as a 'movement', as an interpretative attitude that can potentially be applied to any individual song, whatever its original genre. As bossa nova veteran Carlos Lyra put it:

There's an old mistake about Bossa Nova: that of believing it was only concerned with samba. That isn't true. Bossa Nova is *modinha* [a sedate, sentimental love-song dating from the eighteenth century], it's *baião* [a lively urban two-step dance rhythm popularised by northeastern accordionist Luis Gonzaga in the 1940s], it's *samba-canção* [a slower, melodic and sentimental version of samba at its height in the 1950s], and it's all those things. Bossa Nova is the spirit of the thing.[4]

Consider the variety of genres featured on the *João Gilberto* album (1973), from samba hits of the 1930s ('Na Baixa do Sapateiro', by Ary Barroso) and especially the 1940s ('Izaura', by Herivelto Martins and Roberto Roberti, 'Falsa Baiana', by Geraldo Pereira, and 'Eu quero um samba', by Janet de Almeida and Haroldo Barbosa) through the northeastern *baião* and the waltz, in the artist's original compositions ('Undiú' and 'Valsa (como são lindos os youguis) (Bebel)', respectively)), to post-bossa compositions ('Águas de março', by Tom Jobim, 'É preciso perdoar', by Carlos Coqueijo and Alcivando Luz, 'Avarandado', by Caetano Veloso, and 'Eu vim da Bahia', by Gilberto Gil).

If, as we have seen, both the individual compositions of the bossa nova repertoire and their performances enact, and unfold in, that state of dynamic tension I called 'suspended animation', between reiteration and transformation, potentiality and movement, then João Gilberto could be said to elevate this into an entire artistic attitude, of which the 'white album' of 1973 is exemplary.[5] It is perhaps not coincidental, in this regard, that it was recorded in the u.s. at a crucial moment in the artist's career, a certain 'between-place' or hiatus of reconcentration and renewal, during a succession of overseas stays dating from the mid-1960s, following the euphoric success of the movement's first phase. There is a common denominator across the album's variety of genres and compositions: the model of singing and playing that Gilberto had been testing out and refining up to this point is now taken to a new extreme of intensification and distillation. The elimination of all the 'modern' accompanying instrumentation heard on his previous records, such as wind, brass, string orchestra and piano, heightens the impression that we now are inhabiting the artisanal world of the modal era, its performative elements pared down to the essential partnership between voice and guitar, reinforced by Sonny Carr's minimal percussion (brushes on a high-hat and on a wicker basket).[6] Conditional on an extraordinary level of vocal and instrumental discipline on Gilberto's part, this newly concentrated intensity is achieved largely by exploiting the principle of repetition.

Repetition is evident, not only in the often near obsessive consistency with which João Gilberto executes the *batida* of the right hand and the vocalizations of each melody – here, alone, attaining an impressive degree of uniformity – but also in the high number of reiterations which the song-cycle undergoes. It is worth noting João Gilberto's decision to perform on this album a significant number of compositions already character- ized by reiterative themes, which intensifies still further the effect of reduplication when performed more than once in their entirety. Thus, with only one additional reprise, 'Águas de março' (whose structure comprises as many as 46 lines, many of them internally repetitive) reaches 5′23′′; 'Valsa', 'É preciso perdoar' and 'Undiú' are all reiterated three times, the latter occupying 6′39′′ of playing time, while 'Eu quero um samba' and 'Izaura' complete four cycles, and 'Eu vim da Bahia' five. Compared to an average track length of under two or three minutes on the previous albums, therefore, these recordings end up varying between 3′20′′ and 6′40′′.

This feature of João Gilberto's approach to performance reinforces one of the already inherent characteristics of the bossa nova repertoire: the recourse to repetitive figures in the melodic line, as found in 'Garota de Ipanema', 'Insensatez' and, on this album, 'Águas de março' and 'É preciso perdoar', among many other compositions. Taken together, this tendency to extend the overall duration by redoubling the songs' already reiterative structures has at least two consequences. First, it serves to highlight, in real time, the interpretative core and performative dynamic of the song, laying bare its melodic-verbal structure and revealing its simultaneously concrete, material and symbolic character, as *movement*.

Second, as far as the listening experience is concerned, these extended, reiterative performances take on the hypnotic quality of enchantment or fascination that liturgical forms of music can exert, as they capture the listener's psychosomatic attention and transport him into another state of consciousness. At this point, the semantic, discursive function of the lyrical verses, as language, can become extenuated so as to give way to a chiefly sonic function, as the bearer of melodically and rhythmically intoned refrains. It is significant that João Gilberto – who had already tested out the option of pure verbal sonority, the 'non-lyric', in early original compositions such as 'Bim bom' ('É só isso o meu baião / E não tem mais nada não' – That's all there is, just my *baião* / That's your lot, it's all you got) and 'Hô-bá-lá-lá' ('Vem ouvir / O hô-bá-lá-lá / Hô-bá-lá-lá, esta canção – Come and hear / The oh-ba-la-la / Oh-ba-la-la, that's this song), and in João Donato's 'A rã' (The frog) – performs two songs on his 'white album', 'Undiú' and 'Valsa', which also dispense with words altogether. The only instrumental track on the album, 'Na Baixa do Sapateiro', almost seems to insist on the same point by substituting the guitar for the sung voice, as if meaning precisely to eliminate the boundaries between instrument and voice, which somehow still remains tacitly present. 'Undiú', meanwhile, with its endless, mantra-like repetition of a single, semantically empty vocable, can be heard as a kind of incantatory hymn to the modal impulse within Brazilian music; while the syllable 'Und-' sounds the unchanging, drone-like root of D, which is also heard on the bass string of the guitar, underpinning the entire piece, the second syllable '-iú' leaps to different successive intervals, falling back to the root each time, as if in a meditative movement around, and regression to, the 'magnetic' centre of things.

This same principle of hypnotic, incantatory fascination is the key to the seemingly irresistible appeal of Jobim and Moraes's 'Garota de Ipanema' (Girl from Ipanema); it is, in fact, the musical correlative of the song's central theme, that state of entrancement in which the vocal subject contemplates the girl on her way to the sea, as if mesmerized by the grace and poetry of her movement. The key to that state of entrancement lies in its opening melodic-discursive phrase, a paradigmatic example of 'suspended animation': in a swinging dactylic metre of one strong and two weak beats (– · ·), the words 'olha que **coi**sa mais **lin**da, mais **chei**a de **gra**ça, é **e**la menina, que **vem** e que **pa**ssa . . .' (**look**, was there ever a **love**lier **sight**, or more **grace**ful? That **girl**, she's the **one**, here she **comes**, going **by** now . . .) intone the familiar reiterative three-note, modal theme which, heard unaccompanied, sounds so banal; only in relation to the harmonic ground and syncopated accents that shift beneath it, does it magically acquires its meaning:

| | |
|---|---|
| *Olha que coisa mais linda* | Oh, was there ever a lovelier |
| *Mais cheia de graça* | sight, or more graceful? |
| *É ela, menina,* | That girl, she's the one, |
| *Que vem e que passa* | Here she comes, going by now |
| *Num doce balanço* | And swaying so gently |
| *A caminho do mar* | On down to the sea. |
| | |
| *Moça do corpo dourado* | Body so golden, a child |
| *Do sol de Ipanema* | of the sun of Ipanema, |
| *O seu balançado* | Her swing makes me smile, |
| *É mais que um poema* | It's all poets dream of, |
| *É a coisa mais linda* | I've seen no-one lovelier |
| *Que eu já vi passar.* | Walk by to the sea. |

On first hearing (as we are invited to share in the sense of entrance-ment), rhythm, melody and harmony are held in a curious state of tension and dissonance, as the dancing three-note phrase (pre-figured in the wordless introduction to the João Gilberto / Stan Getz recording) hovers around, but never quite settles on, the harmonic root, the tonal centre or 'home' that the song inhabits, generating a disguised but subtly unsettling dissonance (see Fig. 6). Only on the word 'graça' (grace) is that suspended dissonance between melody and harmony resolved, as the chord moves up a whole tone and adjusts the relationship to a state of consonance; but then the bright mood of 'that girl [who's] the one' darkens from major to minor as she walks by ('passa'), and we're returned to the initial state of suspension, of her 'sweet swaying walk, heading on down to the sea' – she seemed so close, but now she's impossibly out of reach again.

Figure 6 Opening theme of 'Garota de Ipanema' – the reiterated three-note figure first dances dissonantly about the root or fundamental tone before becoming resolved magically on the word 'grace', only to descend on 'passa' into the darker minor key, as the girl walks by.

| *Olha* | *linda* | **graça** | *-nina* | | | |
|---|---|---|---|---|---|---|
| ----------------------ROOT--- | | | | **passa** | | |
| *Que coisa* | *Mais cheia* | *É ela* | *Que vem* | | *-lanço* | |
| | *Mais* | *de* | *me-* | *que* | *Num doce* | |
| | | | | | *Ba-* *caminho* | *mar* |
| | | | | | | *do* |

As if this weren't enough, the middle section offers us another re-iterated motif, but here we leave the mesmerized fixation on the girl's receding passage horizontally across our field of vision, to concentrate on the inward emotional response to this:

| *Ah, porque estou tão sozinho?* | Why do I feel so alone now? |
|---|---|
| *Ah, porque tudo é tão triste?* | Why does this sadness surround me? |
| *Ah, a beleza que existe* | Why does her beauty confound me? |

| | |
|---|---|
| *A beleza que não é só minha,* | All she needs is to live, just to be, |
| *Que também passa sozinha.* | As she walks so alone, and so free. |

The falling movement of the new melodic theme, set against an anxiously rising sequence of clashing chords, raises the state of perplexity and frustrated desire to a new pitch of tension. As well as the conflict between the descending melodic figure and its ascending reiteration, this is achieved by setting the first, distressed tone of each repeated phrase – 'Ah, porque estou tão sozinho?' (Oh why do I feel so alone now?) – just beneath, and against, the root or keynote of the underlying chord, so as to produce the narrowest and most unstable interval in our musical vocabulary, a subtly clashing semitone (see Fig. 7).

Figure 7 Middle section of 'Garota de Ipanema' – the successive reiterations of the falling pattern, each at a higher pitch of anxiety than the last, set the emotive cry 'Ah!' dissonantly against (just below) the root of the chord.

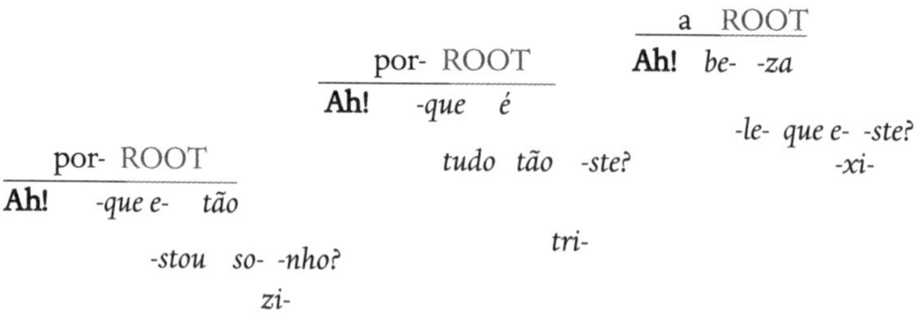

When, to our relief, we are restored to the original swaying theme, the return to that suspended, floating three-note phrase is associated with a new idea – 'Ah, se ela soubesse que quando ela passa, o mundo sorrindo se enche de graça, e fica mais lindo por causa do amor' (Oh, if only she knew how that walk full of grace turns the world into laughter, a magical place, that's made even lovelier because of love) – in other words, that entrancing, self-possessed unattainable ideal, the elusive beauty of the woman who 'walks so alone and so free', has transcended the visual and emotional field of the male gaze, to infuse and enchant the whole world in a kind of erotic state of grace:

| | |
|---|---|
| *Ah, se ela soubesse* | Oh, if only she knew how |
| *Que quando ela passa* | That walk full of grace |
| *O mundo sorrindo* | Turns the world into laughter, |
| *Se enche de graça* | A magical place |
| *E fica mais lindo* | That's made even lovelier |
| *Por causa do amor.* | Because of love. |

In 'Garota de Ipanema', then, Tom Jobim and Vinicius de Moraes dramatized the paradox of erotic longing, lingering suspended at the threshold between desire and its gratification, between the onlooker's passive gaze and the animated movement of its object. Syncopation, oscillating melodic figures and harmonic dissonance all hold that state of erotic desire at its point of imminence, of dynamic tension, which is the very essence of time present, the *becoming* of time.

The other masterpiece of the Jobim/Moraes songwriting partnership to capture this between-place of the present, of time in its unfolding from *before* to *after*, is 'A Felicidade' (Happiness). The refrain that opens the song is intoned by a phrase – 'Tristeza não tem fim' (Sadness has no end) – whose corresponding notes, when intermeshed with those of the first chord typically heard on the guitar, set up an unsettled harmonic mood that disorientates our sense of tonal location. For one thing, the melodic phrase avoids the root of the chord, the note C, rising and hovering above it, briefly touching the octave above before falling back to the word 'fim' (end). And the second syllable of the word 'sadness'

('Tri-ste-za') is extended, held suspended on the sixth note of the scale, an unusual choice for such a significant moment in the melodic and lyrical argument of the song (see Fig. 8).

Figure 8 'A Felicidade' – the key, opening theme arches above the root or fundamental tone of the home key, hovering suspended on the prolonged second syllable of 'tris-teza' (sadness), at the disorientating sixth interval of the scale.

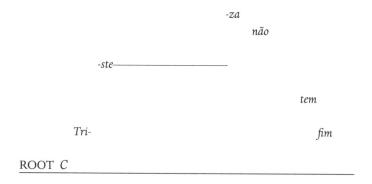

The impression created is that we are momentarily adrift, in a limbo, caught in the suspended time of the eternal sadness that is the song's theme – before starting on the forward-moving harmonic sequence impelled by the phrase 'Felicidade sim' (literally 'Happiness does [. . . have an end]'), which returns us to the sphere of the present, of transience. A more adventurous melodic journey structured by a series of harmonic modulations now leads us through various poetic examples of the theme of *tempus fugit*, the fragile brevity of life's successive moments, epitomized by the transition between Shrove Tuesday and Ash Wednesday, between the euphoria of Carnival and its anti-climactic aftermath.

In its dialogic tension between the reiterated refrain 'Tristeza não tem fim' and these extended verses, the song therefore enacts a musical realization or embodiment of the infinitesimal threshold of the present, of those transient moments which seem somehow intent on resisting the onward logic of real time, stretching their duration and eternally deferring their end, like the dewdrop trembling tantalizingly on the flower's petal, the feather floating in the air, or kisses hovering at the margin between night and day, within a limbo of infinite cyclical repetition:

| | |
|---|---|
| *Tristeza não tem fim* | How long must sorrow last |
| *Felicidade sim.* (repeat) | When joy so soon is past? |
| | |
| *A felicidade é como uma gota* | Happiness is like a drop of dew |
| *De orvalho numa pétala de flor* | Clinging to the petal there, above |
| *Brilha tranqüila* | So still, you see it glimmer |
| *Depois de leve oscila* | It barely seems to shimmer |
| *E cai como uma lágrima de amor* | And falls just like the tear we shed for love |
| | |
| *Tristeza não tem fim* | How long must sorrow last |
| *Felicidade sim.* | When joy so soon is past? |
| | |
| *A felicidade do pobre parece* | The poor man only gets his glimpse of happiness |
| *A grande ilusão do carnaval* | That fleeting day when carnival comes round |
| *A gente trabalha* | For twelve long months you labour |
| *o ano inteiro* | Just so that you can savour |
| *Por um momento de sonho* | The dream that lives for a moment |
| *Pra fazer a fantasia* | While you pretend to be |
| *De rei ou de pirata ou jardineira* | A king, a pirate or a casanova |
| *Pra tudo se acabar na quarta-feira* | Then Wednesday comes and all your joy is over |

| | |
|---|---|
| *Tristeza não tem fim* | How long must sorrow last |
| *Felicidade sim.* (repeat) | When joy so soon is past? |
| | |
| *A felicidade é como uma* | Happiness is like the lightest |
| *pluma* | feather |
| *Que o vento vai levando pelo ar* | That's carried by the breeze |
| | upon the air |
| *Voa tão leve* | It glides without a sound |
| *Mas tem a vida breve* | And then falls floating to the |
| | ground |
| *Precisa que haja vento sem parar* | It only lives while there is |
| | breath to spare |
| | |
| *A minha felicidade está sonhando* | This happiness of mine seems |
| | to be dreaming |
| *Nos olhos da minha namorada* | Deep within my darling's |
| | sleepy eyes |
| *É como esta noite* | It's like the night that's moving |
| *Passando, passando* | Towards the light of dawn |
| *Em busca da madrugada* | Soon the sun's going to rise |
| *Falem baixo, por favor* | So whisper softly as a dove |
| *Para que ela acorde alegre com* | Then she will wake tomorrow |
| *o dia* | smiling sweetly |
| *Oferecendo beijos de amor* | With kisses poised like |
| | offerings of love |
| | |
| *Tristeza não tem fim* | How long must sorrow last |
| *Felicidade sim.* (repeat & fade) | When joy so soon is past? |

It is striking how many compositions selected by João
Gilberto for his 'white album' dramatize, in some form or other,
the musical-discursive theme identified above, which seems also
to constitute such a central principle of Tom Jobim's work, both

in collaboration with Vinicius de Moraes and alone; whether through the purely musical movement of circular reiteration and perpetual return, as in Gilberto's own 'Undiú' and 'Valsa', or in the scenario of the between-place of vacillation or exile – the exile of the singer who 'came from Bahia, but will one day go back' ('Eu vim da Bahia', Gilberto Gil); or even in a lighter, more comical register, the dilemma of Izaura's lover who, one minute, feels compelled to obey the call to work until returning to her arms next Sunday and, the next moment, allows himself to be seduced by the non-time of pleasure and leisure, where 'There's no alarm-clock that can wake me' ('Izaura', Martins/ Roberti). In Caetano Veloso's 'Avarandado', as in 'É preciso perdoar' (Coqueijo/Luz), discussed in the previous chapter, Gilberto again explores the threshold moment of transition between the night's end and daybreak, this time as a celebration of the deliciously fragile interval that is to be savoured and lived. Slowing down the pace and stretching the vocal articulation, he exploits to the full the song's moments of melodic and harmonic suspension, especially prolonging the vowels 'a', 'e' and 'i', as if himself trying to postpone the dawn's arrival: 'Qualquer canção, quase nada/ Vai fazer o sol levantar/ Vai fazer o dia nascer' (Any song at all, the slightest thing/ Is going make the sun rise/ Is going to make the day break).

Finally, in Tom Jobim's extraordinary solo composition 'Águas de março', we experience the endless unfolding of cyclical time within the rhythms of natural and human growth and decomposition, life and death, renewal and decay. These rhythms have their musical counterpart in the essentially modal, melodic oscillation between the first and third notes of the scale (sometimes via the second), and between the fifth and the octave, and an eternal cycle of return to the root (Fig. 9):

Figure 9 'Águas de Março' – the theme oscillates between the principal intervals of the scale, leaping from the tonic to the third, the fifth, the octave, but always falling back to the root.

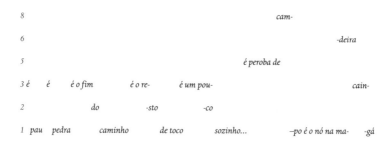

| 8 | | | | | | cam- | | |
| 6 | | | | | | | -deira | |
| 5 | | | | | | é peroba de | | |
| 3 é | é | é o fim | é o re- | é um pou- | | | | cain- |
| 2 | | do | -sto | -co | | | | |
| 1 pau | pedra | caminho | de toco | sozinho... | | –po é o nó na ma- | | -gá |

The song's ritualistic, liturgical character, as suggested by this endlessly repetitive circularity was, it seems, explicitly in evidence to Tom Jobim, who was inspired by a *ponto*, a verse and melodic theme from the syncretic Afro-Brazilian religion of *macumba*. The quality of temporal suspension takes on an added intensity due to the tension between the reiterative melodic figure and the harmonic sequence, following the unresolved, inverted seventh chord which opens the song as a lone pulse, before the voice enters to begin the cycle. The unstable element of the seventh note of the scale, which we might expect to find in the higher registers, is heard instead on the guitar's bass string, in the root, seeming to invite its own resolution from the very start. The effect is to give the impression that the song has not exactly 'started' at our moment of listening, but rather that we have just stepped into a *moto perpetuo*, an already endlessly turning *roda* or circle.[7]

Once combined with the lyrics' strikingly liturgical structure – consisting of a lexical store of remarkably rich sonic as well as semantic potential, and organized, not along narrative or discursive lines, but as a series of substantive enunciations using the device of anaphora ('It's a stick, it's a stone, it's the end of the road . . .') – the musical movement is revealed as an organic fabric of contradictory and complementary tendencies, in a permanent state of flux, of ebb and flow, growth and renewal. Amid the many strands out of which this dynamic texture is woven (including a dialogue between the natural and the human, and between the fragment and the whole), one that stands out is a spatial dimension: the musical, as well as thematic, play between the horizontal and the vertical, between land and air. If the melodic figure is always striving to leap, via other intervals, from the tonic to its octave, so as to overcome the inertia, the gravitational force of the ground, and reach the 'heights' (the same word, *altura*, translates musical pitch and 'height' in Portuguese), the logic of the harmonic sequence insists on always falling, sinking into the earth's roots. At the same time, the poetic images, too, shift between the ground and its mineral and vegetable matter ('stick . . . stone . . . the remains of a stump . . . the knot in the wood'), the urge to fly like 'a bird in the sky', and that intermediate or mediating realm of water, rain and currents which mobilizes the power of communication, fluidity and the rebirth of nature's creative, restorative powers: 'São as águas de março fechando o verão / É a promessa de vida no teu coração' (It's the waters of March bringing summer to an end / It's the promise of life in your heart).

Out of that tension between, on the one hand, the pole of inertia, immobility and groundedness, and, on the other, the upward flight towards the realm of transcendence, we do not exactly arrive at a state of conciliation, resolution or the cancelling out of both tendencies; rather, by means of the vitalizing symbolic power of water, we reach a dynamic, eternally suspended equilibrium which hovers about the magnetic centre, the root, without ever settling on it. In the wake of João Gilberto's extended, masterfully controlled performance, this is all experienced, not so much as a narrative unfolding, but rather as incantation, as something approaching prayer.

In the light of the artistic and personal commitment that this
and other performances by João Gilberto seem to invest in a quasi-
spiritual, contemplative attitude of harmonization between the
self, the world and the other, and in the value of human solidarity
and community, we can perhaps make sense of a rather surprising
anecdote recounted by Sérgio Ricardo, as recorded in the documentary history of bossa nova, *Coisa mais linda – história e casos
da bossa nova*. In the early 1960s, in the midst of a period of fervent
political radicalization, when the future left-wing activist Sérgio
Ricardo was still studying yoga and other 'spiritualist stuff', he
claims that the person who shaped his political thinking was
none other than João Gilberto, not someone we would normally
suspect of left-wing evangelism. Commenting on his generation's
search for individual wellbeing and fulfilment, but recalling too
the immense reality of social deprivation and misery in a country
such as Brazil, João Gilberto turned to Sérgio Ricardo and said:

> 'Right, that's all very well, but . . . It's very nice, it brings
> you happiness and all, but real, full happiness is when you're
> connected to your fellow human beings, and you're all in the
> same situation of happiness' . . . And he started talking about
> Marx! About Marx, communism and such like. . . . And it was
> he who opened my eyes for the first time to what socialism
> was about.[8]

While many of his generation may have shared a common
utopian vision of Brazil's future, the direction popular music
was to take over the next few years implied a radically different
interpretation of the relationship between music and politics
from that envisaged by João Gilberto. It would also transform
bossa nova almost beyond recognition.

# 4 GUNS AND ROSES: BRAZIL'S MUSIC OF POPULAR PROTEST, 1958–68

| | |
|---|---|
| *Pelos campos a fome em* | Hunger spreading across |
| *grandes plantações* | huge plantation fields |
| *Pelas ruas marchando* | Carnival-goers marching |
| *indecisos cordões* | hesitantly down streets |
| *Inda fazem da flor seu* | They still make the flower |
| *mais forte refrão* | their strongest refrain |
| *E acreditam nas flores* | and believe that flowers |
| *vencendo o canhão . . .* | can defeat the gun . . . |

From Geraldo Vandré's 'Pra não dizer que não falei das flores
(Caminhando)'

## POLITICIZING SONG IN THE ERA OF MASS CULTURE

Just a few years after its emergence in the late 1950s, long before
bossa nova acquired its international connotations as the arche-
typal 'background' muzak of airport lounges and shopping malls,
questions were being asked about its popular status and its social
relevance by some of the very performers and songwriters whose
musical education had been steeped in the new wave established
by Tom Jobim, Vinicius de Moraes and João Gilberto. These were
years of political radicalization, when increasing numbers of
people became mobilized in trade unions, peasant leagues and
student organizations, influenced by anti-imperialist and socialist

ideas and especially the example of the overthrow of the Batista regime in Cuba in 1959. Culture, including song, was now required to play a conscious, active role in expressing the interests and aspirations of the movement for social and political change.

Indeed, the notion of a revolutionary 'popular culture' was the subject of both theoretical discussion and practical activity by the organized Communist left and its periphery. The starting-point of this intervention was a critique of the optimistic, development-alist culture of the Kubitschek years (1956–61), whose promise of 'fifty years' development in five' had been publicly endorsed in the celebration of avant-garde innovations in architecture, interior design, fashion, the media, technology and the arts.[1] For among the social consequences of the development boom was the influx of massive numbers of the country's predominantly rural population, especially those forced by landlessness, drought and violent conflict to emigrate from the impoverished northeast into the southern cities with their new manufacturing industries and construction projects, such as the futuristic new capital, Brasília. It was these peasants and workers, the 'victims of the economic miracle', as they would be known in later decades, who were to become the protagonists of the Marxist-influenced cultural projects such as the Cinema Novo movement, the Arena, Oficina and Opinião theatre groups, the Street Guitar poetry movement and the new forms of political songwriting that were grouped under the name 'canção de protesto' or 'protest song'.

Indeed, while an organizational and theoretical focus for these various initiatives was provided by the Communist-led Popular Culture Centres, music arguably acted as an equally cohesive force at an artistic level. Politically sympathetic musicians who had gained a reputation as songwriters and performers in their own right were now also typically called upon to provide the musical soundtracks or scores for films and plays. Through this political apprenticeship many former practitioners of bossa nova made their own critique of the musical avant-garde, renouncing what they saw as the style's 'foreignness', its ideological conformism and its alienation both from the country's 'authentic' popular musical traditions and the experiences of the rural and urban poor at this moment of traumatic socio-economic upheaval.

Such arguments were given added intensity by the coup that brought a military dictatorship to power in 1964, further opening up the economy and society to the influence of multinational capital. On the one hand the regime sought to enforce a 'nationalist' loyalty to its developmentalist aims by political and ideological means: outright repression of organized labour and the political opposition and, simultaneously, the projection of a propagandist self-image of well-being and unanimity through the celebration of mass cultural events like football and carnival, and slogans such as 'Brazil – love it or leave it'. On the other hand, the effect of the state-led boom, known from 1968 onwards as the 'Economic Miracle' for its annual growth rates of 10 per cent, was to internationalize Brazil's culture and society, exposing the new consumer market to North American lifestyle models through the channels of the mass media.

Television, in particular, played an instrumental role in shaping the ambivalent character of mass culture in its national and international dimensions and also, consequently, of the evolution of popular music, as it was forced to respond to the challenge of the new medium. The importance of television between its appearance in Brazil in 1950 and the end of the period under consideration here cannot be compared with that which it holds today, when TV Globo is considered the world's fourth largest commercial network. It was precisely from the late 1960s, the beginning of the 'Miracle' itself, that a sufficiently mass audience for consumer goods began to attract major advertising revenues, and the dominance of this mass audience by TV Globo only became evident from the late 1970s. Nevertheless, the 1960s were the crucial decade in the emergence and official promotion of the first televisual medium with truly national scope.

Radio had been organized chiefly at local and regional level, and was, therefore, more directly expressive of popular cultural interests. Music programming reflected this, with both live and recorded broadcasts promoting local, traditional forms and 'popularizing' them across the country as rural northeastern music travelled southwards with the flux of internal migration. By contrast, the development of an elite-dominated general tele-communications system served government needs to radiate its messages of economic developmentalism and nationalist propa-ganda outwards from the centre to the periphery, reinforcing an identification between regional interests and those of the state.[2] The lifestyle aspirations that it projected were for much of the decade those of the middle-class consumers with the necessary purchasing power to acquire television sets – these still only num-bered three-quarters of a million in 1960, when the first televised song festivals were broadcast.

Song contests, in which compositions and performers were awarded prizes by a voting audience, had first enjoyed popularity in the 1920s and '30s, before radio broadcasting began to offer widespread access to live performances. By the 1940s and '50s, however, the role of mobilizing the listening public in favour of commercially recorded songs had passed to fan-clubs organized through the major music programmes. It was the new promo-tional possibilities opened up by television which led to the revival of live competitive festivals in the 1960s, especially from 1965 onwards, when the TV Excelsior network and the newly created TV Globo began systematically to target the urban middle-class youth of São Paulo and Rio de Janeiro. Photographic records of the period reveal a markedly white, middle-class attendance at the live televised festivals, by contrast to the poorer, black and mixed-race presence at the radio contests of previous decades.[3]

At the same time, the interests of advertising sponsors, broadcasters, recording companies and venue promoters, facing the challenge of imported forms of mass music, including rock, converged in imposing a demand for musical arrangements that conformed to an undifferentiated, generically 'international' sound. Such pressures were built into the structure of the annual International Song Festivals that the state tourist office of Rio de Janeiro (at that time the State of Guanabara) was persuaded to organize in the city's Maracanãzinho arena from 1966 onwards. Modelled on the San Remo Festival, the event was divided into two parts: 'the first, intended to choose the Brazilian song which will compete with the songs representing the other participating countries; the second, intended to choose the best international song, including the Brazilian entry, out of the countries registered'.[4]

The challenge faced by the protest song movement was not merely the need to offer an ideological alternative to the state's developmentalist rhetoric and its conception of popular and national identity. The new media and commercial conditions in which musical production now operated placed more formidable barriers in the way of constructing a cultural alliance or community between the politicized vanguard of musicians and their imagined 'popular' audience. Paradoxically, the orthodox left's reaction to the modernization and internationalization of Brazilian culture was symptomatic of an idealistic isolation from the realities of the 1960s, which prevented it engaging critically and creatively with the new mass culture. Repudiating the cosmopolitan sophistication and modernity of bossa nova, the protest songwriters aimed to project a public message of denunciation and resistance drawing on the traditions and experiences of those very sectors of the population most severely victimized by the country's industrial revolution and later on by the dictatorship. Urban and rural musical traditions such as *samba de roda* (circle-dance), the rural folk ballad and the playing of the *berimbau* (a tuned, percussive bow used to accompany the combat game of *capoeira*) were to be employed to restore a national-popular authenticity to the song of political protest, against the imported, 'Americanized' culture that bossa nova, and increasingly rock, were held to represent.

Ironically, though, the vehicles through which this music of popular, anti-imperialist protest was heard were increasingly the very media that the modernizing regime had been responsible for promoting and organizing – in particular the televised shows and song contests. At the same time, the exclusion of the vast majority of workers and peasants from participation in this new culture industry exposed a contradiction at the heart of the protest movement: between its essentially middle-class constituency and the 'popular' classes in whose name it claimed to speak.

In September 1968 these contradictions were brought to a dramatic climax. In Rio de Janeiro's Maracanãzinho arena an enraged audience of 30,000 joined in the encore of Geraldo Vandré's 'Caminhando' with spectators leaning from their apartment windows outside. They had just learned of the decision of the jury of the 3rd International Song Festival, organized by the TV Globo network, to deny it first place in the face of overwhelming audience approval. Thereafter commercial distribution of the live recording of that performance of the song was banned on account of its 'psychologically damaging message of revolutionary war against the Brazilian regime'. Called to answer an inquiry for ' activities contrary to National Security', Vandré found himself among those forced to leave the country by the end of the year, as a wave of strikes, demonstrations and left-wing guerrilla activity against the military dictatorship was answered with the closure of Congress and the suspension of political and civil rights, heralding a new and brutal phase of authoritarian rule.[5]

But what kind of challenge, revolutionary or otherwise, did this collective performance of Vandré's protest anthem really pose to the regime, to its developmentalist agenda and repressive aims,

Geraldo Vandré, Rio de Janeiro, 1967.

or to the forms of song which had preceded it? Certainly, 'Caminhando' – with its simple, sombre melody, solemnly pedestrian chords
and its call to 'Come, let's get going/ For by waiting we'll never
know/ If you know then you make your time/ You don't wait for
it to come' – was a far cry from the sophisticated, conversational
intimacy and playfulness of the bossa nova recordings which
had, in their own way, revolutionized Brazilian popular music just
a decade before. In almost every respect – melodically, harmonically, rhythmically, vocally, instrumentally and lyrically – Vandré
had broken with the ten-year-old bossa nova tradition. As such,
'Caminhando' represented the logical outcome of efforts to

politicize a music that was considered, at best, to have abstained from the struggles preceding and following the 1964 coup and, at worst, to have endorsed the spirit of post-war capitalist modernization. But to what extent was the new song actually capable of mobilizing the imagination and sensibility of a broadly 'popular' audience towards conscious political action?

Writing in 1968, the Brazilian critic Walnice Nogueira Galvão arrived at a disturbingly pessimistic assessment of the output of the 'protest song' as represented by the work of Geraldo Vandré and of contemporaries such as Edu Lobo, Caetano Veloso, Gilberto Gil and Chico Buarque. For Galvão, despite the new song's commitment to 'an everyday, present reality, to the "here and now"', it did little more than replace the obviously ideological, 'escapist complacency' of bossa nova, and its mythology of 'sun, sea and sand', with a new and equally reassuring mythology. Its ubiquitous theme, 'The day will come', substituted the redemptive power of the song itself for any kind of real action, which was postponed to some hypothetical, utopian future. The 'people' were thus consigned to passivity as 'listeners', absolved of responsibility and denied any agency as the subjects of their history.[6]

Galvão makes an indisputable case for this argument, marshalling an overwhelming body of textual evidence in support of her analysis. However, popular song is clearly much more than simply text or ideological 'message'. First and foremost, and this is crucial to the specific period under consideration, like all forms of music it is the performance of organized sounds, including those of vocalized language. The significance and communicative power of these sounds are only realized as a social process in so far as the performative act is capable of articulating and engaging a community of musicians and listeners in a form of social intercourse.[7] If we are to understand the trajectory of Brazilian popular music from bossa nova to the 'protest song' of the late 1960s, then it must be with this perspective on the evolution of the tradition as social practice. For a central feature of cultural debate and activity through this decade was precisely the assumption that 'popular culture', including song, constituted a terrain of dispute within which rival voices and stylistic traditions were competing for the loyalties of a heterogeneous population of potential listeners. In the balance of forces between the authoritarian, developmentalist state and the left-wing, reformist movement, music offered one important means of constructing alternative forms of community, defining and redefining notions of what was a shared 'popular' or 'national' culture.

The 'players' in this arena of competing voices and listeners were, first, the professionalized middle-class youth of Brazil's major cities. This generation was a product and beneficiary of the 1950s modernization drive, and it provided bossa nova with its songwriters, performers and initial audience. Second, emerging from the intellectual and student wing of this new middle class, was a group of politicized left-wing cultural activists. In the apparently favourable climate of João Goulart's reformist government (1961–4), these activists aimed, in a variety of projects, to reflect the experiences and aspirations of the rural and urban workforce, which was now being organized and mobilized in the defence of its demands. Third, there were the working-class and peasant communities themselves, which the projects associated with the Popular Culture Centres and their theory of a revolutionary culture sought to engage as allies in a broadly 'popular' movement of social and political transformation.

By 1968, however, the idea of such a movement, and the popular alliance of progressive middle-class, intellectual and mass interests that it implied, had become especially problematic. The military dictatorship which came to power in 1964 had systematically severed the organized political links between workers, peasants, students and intellectuals that had emerged since the beginning of the decade. The key activists responsible for building these links between the grassroots popular movement and the political vanguard were eliminated through imprisonment or worse. Isolated from the revolutionary classes on whose behalf it claimed to speak, the left-wing intelligentsia was considered innocuous enough by the regime to be permitted to continue its theoretical and cultural activities relatively unimpeded, for the time being at least. At the same time, the regime's strategy of investment and state intervention in the culture industry aimed to demobilize the movement on a different level by creating a compliant, passive population of consumers for the new nationalist propaganda and its vehicle, the mass media industry, which was to be dominated by television.

The musical history of the decade up to 1968 dramatizes the efforts to construct new forms of audience/performer community against this background of socio-economic, political and cultural upheaval. Not only the songs' lyrics, but also their musical structures, instrumental styles and modes and conditions of performance, express in their 'posture' or idiom different possibilities for the 'socialization of the self',[8] and for constructing alternative kinds of subjectivity within the new middle-class urban community and beyond its ranks. In the account which follows, we shall see how the evolution of these musical idioms was also shaped by objective factors. If, on the one hand, they represented different ways of responding to the demand for cultural practice to perform a conscious political intervention, they were, on the other, equally influenced by the economic pressures of commercial competition, in the form of Brazil's nascent rock industry, and by the other cultural activities through which they were often mediated, such as theatre, cinema and the television song contest.

## ROCK AND REVOLUTION: FROM THE CITY-STAGE TO THE FAVELA

As early as 1960, whatever spirit of consensus and community the bossa nova movement had momentarily been able to sustain was showing signs of strain. The first symptom of this was a celebrated rift between composers Carlos Lyra and Ronaldo Bôscoli. Whether, as has been suggested, the split reflected Lyra's jealousy of the songwriting partnership between Bôscoli and Roberto Menescal, or his objection to Bôscoli's political conservatism,[9] it seems that personal and ideological differences had coincided or were reinforcing each other. Lyra was by now participating with another longstanding member of the bossa nova fraternity, Sérgio Ricardo, in meetings at the National Students Union headquarters that led to the creation of the Centre of Popular Culture, subsequently renamed the Popular Culture Centre (CPC). Echoing Ricardo's concern that bossa nova had distanced itself from the country's local, popular traditions, Lyra argued that the preoccupation with musical form had left the question of ideological content unclear.[10] By November 1962, with the benefit of hindsight, he was able to claim somewhat prematurely that

> Bossa Nova was destined to live only for a brief time. It was just a musically new way of repeating the same romantic and inconsequential things that were being said long since. It didn't alter the content of the lyrics. The only path is nationalism. Nationalism in music isn't provincialism.[11]

However, it is clear that well before a precise definition of this notion of musical nationalism had been worked out, other, commercial pressures had come into play. Lyra and Bôscoli had signed recording contracts with the Philips and Odeon labels respectively, and the rivalry between them was thus transferred to the marketplace. In the live arena, too, the competition for audience loyalties was opening up. May 1960 saw two shows on the same evening: Bôscoli's 'Night of Love, Smiles and Flowers', staged in Rio de Janeiro's Faculty of Architecture, and Lyra's 'Sambalanço Night', at the Catholic PUC University.[12]

This more aggressive projection of bossa nova into the commercial market was in part a conscious response to the challenge posed by U.s.-style rock'n'roll, which had offered an alternative pole of attraction to Brazil's middle-class urban youth since the mid-1950s. The first local recording was Nora Ney's English cover of 'Rock Around the Clock', released in November 1955, and the film of the same title was screened in São Paulo the following year. When reports emerged of cinema audiences dancing in the aisles and 'rioting', State Governor Jânio Quadros ordered the police to intervene and restore order. In May 1957 the first Brazilian rock composition, Miguel Gustavo's 'Rock and Roll em Copacabana', recorded by Cauby Peixoto, was released and the industry took off with local artists covering originals in English to supplement the import market.[13]

Until 1958, however, there were no specialized musicians, only popular singers who also performed rock compositions, such as Cauby Peixoto, Agostinho dos Santos, Lana Bitencourt and Nora Ney. The case of Sérgio Murilo illustrates the vacillations within the performing community in its divided musical loyalties. In 1960 Murilo was still hesitating between bossa nova and rock, having recorded his own version of 'Chega de saudade', when the success of 'Marcianita' made him turn definitively to rock.[14] A similar path was followed by the now legendary romantic pop singer Roberto Carlos, who, in these early years, had been performing both sambas and rock. After a row between Sérgio Murilo and his recording company, Columbia/CBS, the latter targeted Roberto Carlos, who shifted lock, stock and barrel to the new music and went on to make his name in Rio.[15] In the guitar 'academies', too,

which had been an important training-ground for the bossa nova
generation, young middle-class women were both learning the pre-
bossa compositions of Maysa and Dolores Duran and attempting
the style of the new rock'n'roll.[16]

In 1960, for the first time, the media gave full publicity to
a homegrown rock star, Celly Campello, the 'Darling of Brazil',
whose music was played extensively on the radio, and who
collaborated with the promotional mechanisms that were being
developed for the consumer market, recording advertising jingles
and lending her name and endorsement to a children's doll. The
appearance of the first Brazilian rock magazine in August 1960
marked the consolidation of the industry, which, by early 1962,
boasted an extensive repertoire of covers of U.S. hits as well as
original material, a domestic pool of specialized instrumentalists,
and films, radio and TV shows.[17] This was the same year in which
bossa nova made its first venture into the international market,
following a legendary concert at New York's Carnegie Hall on
21 November. Despite poor organization, it was a sell-out, acting
as a showcase for some of the leading bossa novistas, such as João
Gilberto, Luís Bonfá and Oscar Castro-Neves. With the enthusi-
astic presence of local jazz musicians such as Stan Getz, Charlie
Byrd and Gary Burton, it exposed the new style to a wider, international musical audience, winning recording contracts for a
number of Brazilian artists.

The competition between bossa nova and rock within the
Brazilian market was summed up by Ronaldo Bôscoli: on the
advice of Odeon label's musical director, André Midany, he and
Carlos Lyra composed 'Lobo bobo',

> to see if there was any identification with people. We created
> the bossa nova movement to defend Brazilian music from the
> phantom of Rock, which at that time was selling 70 per cent
> of the market. In 1962, I heard that same man, Midany, say:

'Ronaldo Bôscoli, your movement has now taken Brazilian music to the point where it's selling half and half, 50 per cent.'[18]

The market was thus divided down the middle between the Dionysian appeal of rock, with its celebration of sonic intensity and movement in all its physical, bodily ecstasy (suggesting, in this sense, a modern, cosmopolitan and industrial alternative to the music of carnival) and the Apollonian rationality and intimacy of bossa nova.

Now, however, amid the political ferment of Goulart's reformist administration, popular music was required to mobilize its audience towards a different purpose, according to a new, consciously ideological rationality. In December 1961 the Popular Culture Centre (CPC) launched a series of projects under the leadership of film-maker Leon Hirszmann, dramatist Oduvaldo Viana Filho and Carlos Estevam Martins. The movement's pre-*Manifesto*, drawn up in the following year, dictated the principles by which a revolutionary, popular art might transform the political consciousness of its audience so as to challenge the prevailing ideas:

> Instead of man isolated in his individuality, lost forever in the intricate meanderings of introspection, our art must carry to the people the human meaning of oil and steel, political parties and class associations, rates of production and financial mechanisms.[19]

The precondition for this possibility was the relative autonomy of art, in the Marxist language of the time, as an element of the social superstructure, and its capacity to produce substantial effects in the base, that is to say, in the less advanced material structures of society: 'If it were not possible for consciousness to overtake the social being and become, to a certain degree, a modifying force on the social being, neither revolutionary art nor the CPC would be feasible.'[20]

The CPC's interpretation of the role of vanguard leadership, as an ideologically advanced political consciousness at the head of a mass audience, points up the central problem facing what was essentially an intellectual movement, one which lacked organic roots within the popular classes it was claiming to speak to, as well as for. If, as was assumed to be the case, this self-appointed leadership was the bearer of a more evolved political understanding of the world, then a voluntaristic ideological leap of social consciousness would be necessary for the revolutionary artist to shrug off his petty-bourgeois assumptions, and identify with the 'people'. Thus 'the members of the CPC have opted to be of the people, to be an integral part of the people, detachments of its army on the cultural front'.[21] At the same time, there must be no 'romantic' concessions to the popular consciousness in its backward state of cultural development; a revolutionary popular art could not simply be the 'formalization of the spontaneous manifestations of the people'. Rather its *popular* legitimacy would reside in the ability to 'popularize not the work or the artist who produces it, but the individual receiving it and in making him the politicized author of the polis'.[22]

The challenge of overcoming this disparity between the cultural and political development of the revolutionary artist and that of his popular audience was addressed in the pre-*Manifesto*'s analysis of the relationship between form and content. On the one hand, a popular revolutionary art 'aspires . . . to intensify in each individual his awareness of belonging to the social whole; it seeks to invest in him the possession of common values and collective aspirations, thus consolidating his spiritual insertion into the entirety of communitary interests'.[23] But while this revolutionary consciousness must be 'brought' to the people from beyond its ranks, the materials, forms and aesthetic criteria required for its artistic expression would have to meet the need for accessibility and would therefore be drawn from the cultural traditions of the popular audience itself. The revolutionary artist would have to place formal limits on his own creative initiative so as to match the relatively primitive cultural resources available to the popular audience in responding to its experiences, 'rendering dynamic the stereotypes it uses and obliging them to yield the maximum eloquence possible'.[24]

The CPC pre-*Manifesto*'s theoretical formulation was thus an attempt to address the broad challenge facing all the revolutionary, left-populist projects of the next seven years, including the protest-song movement: how to bridge the social and cultural distance that the new political situation had exposed between the post-bossa artistic vanguard and the mass of urban and rural workers and their traditions. Yet while there seems to have been a degree of consensus about the need to reclaim some of the stylistic and technical resources of pre-bossa traditions in popular music, the CPC formula, combining 'popular' form with revolutionary content, was not adopted uncritically or unproblematically by the movement's adherents.

Former architecture student Carlos Lyra and law student Geraldo Vandré made their first contact with left-wing political ideas during a visit to São Paulo to record a bossa nova show. Together they composed the song 'Quem quiser encontrar o amor' (If you want to find love) for new-wave film-maker Joaquim Pedro de Andrade's documentary short *Couro de gato* (Cat-skin, 1960). Lyra also went on to write the music for the Arena theatre production *A mais valia vai se acabar* (There'll be no more surplus-value), by Oduvaldo Viana Filho, when it was brought from São Paulo to Rio. However, Lyra soon opposed that faction within the CPC which 'believed they should make music with lyrics by educated guys talking about political realities and truths. I was against that because then it would just be

Zé Kéti was one of the key roots samba performers who collaborated with the second generation of politically committed bossa nova artists.

pamphleteering.'[25] Vandré soon left the movement altogether, protesting along similar lines: 'Art isn't a pamphlet!'

With the support of poet Ferreira Gullar, Lyra had won the argument to change the original name, Centre of Popular Culture (CCP), to Popular Centre of Culture (CPC). This apparently minor modification actually stood for an important political distinction, reflecting Lyra's preference for a broadly inclusive project open to all tendencies, as against the narrowly workerist position of the more idealist, would-be slum-dwellers among the revolutionary intellectuals: 'I'm a bourgeois, I don't make popular culture, I make bourgeois culture, there's no avoiding that.'[26] To identify with, or take inspiration from, the roots traditions of the *samba de morro* (shanty-town samba) did not necessarily mean taking up residence there. Lyra's statement was an honest recognition that the social and cultural divide between the hillside slums and the middle-class apartment blocks below could not be abolished overnight by a voluntaristic effort of will or imagination.

Lyra's approach instead insisted on incorporating the technical innovations of the classical bossa nova style within a more socially conscious and critical idiom. As Vandré put it, the success of 'Quem quiser encontrar o amor' 'coincided with a moment when Lyra's group was making an attempt to use the artisanal resources of an essentially jazz culture in the service of a national culture'.[27] Gilberto Gil later observed that Lyra's contribution to the debate was the elaboration of a dramatic musical texture: 'It was that idea of the music incorporating or trying to incorporate, explicitly, elements of theatricality, the specific colours of the people.'[28] This solution, shaping the textural possibilities developed within the bossa nova tradition to a new cultural landscape, was also pursued by Lyra's fellow traveller Sérgio Ricardo.

In Ricardo's case, though, this development was stimulated particularly by his involvement in cinema, and the need to integrate the musical soundtrack into a dynamic visual fabric. As early as 1960 he had been criticized by bossa nova purists for his dramatic composition 'Zelão', which used a solo/chorus dialogue to depict a shanty-town's collective grief for the *sambista* whose shack is swept down the hillside by a flood. This precipitated Ricardo's departure for the CPC, where he met the film-maker Ruy Guerra.[29] But, as he recalls, his blend of bossa nova lyricism and social comment sat just as uncomfortably with the CPC's orthodox formula of popular form and revolutionary content.[30] 'A Fábrica' (The Factory), from the film *Esse mundo é meu* (This world is mine), which was screened on 1 April 1964, the first day of the military dictatorship, was a daringly orchestrated arrangement for its time.

The polyrhythmic beat and instrumental colouring of the bossa nova idiom were shaped to reproduce the rhythms and noises of life in an automobile parts factory, with its interplay of human and mechanical sounds. The worker's brief daydream fantasy of a world of pleasure and plenty is abruptly ended by the factory whistle, awakening him once more to the reality of his daily routine.

In Carlos Lyra's work, meanwhile, the dramatic intention took the form of a kind of musical dialogue between the bossa nova and samba traditions, which echoed the problematic relationship between the cultural vanguard and its popular counterpart, between the city and the *favela*. Lyra's 1962 composition 'Influência do jazz' was a musically enacted obituary for the traditional samba, which had 'been mixing and modernizing and got lost' under the sway of jazz-influenced rhythms. After a central pastiche of the 'twisting, complicating' Afro-Cuban dance style that was supposedly killing the 'side-to-side' swing of the samba, the song returns to its roots in the *favela* for help, 'So it won't be a samba with too many notes, a front to back twisted samba'.

Between 1961 and 1964, Lyra's musical dialogue with the *samba de morro* was transferred to the stage in the compositions he produced for the Arena project. For example, 'Feio não é bonito' (Ugly ain't pretty), co-written with dramatist Gianfrancesco Guarnieri, reproduced the familiar bossa nova structure of a melodic pattern repeated in different registers over a descending chromatic harmony. But its theme, in a sombre minor key, was the title's anti-romantic depiction of the *favela*, which 'is brave and never lets itself be broken', yet which also cries out for 'a different [hi]story'. The song's other innovation was to counterpose this solo statement of love of, and for, the *favela*, against an ironic pastiche of the nationalistic *samba-exaltação* sung by a chorus in a cheerful major key: 'Hooray for the beauties of this my Brazil/ With its past and tradition/ And hooray for the shanty full of glory / With its schools that speak of its history of samba.' In a somewhat moralistic and sentimental gesture of solidarity, 'Love the *morro*, love', the old national-populist mythology of the 1930s and '40s is usurped by an 'authentic' populism, the 'true story' as told by the soloist.

The hybrid structure and style of the song, however, left its contradictions curiously intact: solo and chorus, bossa nova and samba, reality and mythology, continued to inhabit separate sides of the social, cultural and ideological divide. Like the 'poor little rich girl' of the Lyra / Moraes musical comedy *Pobre menina rica*, the radicalized bourgeois intellectual-artist was trapped inside an inescapable social identity of illusory wealth and privilege, which were, of course, not illusory at all, but constituted real obstacles in the way of a genuinely classless, 'popular' solidarity.

Vocalist Nara Leão dramatized this dilemma in her musical interventions on and off the stage, as both singer and militant CPC activist. While still a teenager she had met the leading figures of the bossa nova fraternity and became known as the 'muse' of the movement (although she was much more than this), with her parents' Copacabana apartment serving as a frequent venue for its meetings. In 1963, at Vinicius de Moraes's invitation, she played the 'poor little rich girl' herself in the stage musical. Then, in the same year, Carlos Lyra introduced her to the old-guard *sambistas* Cartola, Nelson Cavaquinho and the Portela samba-school's composer, Zé Kéti. The outcome of these collaborations was two albums, *Nara* (1963) and *Opinião de Nara* (1964), the second of which definitively split the bossa nova movement just months after the military coup of 31 March 1964. It was an anthology of the songs produced for Oduvaldo Viana Filho's show *Opinião* (Opinion), which voiced the orthodox left's protest against the dictatorship through the themes of urban poverty and the rural struggle for land reform. Leão publicly disowned the 'bourgeois introspection' of bossa nova to take on the voice of popular tradition and protest:

Enough of Bossa Nova. No more singing some little apartment song for two or three intellectuals. I want the pure samba, which has much more to say, which is the expression of the people, and not something made by one little group for another little group . . . I don't want to spend the rest of my life singing 'The Girl from Ipanema' and, even less, in English. I want to be understood, I want to be a singer of the people.[32]

Nara Leão's performance of Zé Kéti's 'Diz que fui por aí' (Say I've gone over there) captured perfectly this voluntaristic populism, with a classic, soft-spoken bossa nova melody announcing her departure for the *favela*: 'Carrying a guitar under my arm / I stop at any corner / I walk into any bar / If there's a reason / It's one more samba for me to play.' The surely redundant claim, 'I've got lots of friends, I'm popular', smacks self-consciously of wishful thinking rather than fact, the longing of someone inhabiting a cultural and social limbo between Rio's beachside residences and the hillsides above: 'If they want to know / Whether I'm coming back, say that I am, / But only after this longing leaves me . . . / I'm in the city, I'm in the *favela* / I'm over there, always thinking of the *favela*.'

In December 1964 Nara Leão was replaced in the *Opinião* show by Maria Bethânia, who had arrived from the northeastern city of Salvador da Bahia with a new generation of musicians who would become known as the *baianos*, and who included Gal Costa, Gilberto Gil, Tom Zé and Caetano Veloso. By contrast to Leão's more fragile, girlish delivery, Bethânia's richly sonorous voice represented a radical new departure in the projection of the music's political message, which reflected more closely the thinking of the CPC:

Our greatest contradiction as artists is that of going for an aesthetic and formal development for which the people we

Album cover for Nara Leão's *Manhã de Liberdade*, 1966.

are addressing are not ready . . . I have the impression that
it would be a mistake for us to go back to João Gilberto.
We have to face reality. And the present reality is one of
stridency. Today's youth loves stridency, because it represents
modern civilization. Maria Bethânia is herself the negation
of João Gilberto.[32]

Bethânia's performance of the João do Vale composition 'Carcará'
epitomized this new style of vocal projection. The song, which
took as its theme a bird of prey in order to celebrate the resilience

of the northeast's legions of peasant migrants, courageously fighting for their sustenance, was prohibited by the censor in São Paulo:

> In vain. The authors of the show, in order to obtain its release, replaced the figures about northeastern migration with others about the successes of the country's textile industry. But the rage with which Bethânia recited the new figures was a protest in itself. The audience understood and applauded on their feet. The single of 'Carcará' that she recorded in São Paulo sold out in three days.[33]

Her singing, too, reinforced that aggressive message by emphasizing the irregular stresses of the bossa nova rhythm in a semi-shouted delivery. Bethânia herself identified an additional stylistic problem, which was to mark a further shift in the new protest music away from its avant-garde predecessor:

> I believe that Bossa Nova addicted composers to something which has got lost in protest music: dissonant chords. That's something that protest music broke with completely. The dissonant chord is a very wishy-washy kind of thing and for protest music you need something more aggressive.[34]

Once again these changes must also be seen in large part as a response to a renewed challenge from the aggressively commercial rock industry, which, in the wake of the military coup, was seeking to occupy an expanded mass market. Up to this point, the promotion of rock, or 'iê-iê-iê; as it became known (mimicking The Beatles' refrain 'Yeah, yeah, yeah'), had been hampered by limited television and radio coverage, and by taxes and other restrictions affecting the phonographic industry. The TV rock programme *Reino da Juventude* (Kingdom of Youth) was confined to a daytime slot, while the bossa nova shows *O Fino da Bossa*

(The Cream of Bossa) and *Bossaudade* (Bossalonging) enjoyed prime-time evening exposure. And so, on 16 July 1964, the 'Clube do Clan' (Club of the Clan) was founded in São Paulo to (first) 'defend intransigently the interests of every young music artist in all their forms' and (second) 'organize festivals at a national and international level'.[35] The Club acquired its own exclusive programme on São Paulo's Rádio Nacional every Saturday at 7.30 pm, attracting members via publicity in the Brazilian magazine *Intervalo* and its American stablemate *Cash-box*. Opposition from popular music traditionalists and bossa nova loyalists turned to protest, especially when the Clube do Clan attempted to end the practice of free air-time for disc jockeys promoting 'national', that is, traditional, non-rock artists. Pressure from broadcasters and journalists forced the Club to retreat and, from a position where it boasted 80 per cent audience support, it had virtually disappeared by early 1965.

Despite this initial setback, the rock industry continued to make great strides. After a successful run of international festivals, the annual 'Chico Viola' prize was awarded by TV Record (the Globo Network of its day) in 1965 to Ronnie Cord for 'Rua Augusta' (Augusta Street), to Demetrius for 'Ritmo da Chuva' (Rhythm of the Rain), and Roberto Carlos for 'É proibido Fumar' (No smoking allowed). As The Beatles rose to international fame, Carlos enjoyed a long run at the top of the hit parade with his LP *Canta para a Juventude* (Sing for Youth) and the single 'A história de um homem mau' (Story of a bad man).[36] The rock programme *Jovem Guarda* (Young Guard) went on the air every Sunday afternoon from 1965 to 1968 on TV Record's Channel 7 and shot to national prominence. With the promotional machinery set in motion by the Magaldi, Maia & Prosperi advertising company, the programme became a vehicle for the marketing of consumer goods under the brand names of Calhambeque (trousers), Tremendão (amplifiers) and Ternurinha (dolls, perfumes, clothes and records.)

The softening of the initially more offensive aspects of live rock performance made its acceptance possible by people of all ages, so the new rock artists achieved the kind of national popular impact that their bossa nova counterparts never could.[37] More important still, Roberto Carlos and the *Jovem Guarda* fulfilled a crucial ideological role in winning away its middle-class youth audience from a conscious political reflection on the nature of the regime: 'In this respect, the Jovem Guarda, as a thermometer of changes in young people's behaviour, channels the interest of the youth, alienating him from the political crisis into which the country was sinking.'[38] Roberto Carlos et al. were a reassuring symbol of rebellious youth that had adapted to respectable values and were capable of being loved by 'heads of family'; they had been divested of its more threatening expressive features. Consequently, it has been argued, 'Brazilian iê-iê-iê doubtless helped to suffocate the protest movement into which Bossa Nova had drifted.'[39]

## GOD AND THE DEVIL IN THE LAND OF THE SUN: PRAYER, EPIC AND THE TV CONTEST

Two factors became apparent in the wake of the coup of 1964 and the reinvigoration of the rock industry. First was the surprising realization that, as Roberto Schwarz put it, despite the political dictatorship of the right there was a relative cultural and intellectual hegemony of the left in the country.[40] The socialist intelligentsia, which had been preparing itself for prison, unemployment and exile, was spared for the time being, while torture and prolonged imprisonment were reserved exclusively for those who had organized contact with workers, peasants, sailors and soldiers:

> Whereas on that occasion the bridges between the cultural movement and the masses were severed, the Castelo Branco

government did not prevent the theoretical or artistic circulation of leftwing thinking which, although within a narrow area, flourished to an extraordinary degree.[41]

The viable 'popular' audience for the cultural left was now much more clearly confined to its immediate social periphery, the middle class.

Second, it was clear that the urban idioms of samba and bossa nova were losing the battle to compete for the attention of that audience with the industrial vigour of electrified rock. It was with this understanding that the new-wave film-maker Glauber Rocha, the director of *Deus e o Diabo na Terra do Sol* (God and the Devil in the Land of the Sun, 1964), approached Carlos Lyra, Geraldo Vandré and Sérgio Ricardo with a new proposition: a music that would draw its expressivity from the technologically raw primitiveness of rural traditions and instrumentation:

> One of the things that Glauber defended greatly was this: if technically we wanted it to be nice and pretty, nicely made, nicely finished off, we would end up urbanizing it. The important thing was to be able to draw out that anguish from the Brazilian people, which comes from the underdeveloped form of its laments. If we gave the process of communication an evolved form, it would sound false.[42]

The decisive step in this direction came with Vandré's recording in 1966 of 'Disparada' (Stampede), which he composed with Théo de Barros for the film *A hora e vez de Augusto Matraga* (Roberto Santos, 1965), a depiction of the harsh violence and religiosity of the rural interior. Vandré himself explained the significance of the song in terms of its ability to project the 'sound' of this mass rural experience onto a national stage:

Any manifestation of a national culture that has no support amongst the urban middle class, which will stand up for itself and its interests, has no way of asserting itself within the national mentality. The *moda de viola* [guitar-accompanied rural folk-song] is the most proletarian of these manifestations. *Disparada* broke that middle-class prejudice, but not by virtue of its harmonic or poetic poverty. Harmonically and poetically, the American hillbilly folksong is as impoverished as our own, yet is accepted throughout the world. But a whole line ought to follow from *Disparada*. If it hasn't it is just through a lack of investment and the low regard of middle-class musicians for a manifestation of culture which, whether they like it or not, represents the only way of singing for 60 or 70 per cent of the Brazilian population, rural populations of the states of Mato Grosso, Goiás, Minas, Paraná, Santa Catarina and Rio Grande do Sul.[43]

Caetano Veloso agreed that Vandré's adoption of the *moda de viola* constituted a turning-point in the elaboration of a more vigorous formal vehicle for the protest message:

With its epic lyrical structure, its narrative literature tending towards violence, and its simple musical structure as the basis of a banal style of song . . . and its artisanal approach to presentation . . . *Disparada* is the first clear attempt to make a strong, industrial Brazilian music, something like 'iê-iê-iê'.[44]

But before this complete rupture with the bossa nova idiom, other options were being explored to inject into the latter's modern rationality something of the spirit of the pre-urban, regional traditions of popular culture. Whereas the epic narrative approach based on the peasant ballad encouraged a didactic, even antagonistic posture, this alternative current sought to recuperate the

Baden Powell performing in 1963.

communitarian spirit associated with Afro-Brazilian religiosity. Rhythms linked to dance, worship and physical combat became the central structural elements of songs that invoked solidarity and action through prayer and movement.

The first key instigator of this development was the mixed-race guitarist and bossa nova composer Baden Powell, who had been raised in Rio de Janeiro's hillside community of Pedregulho, in the famous neighbourhood of Mangueira. In 1961 Baden Powell was introduced by Vinicius de Moraes to recordings of several Afro-Brazilian forms from the northeast: the *samba de roda*, a circle dance accompanied by handclapping and percussion, and one of the oldest forerunners of modern samba; the heavily percussive music of *candomblé*, the West African-derived animist religion centring on trance and possession; and the music of the *berimbau*, a stringed wooden bow amplified with a gourd, played by striking a metal or rubber string with a stick, and used as the tuned rhythmic accompaniment to the combat game of *capoeira*. In early 1963, after visiting Bahia to experience the sounds directly, Baden Powell began to compose with Vinicius a series of 'Afro-sambas' and other songs based on these rhythms.

The composition simply entitled 'Berimbau', now a classic, illustrates how melody, lyrics, harmony and instrumentation had now become subordinated to the rhythmic theme, whose functions combined incantation and initiation. Against a constant bass, Baden Powell reproduces on the upper guitar strings the two-tone figure of the *berimbau*, which is matched by what is essentially a vocalized inflection of the same two-note pattern, supported by a much reduced harmonic repertoire of two alternating chords (Dm7 and Am7). The movement is no longer the cycle of dissonance and harmonization found in the classic model of bossa nova. Rather, it is a single, reiterated pattern fixed on a stable centre towards which the listener is drawn hypnotically, as if to be educated in the art. It has its lyrical counterpart in a series of aphoristic lessons in the struggle of life, which argue against betrayal and injustice in favour of the values of integrity and solidarity:

| | |
|---|---|
| *Quem é homem de bem não trai* | The man who's good won't betray |
| *O amor que lhe quer seu bem...* | The love that only wants the best for him ... |
| *Quem de dentro de si não sai* | Whoever won't come out of himself |
| *Vai morrer sem amar ninguém* | Will die without loving anyone |
| *O dinheiro de quem não dá* | The money that belongs to one who won't give |
| *É o trabalho de quem não tem* | Is the labour of the one who has none |
| *Capoeira que é bom não cai* | The capoeira who's good won't fall |
| *Mas se um dia ele cai, cai bem* | And if one day he falls, he'll fall well. |

The only departure from this oscillating pattern is a dramatic coda in a more familiar melodic and harmonic style, which announces the *capoeira* player's arrival to fight for love.

'Samba da bênção'(Samba of blessing, 1965), meanwhile, though based on an equally simple two-chord pattern and inflected melody, takes up the more relaxed, swinging rhythm of the Bahian samba. Its balanced aphorisms celebrate the equilibrium of the 'prayer-like' samba, a combination of melancholy and joy, the 'dark' oppression of its historical origins and the 'white' optimism of its lyricism (or more questionably, as we saw in chapter One, between the sensual 'heart' of the black body, and the white domain of reason and language):

| | |
|---|---|
| *Porque o samba nasceu lá na Bahia* | For samba was born up there in Bahia |

| | |
|---|---|
| *E se hoje ele é branco* | And if today it's white in |
| *na poesia* | its poetry |
| *Ele é negro demais no coração* | It is black, so black in its heart |

'Canto de Ossanha' (1966), a 'chant' for the Yoruba orisha or divinity Ossanha, returns to the format of 'Berimbau' with, this time, a three-note figure reiterated over a relatively simple descending sequence of chords. Again, a series of aphorisms denounces the man's words of treachery, dishonesty and cowardice, challenging him with a physical, rhythmic force to resist or yield to the spell that invites him to risk the pain or joy of love:

| | |
|---|---|
| *Coitado do homem que cai* | Pity the man who falls |
| *No canto de Ossanha, traidor!* | into the chant of Ossanha, traitor! |
| *Coitado do homem que vai* | Pity the man who goes |
| *Atrás de mandinga de amor* | After the spell of love, |
| *Vai! Vai! Vai! Vai!* | Go! go! go! go! |
| *Não Vou!* | I won't go! |
| *Vai! Vai! Vai! Vai!* | Go! go! go! go! |
| *Não Vou!* | I won't go! |

Thus the incantatory power of Afro-Brazilian rhythms served both to invoke a sense of collective identity in the communion of prayer, and to mobilize its initiates for the struggles of life. These themes were developed in a more dramatic and explicitly political way by Edu Lobo, a law student from Ipanema who acquired his musical education informally from his father, Fernando Lobo, and through bossa novista artists such as Carlos Lyra and Baden Powell, as well as the northeasterner João do Vale. In 1963 he had worked on CPC dramatist Viana Filho's uncompleted musical *Os Azeredos mais os Benevides* (The Azeredos plus the Benevides).[45] Their collaborative composition 'Chegança'

(Homecoming) is the only surviving piece from the show, and typifies the structural formula adopted by Edu Lobo in much of his subsequent work.

The title makes reference to several traditional practices bearing the name, all related to its etymology of 'arrival', including the celebration of a ship's safe arrival in port, and the Christmas house-to-house visits akin to 'first-footing'. However, here the theme has been adapted to the political question of agrarian reform and land occupations. An introductory and concluding figure on alternating adjacent minor seventh chords and notes (including the distinctively northeastern augmented fourth) intones the ritualistic rhythm of the *samba de roda*. This serves to announce the gathering of the people and their occupation of the land, which will 'set the world spinning'. It is left to the song's intervening passages, in a more classic bossa nova harmonic and melodic style, to provide a lyrical 'interpretation' of this action, its promise of renewal, fertility and hope:

| | |
|---|---|
| *Trazendo na chegança* | Bringing as they come |
| *Foice velha, mulher nova* | Old scythes, young women |
| *E uma quadra de esperança . . .* | And a parcel of hope . . . |
| *Chegar sem parar* | Arriving endlessly |
| *Parar pra casar* | Stopping to marry |
| *Casar e os filhos espalhar* | To marry and scatter their children |

Lobo's use of these regional African traditions, and especially their religious associations, moved ahead following his work with the dramatist and film-director Ruy Guerra, and particularly his collaboration on the *Arena conta Zumbi* project, depicting the seventeenth-century maroon slave kingdom of Palmares. The Lobo / Guerra composition 'Reza' (Prayer) combined – like 'Chegança' – the bossa nova idiom, with its extended lyrical expression of desire and promise, and the ritual evocation of

prayer, in the rhythmically repetitive and choral style of the
Afro-samba. 'Canção da terra' (Song of the land) reproduced the
same hybrid structure, opening with a mysterious Yoruba invocation – 'Olorum bererê / Olorum bererê / Olorum ici beobá'
– voiced in parallel moving parts. This then leads into a more
bossa-like solo chromatic melody on the theme of privation, the
landless, loveless, voiceless son struggling to regain everything
he has lost by summoning up the power of faith. In 'Borandá'
(Let's go away), meanwhile, it is in spite of so many prayers that
the migrant is forced to flee the drought. The song moves between
the rhythmic urgency of the call to depart, the dissonance of
despair at the failure of the promises offered up, and an extended,
lyrical regret, in half-time, for the land left behind. This multi-
layered dramatic structure was also applied in 'Arrastão' (Drag-
net), composed with Vinicius de Moraes and shifting the scenario
to a maritime setting. The swelling tide and movement of the
fishing-raft are suggested by an arabesque figure reiterated in
ascending registers over a galloping rhythm. A descending scale
in triplets links this mood of excitement and expectation to the
invocation of Iemanjá, the goddess of the sea. As in 'Borandá',
a slower prayer-like passage follows, appealing for the blessing of
the queen of the sea, and her hand in marriage, in a celebration
of abundance and fertility.

If Edu Lobo's exploration of the possibilities of combining
modern and traditional musical idioms marked a development
of Carlos Lyra's approach, it arguably resulted in a richer dramatic
texture. Furthermore, it moved beyond Lyra's *enactment* of a
dialogue between urban avant-garde and popular traditions to
a more integrated musical landscape, which was unified and
mobilized by the ritual and mystical sound of Afro-Brazilian
rhythms. It was doubtless this enriched rhythmic texture and
colour which accounted for the success of Lobo's 'Arrastão' in
1965, as the winner in the first of Brazil's international festivals of

Edu Lobo, São Paulo, 1967.

popular music, where the competition between different musical idioms was soon to be projected onto the television screen.

The rise of the mass media industry as an arena for the performance of this rivalry coincided with an atmosphere of renewed political ferment. The year from 1965 to 1966 saw anti-military demonstrations across a number of states, strikes in eighteen university faculties and barricades erected in front of São Paulo University's philosophy faculty. The convergence between this atmosphere of political agitation and the new dramatic colour and rhythm of Baden Powell's and Edu Lobo's Afro-sambas found its ideal exponent in the singer Elis Regina. It was she who, with her theatrical, extroverted style of performance, won first place together with Jair Rodrigues for Lobo's 'Arrastão' in TV Excelsior's Brazilian Popular Music Festival in April 1965. She went on in the following month to front a weekly show, *O Fino da Bossa* (The Cream of Bossa), which was broadcast by TV Record every Wednesday, sent out to other states and repeated in São Paulo on the following Saturday.[46] After three months the show became known simply as *O Fino*; paradoxically, though, while this exposed the veteran figures of bossa nova to their first truly mass audience, Carlos Lyra argued that it was precisely the televisual medium which brought the classic, 'cool' phase of the movement to its end.[47] By early 1966 the show's ratings were in decline as *Jovem Guarda* went into the ascendant, rivalling *O Fino* with its simplicity and vigour.

Once again the new tradition of songwriting and performance was obliged to reinvigorate itself by turning further away from the idiom which had revolutionized the form in the mid-1950s. The last years of the decade now saw a wholesale return to a number of familiar regional and popular styles – samba, *frevo*, *marcha*, *ciranda*, *moda de viola*, *desafio* – which dispensed altogether with the dissonant subtlety and conversational posture of bossa nova. Interestingly this reversion to tradition was mirrored, in the form of the *sambão*, by the work of a number of performers who were at best uncritical, at worst supportive, of the dictatorship's ideological aims. Antônio Carlos, Luís Airão, Benito de Paula, Gilson de Souza, Jorginho do Império and Martinho da Vila reappropriated the symbols of national-populist exaltation – the samba schools, football, the deities of candomblé and the 'people' itself – in the service of the regime's propaganda machine.[48] Thus the notion of 'the popular' became an even more heterogeneously disputed terrain for both left and right, now dramatized within the increasingly pugnacious arena of the televised song contests.[49]

The proceedings of TV Record's 2nd Festival of Brazilian
Popular Music in September–October 1966 typified this atmosphere, with the partisanship of sections of the audience described
as reminiscent of that of a soccer stadium. Ironically Sérgio
Ricardo's 'Beto Bom de Bola', a protest against the pernicious
influence of the football industry itself, was booed until he
exploded, shouting 'You're a lot of animals!'; he then smashed
up his guitar and threw it at the audience.[50] The first prize was
shared by Chico Buarque's march, 'A Banda' (The Band), and
Geraldo Vandré's 'Disparada' (Stampede), co-written with Théo
de Barros and performed by Jair Rodrigues with the Trio Novo and
Trio Marayá. The uncompromisingly rural format of 'Disparada'
and its energetic, northeasternized adaptation of the bossa nova
instrumental line-up – combining the widely used guitar with its
smaller rustic counterpart, the metal-strung *viola*, a flute, piano
and a wide range of percussion, including a mule's jaw – daringly
challenged the expectations and conventions of the contests as
staged until then.

Born in the northeastern state of Paraíba, Vandré began
his singing career in his childhood, when he heard the semi-
improvised ballads of the *cantadores* or troubadours who performed at fairs and markets. His first solo songwriting success
was 'Fica mal com deus' (You'll fall out with God, 1963), whose
epic *galope* rhythm broke completely with the domestic intimacy
of bossa nova, and its magical equilibrium and 'grace', to carry
the rider on his defiant adventure across the backlands:

| | |
|---|---|
| *Quem quiser comigo ir* | Whoever wants to go with me |
| *Tem que vir do amor* | Must come from love |
| *Tem que ter pra dar . . .* | Must have something to give . . . |
| *Vida que não tem valor* | A life without courage |
| *Homem que não sabe dar* | A man who cannot give |
| *Deus que se descuide dele* | Will be abandoned by God |

Vandré went on to win TV Excelsior's June 1966 Excelsior festival with 'Porta-Estandarte' (Standard-bearer), which, at a time when street demonstrations were banned, took up the theme of the samba schools' carnival parade as a metaphor for the people's struggle to reappropriate the avenue. 'Disparada' emerged from his experience of producing the soundtrack for Roberto Santos's film *A Hora e Vez de Augusto Matraga*, and was composed during a trip through the northeast with Airto Moreira, his co-writer Théo de Barros and Heraldo, who went on to form the Trio Novo.

For this composition Vandré adopted wholesale the simple narrative form of the *toada*, the four-, five- or six-line stanza and refrain which is the typical vehicle for the *cantador's* self-improvised stories of hinterland life. Gone is the polyrhythmic syncopation of the bossa nova or Afro-samba, with their emphasis on ritualistic reiteration, circularity and incantation. Gone, too, is the tension and dissonance of those styles' chromatic melodies and harmonies. In their place is a purely functional tonality and binary rhythm which serve primarily to project the storyteller's epic lesson of life. The posture is confrontational, the self-assured voice of experience challenging the listener to choose between enlightenment or ignorance:

| | |
|---|---|
| *Prepare o seu coração* | Make your heart ready |
| *Prás coisas que eu vou contar* | For the things of which I'll sing |
| *Eu venho lá do sertão* | I come from the backlands |
| *E posso não lhe agradar. . .* | And you may not like what I have to say . . . |
| | |
| *Se você não concordar* | If you don't agree |
| *Não posso me desculpar* | I'll not say I'm sorry |
| *Não canto prá enganar* | My story's not told to deceive |
| *Vou pegar minha viola* | I'll take up my guitar |

| *Vou deixar você de lado* | I'll leave you aside |
| *Vou cantar noutro lugar* | I'll sing some place else. |

His tale is one of defiance, about the man who learned to say no, who chose to set a topsy-turvy world to rights, to throw off the beast of burden's yoke and become the mounted horseman of a kingless kingdom. The grand scenery of the backlands, so often the setting in rural mythology for the larger-than-life battles between bandits and gunmen, the latter-day knights of the road, and of family feuds and territorial disputes, has become the stage for an exemplary tale of utopian heroism.

With 'Disparada' the audience was no longer invited to participate in the rhythms of a world of shared, communitarian spirituality, ritual or dialogue. It had become instead the object of a new didacticism, one that seemed indifferent to the 'people's' disposition to 'listen'. Like other new compositions of the time such as Gilberto Gil's 'Roda' ('My people, pay heed . . . If you don't want to listen, you don't have to hear'), 'Disparada' dramatized an increasingly antagonistic relationship between singers and audience that was sometimes even verbalized in aggressive confrontations in the live arena. In the heightened political climate that preceded the 'second coup' of 1968, and in the context of a newly diversified music market, audience loyalties were hotly disputed by competing cultural and ideological forces. Faced with the populist appeal of more familiar urban traditions on one side, and the innovative cosmopolitan styles stimulated by the rock industry on the other, the protest movement increasingly subordinated formal and aesthetic considerations to the rhetorical task of delivering the lyrics' political 'message'. The CPC's strategy had thus apparently been vindicated, but only apparently, because its 'take-it-or-leave-it' posture rendered transparent the relative isolation of the left-wing artistic vanguard within a complex marketplace of cultural styles and attitudes, and its inability to articulate the kind of mass popular consciousness to which it had aspired so optimistically.

Early in 1967, when the 29th Congress of the National Students' Union was obliged to take place in clandestine conditions, Geraldo Vandré's *Disparada* show was just one of a plethora of rival TV programmes representing the musical idioms that the decade had thrown up. Others include *Bossaudade*, with the 'old guard' pre-bossa nova generation of Ciro Monteiro and Elizeth Cardoso;[51] *Pra Ver a Banda Passar* (See the band march past) with *sambistas* Chico Buarque and Nara Leão; and TV Excelsior's *Ensaio Geral* (Dress Rehearsal) with Gilberto Gil and Maria Bethânia. This diversification of the field proved too much for the vehicle of the classic bossa tradition, *O Fino*, which broadcast its last show on 21 June. The 3rd Festival of Brazilian Popular Music began precisely in the month of a new phase of student confrontations with the police, the *setembradas*, and exposed the viewing and listening public to an equally varied range of voices and styles. The first prize went to Edu Lobo/Capinam's 'Ponteio', and second place to Gil's 'Domingo no Parque', third to Chico Buarque's 'Roda Viva', fourth to Caetano's Veloso's 'Alegria, Alegria' (with its outrageous rock support-band, the Mutantes and the Beat Boys), and fifth to Roberto Carlos, whose attempt at a reconciliation with the local tradition of songwriting, in the form of Luís Carlos Paraná's 'Maria Carnaval e Cinzas', was booed by the audience.[52]

The last major landmark in the cycle of televised contests was TV Globo's 3rd International Song Festival, broadcast in September 1968 in the midst of demonstrations, political killings, left-wing urban guerrilla activity and right-wing paramilitary repression, including the violent disruption of the São Paulo stage show, *Roda Viva*, by the anti-communist CCC (Communist Hunter Command). Rather than defending all acts of revolt against the conservative, authoritarian values of the regime, however, the

Sérgio Ricardo confronts booers at the Third TV Record Festival of Brazilian Popular Music, São Paulo, 1967.

response of the orthodox left was to round on those who dared to engage experimentally with the complexities and contradictions of the new cultural climate of the 'Economic Miracle', and its combination of repression and massification.

A particular target of such criticism was the group of artists, including Caetano Veloso, Gilberto Gil, Maria Bethânia, Tom Zé and Gal Costa, who had arrived in Rio de Janeiro from the north-eastern city of Salvador da Bahia in 1964. Known as the Tropical-istas after their pathbreaking album of 1968, *Tropicália ou Panis et Circensis*, the *baianos* defied all existing assumptions of musical and ideological orthodoxy. Uninhibitedly juxtaposing and fusing

elements drawn from rural and urban, local and international,
traditional and modern sources, such as electrified rock and pop,
psychedelia, bossa nova and rural folksong, they dared to reflect
critically and creatively on the bewildering new cultural landscape
over which the military regime was presiding. At the same time
they transgressed and subverted the categories of 'high' and 'low',
of 'bourgeois' and 'popular' culture, of 'alienated' and 'engaged'
art, set up by the theoretical debates within the CPCs; they did this
by combining and juxtaposing the stylistic sources above with influences from the avant-garde art of the period, such as Concretist
poetry and experimental electronic music, as well as with earlier,
commercially popular styles considered *cafona*, in bad taste, or
kitsch, by contemporary aesthetic standards, such as 1950s boleros
or the work of Carmen Miranda. By way of an indication of the
impact of their performances on the sectarian atmosphere of the
Globo festival of 1968, during the competition's qualifying rounds,
as Gilberto Gil shocked the audience by appearing in African dress
and a thick beard to front his inflammatory 'Questões de Ordem'
(Questions of Order), Caetano Veloso and the Mutantes were
drowned out by an enraged crowd that found the libertarian
stance of his psychedelic rock composition 'É Proibido Proibir'
(Forbidden to forbid) – a title inspired by the slogans of the Paris
student demonstrations in May that year – too much to take.[53]

However, although highly charged with political meaning,
there was also something strangely disembodied about this contest of idioms, traditions and discourses, organized as it was by
a mass media network closely allied to the state, and within performance and broadcasting spaces that were still mainly accessible
only to middle-class Brazilians. When Geraldo Vandré came to
perform 'Caminhando', which had by now become the unofficial
anthem of the protest movement, in the Maracanãzinho arena, it
appears as though the ideological battle lines were already clearly
drawn up; composers and performers were expected to assume

the badge of left- or right-wing orthodoxy, to pronounce on behalf of their supporters rather than to engage in an open, critical form of political debate or dialogue. Vandré's comments on and during the live recording of that concert voiced an uncomfortable awareness that these televised events were in danger of staging a theatricalized, make-believe alternative to the political struggles being waged outside in the real world. Fighting to be heard, Vandré appealed to the audience to respect his main artistic rivals, Tom Jobim and Chico Buarque; their common duty as artists was 'to make songs', while there was 'more to life than just festivals'.

The distinction and confusion between political and cultural activism was a crucial one. As Vandré left the stadium he was mobbed by fans and objected: 'This is turning into a mass rally. Please, let me go.' It was precisely at this time that the expression 'esquerda festiva' (festive left) had emerged as a pejorative epithet used by the orthodox Stalinist left to refer to the irreverently heterodox attitude of the new generation of intellectual and artist revolutionaries influenced by the guerrilla movements, libertarian and student protests of the 1960s.[54] At a homage to the Spanish poet and dramatist Federico García Lorca in São Paulo's Municipal Theatre, where a heckler in the stalls accused him of being 'festivo', Vandré replied: 'They want me to dress up in proletarian costume. Well I won't, I won't.'

Vandré's unease reflected both an awareness of the isolation of the protest movement from the urban and rural masses in whose name it was speaking, and the problematic nature of the political intervention that the CPC had demanded of its cultural activists. Yet his song 'Caminhando' itself highlighted Vandré's own hesitancy and ambivalence as regards his artistic and political responsibilities – was he making music or politics? Stripped of all harmonic, rhythmic and textural complexity or distinctiveness, and devoid of any identifiably Brazilian resonances, the song's musical elements functioned purely as a vehicle for a generic,

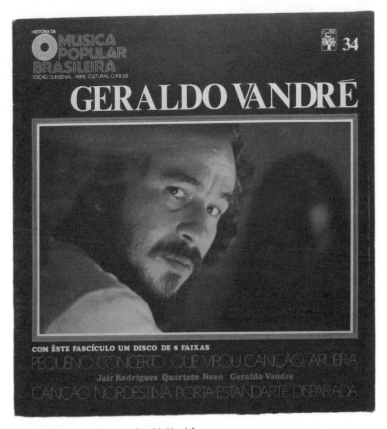

Album cover paying tribute to Geraldo Vandré.

hymn-like expression of solidarity. Paradoxically the song of protest had abandoned all attempts to articulate musically the popular identity of feeling which Lyra, Ricardo, Baden Powell and Lobo had sought in their dialogue and fusion of traditions, rhythms and harmonic textures drawn from modern urban, regional and Afro-Brazilian sources. Instead it took for granted an abstract, 'universal' solidarity symbolized by 'the song' itself, which claims in its self-sufficiency an unquestionable capacity to mobilize around it the anonymous ranks of the faithful:

| | |
|---|---|
| *Nas escolas, nas ruas,* | In the schools, in the streets, |
| *campos, construções* | fields and building sites |
| *Somos todos soldados* | We're all of us soldiers |
| *armados ou não* | whether we're armed or not |
| *Caminhando e cantando* | Marching and singing |
| *e seguindo a canção* | and following the song |
| *Somos todos iguais* | We're all of us equal |
| *braços dados ou não.* | whether arm in arm or not. |

Although extremely simple, poor even, harmonically and melodically, the song derives something of its appeal as both a generic hymn of solidarity and a call to action from a simple rhythmic device which combines these two meanings. This is a 6/8 time signature, a measure or bar of six beats, which has the virtue of being divisible in two ways: as two groups of three, or three groups of two. The song, and its singer, are therefore able to move easily between the binary, marching rhythm exhorting the audience to political mobilization, and the more lyrical, utopian contemplation of future victory in a circular movement in waltz time.

It is not difficult to understand the appeal of such an abstractly 'spiritual' notion of universal solidarity to the grassroots Christian communities (CEBS) who took up Vandré's banned song as their own anthem in the 1970s. A more recent account of the emergence of the Workers' Party (PT), the political expression of the popular movement rooted in the CEBS and a broadly heterogeneous range of other mass-based organizations and left-wing currents, identified its unifying ethos precisely as one founded on a kind of moral solidarity, rather than any clearly defined ideological theory or programme:

To understand this 'open' party, we need to know what it is that keeps the *petistas* [PT members] together, besides a vague

adherence to socialism. It is not a particular definition of
socialism, far less a specific recipe on how to achieve it, but an
ethos, an attitude towards society and political involvement
that combines radicalism, self-denial and moral outrage.
This is the common denominator of all *petistas*, be they
intellectuals, workers, Catholics, agnostic activists, members
of the Landless Peasants Movement or organizers of women's
rights groups.[55]

It was very much this kind of broad, popular front that the student
and intellectual left and its cultural wing, the CPC, had aspired to
lead in the years immediately before and after the 1964 coup. If they
were unable to do so, this was due as much to the shortcomings of
their voluntarist, top-down conception of revolutionary vanguardism and of a revolutionary popular culture, abstractly elaborated
outside the ranks of the mass movement itself, as to the regime's
effectiveness in isolating that movement from the left-wing intelligentsia. The cultural logic of this vanguardism, as we have seen,
was expressed in the shifting relational structures and musical
idioms of the decade's songwriting and performance. Before the
effects of the coup were felt, it took the form of attempts to enact
a dialogue or fusion between the various traditions and musical
sensibilities – urban, rural, modern, pre-industrial, white, black,
bourgeois and working class – that might make up a putative
'popular' alliance of listeners and performers. The aftermath
of the coup saw that artist-audience relationship confined more
acutely to the immediate middle-class periphery of the student
movement, against the background of an aggressively competitive
commercial music industry centred on the televised song contests.
The response was to seek a return to 'pure' traditional forms, or
to the 'universal', generic sound of the protest anthem, as the
vehicle for a more aggressively didactic message, one that was
increasingly abstracted from the complex cultural experiences of

the late 1960s, with the massification and internationalization of the media industry.

To criticize the lyrical content of the post-1964 protest songs for their failure to offer anything more than a vaguely utopian faith in the future, as Walnice Nogueira Galvão did in 1968, was therefore perhaps to miss the point. In the absence of any politically articulated community of interests – that is to say, in the absence of a viable popular movement with its own coherent alternative to the regime's strategy of authoritarian, state capitalist modernization – the traditional left could express little more than its own frustrated idealism and that of its middle-class audience. The challenges posed by the new cultural conditions of the 'Economic Miracle', meanwhile, would have to be addressed by another generation of MPB songwriters and performers, led by the Tropicalistas. It was they who, without political pretensions and freed from ideological orthodoxies and assumptions about musical 'authenticity', were ready to experiment uninhibitedly and imaginatively with the newly diversified range of resources, styles and traditions, local and international, now available to them.

## 5 ORPHEUS IN BABYLON: MUSIC IN THE FILMS OF RIO DE JANEIRO

### BETWEEN THE HILLSIDE AND THE CITY: THE ORPHIC IDEAL

Not surprisingly, the music of Rio de Janeiro's streets and hillsides has played more than a mere supporting role in cinematic representations of the city across the last half-century. The figure of the popular musician is one we might expect to inhabit the scenarios and landscapes of contemporary Brazilian film, with its strong tradition of musical comedy,[1] and its shift in the second half of the twentieth century towards a socially engaged perspective on everyday working-class life and popular culture. But more than that – most explicitly in the two screen versions of the Classical Orpheus myth, one a Franco-Brazilian production (*Black Orpheus*, dir. Marcel Camus, 1959), the other a Brazilian project (*Orfeu*, dir. Carlos Diegues, 1998) – the musician has even been invested with a special, symbolic role of restorative agency, embodying the hopes, dreams and flaws of a city and country traumatically divided along the fault lines of class, culture, state and citizenry.

It is not hard to understand the appeal of the Orpheus narrative, with its drama of the transformative power of music, to the poet and lyricist Vinicius de Moraes, who began considering its dramatic potential as an allegory for the lives of Afro-Brazilians in Rio de Janeiro's *favelas* (shanty towns) as early as the 1940s.[2] The evolution of this idea and its trajectory as a practical artistic project, from Moraes's stage musical *Orfeu da Conceição* (1956) via Camus's *Black Orpheus* to Carlos Diegues's remake *Orfeu* (1998), have been recounted in detail elsewhere, and their representation of the themes of race relations, 'favela life' and national identity have been examined thoroughly by others, so these arguments do not need to be rehearsed here.[3]

Rather, this chapter takes the seminal narrative of Orpheus as a starting-point for interpreting the specific role of music, both symbolic and material, in screen representations of Rio de Janeiro since the 1950s, and especially in the performance of ideas of redemption and perdition for a city in crisis. In doing so it will also take a critical look at one assumption about the shifts in cinematic and musical idiom across this period and their relationship to the realist aesthetic: the idea that the 'harder' soundtracks of the most recent films (centring on hip-hop, soul and a local Brazilian offspring of Miami bass, *funk carioca*, with its bass-heavy electronic beats[4]) correspond to a necessarily more realistic and therefore truthful representation of the city, as opposed to the apparently sentimentalized depictions associated with the musical scores of *Black Orpheus* and *Rio, Zona Norte* (Rio, North Zone, dir. Nelson Pereira dos Santos, 1957), for example.

Taught to play the lyre by his father Apollo, according to classical mythology the Thracian Orpheus was that supremely gifted minstrel whose skill, together with the sweetness of his voice, were such that he could charm wild animals, cause trees to uproot themselves and follow in his steps, and even save Jason and the Argonauts from shipwreck by outsinging the Sirens. Orpheus falls in love with a wood-nymph named Eurydice and enjoys a brief, blissful life with her until one day, pursued through the forest by the minor deity Aristaeus, she steps on a poisonous snake, is bitten and dies. Armed with his musical powers and protected by the gods, the grief-stricken Orpheus descends into the Underworld, where he succeeds in charming the monstrous three-headed dog Cerberus and persuades Hades, the king of the dead, to allow him to return with his wife to the world of the living.

But tragically, Orpheus breaks the one condition imposed by Hades: unable to trust that Eurydice is following him as promised, or impatient to share his joyful anticipation with her, before they emerge into the light he turns to see her, and she is lost to him forever. Swearing that he will never love another, Orpheus mourns Eurydice with his music so intensely and steadfastly that the jealous Maenads, the wild women of Thrace, tear him limb from limb and throw his head into a river. But it goes on singing all the way to the sea, and is thereafter saved by the Muses to remain among the living, enchanting everyone forever with its melodies.

If the spirit of Orpheus was believed to guide the hands of all musicians who sing of lost love, we could say that Brazil's contemporary cinematic imaginary has been animated by a comparable faith in the spirit of music-making as a force for social regeneration and reconciliation. As a disinterested creative impulse, and in its communicative potential as the expression of an inclusive popular identity, music has symbolized the idea of a redemptive, transformative future for the conflict-ridden social world of urban Brazil, in which the power of human creativity and imagination can overcome the spectre of violence and death.

According to musicologist José Miguel Wisnik, for example, the 'poetic-musical wisdom' of popular song, above all since the 1950s, in its especially rich dialogue between the erudite culture of the lyrical text and popular traditions of music-making, has injected a new vitality into the country's literary-intellectual culture, a creative energy derived from the 'innocence of joy' that inhabits the more elemental forms of popular artistic expression, epitomized by the culture of carnival. In this way, music projects an alternative, utopian path for Brazil's destiny as opposed to the social disharmony and alienation that would appear to be its historical legacy.[5]

However, does this idea of music as an interface or terrain of dialogue between antagonistic cultures and social forces –

the erudite and the popular, the *morro* and the *cidade* (the hillside township and the city below) – represent anything more than a merely dreamed-of aspiration of reconciliation for an irremediably divided society? As early as the mid-1930s, the modernist poet Carlos Drummond de Andrade had posed the question, tentatively and ambiguously, in his poem 'Morro da Babilônia' (Babilônia Hill), which evokes a *favela* in the Leme neighbourhood of Rio de Janeiro's south side, occupying a steep ridge separating Copacabana beach from the district of Botafogo:

> At night, down from the hillside
> come voices creating terror
> (urban terror, fifty per cent from the movies,
> and the rest that came from Luanda or got lost in the
>     common tongue).
> When there was a revolution, the soldiers scattered up
>     the hill,
> the barracks caught fire, they didn't come back.
> Some of them got shot and died.
> The hillside became more magical.
> But the voices from the hillside
> aren't exactly mournful.
> There's even a well tuned ukulele
> that overcomes the noises of the rock and undergrowth
> and makes its way down to us, modest and playful,
> like a kindness from the hillside.[6]

The Morro da Babilônia is emblematic of the issues discussed below, as it has been a setting for both real-life and cinematic dramas of encounter and confrontation between different elements of the city. Having its origins as an army observation post in the late nineteenth century, its occupation began in earnest as Drummond was writing, following the construction of the apartment blocks and the tunnels and tramway system linking Copacabana to the older city centre. Extensive sections of Camus's *Black Orpheus* of 1959 were shot in the Morro da Babilônia, and the film's main character, the amateur musician Orfeu, works during the day as a tram driver between the city's centre and this outlying neighbourhood. In more recent years Babilônia, which shares the hill with another *favela*, Chapéu Mangueira, has been controlled by drug traffickers linked to the Terceiro Comando (Third Command) organization. Eduardo Coutinho's documentary *Babilônia* 2000 (1999) followed twelve hours in the lives of the two communities as they prepared for the Millenium New Year celebrations. José Padilha's film *Tropa de Elite* (Elite Squad, 2007) depicts the actions of the BOPE (Special Police Operation Battalion) in the *favela* in 1997, to eliminate the risks to security posed by the drug dealers in advance of the Pope's visit to the city.

Over half a century before this, then, at a key moment in Babilônia's early history during the populist era of Getúlio Vargas's presidency (1930–45), Drummond had glimpsed the possibility of a different kind of relationship between the two worlds 'up there' and 'down here', between the largely Afro-Brazilian and working-class communities of the hillside and the new bourgeoisie of the city's south side, a relationship that might be mediated not by an already long accumulated burden of fear and violence, but by the language of music. It is as if the previously alien, incomprehensible voice of the *favelado* (*favela* inhabitant) were given a modulated intonation, a musical 'tuning' making of it something poetic, ludic and susceptible, if not to comprehension, then at least to recognition. '*Like* a kindness . . .' – with this subtle qualification, Drummond manages to avoid sentimentalizing the relationship, aware of where he stands in the social and cultural divide, and of the power and limitations of the perceptions, mythologies and imaginaries in which he is implicated.

Other depictions of the *morro* and its musical symbols from the same period were not so self-reflective. Kid Pepe's samba 'Se gostares de batuque' (If you like the *batuque*), as recorded by Carmen Miranda in 1935, for example, is an unashamedly paternalistic, middle-class fantasy of the contented poor which invites its listeners to visit an old-style African circle-dance or *batuque* up on the hillside. It thus patronizingly folklorizes the 'rootsy', slave antecedent of the samba, appropriating it as an element of Brazil's national-popular heritage:

Hey, if you like a batuque . . .
There's batuque that's made-in-Brazil
Go up the hill and join the samba
and there you'll see what spry, nimble folk
are dancing samba in the ring
Because all that stuff's real Brazilian
And they lead their lives singing
Forgetting all the rest, that's how they get along
Go up the hill and join the drumming party
and you'll see real humble folk
so happy while they don't have a thing

After the 1930s and '40s, whose official rhetoric claimed to incorporate popular interests and identities into the mainstream of national life, the next instance of musical dialogue between the *morro* and the *cidade* was to have rather different ideological resonances. In his account of the evolution of violence in the city of Rio de Janeiro, *Cidade Partida* (Divided City), Zuenir Ventura points to the mid-1950s, following the suicide of Getúlio Vargas after his return to office by democratic vote in 1950, as a turning point. It was in that atmosphere of generalized political and ideological conflict, and against a backdrop of intense capitalist growth and consumerism (the 'Golden Years' of Juscelino

Kubitschek's presidency), that the symbiotic relationship between violent criminality and repressive policing entered a new phase; one symbolized by the rise of notorious gangsters such as Cara de Cavalo and Mineirinho and their police counterparts Mílton Le Cocq de Oliveira, Amauri Kruel and the Esquadrões da Morte (Death Squads).[7] At the same time, the developmentalist surge of the Kubitschek administration – out of which emerged the new waves in music and cinema, bossa nova and Cinema Novo, respectively – led to a sharpening polarization between the social actors who were claiming the fruits of this prosperity.

By the early 1960s the contradictions of urban life were becoming both deeper and more complex; as we saw in the last chapter, the language of politics turned away from *getulismo,* the old-style populist nationalism associated with Getúlio Vargas, to a new, Left populism, based on a strategy of revolutionary partnership or alliance between the *povo* (masses) and a politicized section of the artistic-intellectual bourgeoisie. Radicalized by the growing mobilization of both rural and urban labour, by the anti-imperialist and revolutionary movements sweeping the Latin American continent and beyond, and by the new president João Goulart's announcement of a programme of grassroots reforms ('Reformas de Base') in September 1961, part of the bossa nova generation of artists and intellectuals committed itself to a partnership with working-class musicians with a view to reinterpreting the notion of 'Popular Culture' as an instrument of revolutionary denunciation and action.

The group's most prominent representatives were Carlos Lyra (co-writer, with Vinicius de Moraes, of the stage musical *Pobre Menina Rica* / Poor Little Rich Girl, 1964), Sérgio Ricardo (singer-songwriter and filmmaker, responsible for the soundtracks to Glauber Rocha's *Deus e o Diabo na Terra do Sol* / Black God, White Devil, 1964, and *Terra em Transe* / Land in Anguish, 1967) and the vocalist Nara Leão, among others. Focusing their activities around the Popular Culture Centres, they sought to unify musically the experiences and aspirations of Brazil's oppressed classes and the vanguardist politics of the new Left by incorporating the compositional and performative innovations of bossa nova within a more militant language of social critique, in collaborations with roots *sambistas* (samba composers) from the hillside *favelas*. In *Pobre Menina Rica*, the musical comedy co-authored by Lyra and Vinicius de Moraes, the lyrical, orphic impulse quite literally brings together the two protagonists – the poor little rich girl and the beggar-poet – in a romantic if ultimately ephemeral encounter on Copacabana beach, mediated by poetry and song. In other cases the friction between romanticism and naturalism, rhetoric and critique, was integral to the aesthetic structure of the new, politically engaged art. *Black Orpheus* and *Rio, Zona Norte* stood at the threshold of this moment of conscious representational rupture, still daring to imagine a city of multiple temporalities where the mythic and the real, the ritual and the everyday, might collide and even converge.

## BETWEEN THE MYTHIC AND THE REAL: *RIO ZONA NORTE* AND *BLACK ORPHEUS*

As early as 1957, some years before the Popular Culture Centre initiatives, Nelson Pereira dos Santos's film *Rio, Zona Norte* was already exploring the theme of the class divide from the point of view of its working-class protagonists, although it was initially criticized for its unwieldy mix of expressionism and social realism and for failing to match the impact of Santos's more consistently neo-Realist debut *Rio, 40 Graus* (Rio, 40 Degrees, 1955).[8] The film's particular thematic focus is the phenomenon of *parceria* – the song-writing partnerships which, on the one hand, opened the way for the professionalization of the careers of many poorer, typically black *sambistas* from the 1930s onwards but, on the other, exposed them to exploitation and the outright theft of their creative material by unscrupulous, ambitious agents and singers. In Pereira dos Santos's dramatization of the relationship, the victim Espírito da Luz Soares (literally 'Spirit of Light Soares', played by the legend of musical comedy or *chanchada*, Grande Otelo) is found dying beside the tracks of Rio's suburban railway, and as his life slips away we relive his dream of artistic success and its cruel destruction.

The soundtrack opens with Alexandre and Radamés Gnatalli's incidental score evoking, in a somewhat traditional Hollywood approach,[9] two contrasting moods – the modernist bustle of the urban landscape and a piano-led romantic interlude suggestive of the tragedy to come. But this soon gives way to the polyrhythmic drumming of a *batucada* or samba percussion ensemble, which connects two contrasting ideas and tempi: the relentless clatter of the commuter train transporting its working-class passengers between the centre and the northern suburbs (where the largely Afro-Brazilian population was forced to resettle at the turn of the twentieth century) and the ecstatic energy of a pre-carnival samba rehearsal, in its most popular version, the improvised *samba de terreiro* or 'dirt-floor samba'.

Although ominously interrupted by a violent gang attack, the scene of the *escola de samba* (literally 'samba school', the term used to refer to Rio's neighbourhood carnival associations) is remarkable as the first of several in which Espírito is seen and heard performing compositions from his (in reality Zé Kéti's and Vargas Júnior's) samba repertoire in their entirety, without any orchestral backing, and in the real-time context of the narrative, rather than simply as extra-diegetic musical interludes. It is as if time and space are given up for the *sambista* and his samba to intervene directly in the drama with a sense of autonomy as agents of creative potential, to voice Espírito's dream of self-realization (to re-marry, be reunited with his baby and wayward son, and make a new home). But it is equally implied that the songs – such as Zé Kéti's 'Mágoa de sambista' (The *sambista's* pain): 'Samba meu, que é do Brasil também' (Samba of mine, and Brazil's as well) – performed by Espírito in their unadorned, raw, 'authentic' state, represent the real soul of popular musicality; by contrast, he laments, once stolen from him by the cynical agent Maurício, his song loses the spirit of its roots in the old-guard traditions of the call-and-response, tambourine-driven *samba de partido alto* ('broken high' samba).

Espírito's illusory, unattainable dream of consummate stardom is symbolized by a cameo performance by the real-life figure of well-known singer Ângela Maria, who hears and offers to record one of his compositions. Espírito takes up the promise of another would-be intermediary and collaborator, the middle-class professional musician Moacir, to have the song transcribed. But on visiting him in his plush south-side apartment, where he is entertaining his fashionable bourgeois friends, he discovers the superficiality and opportunism of Moacir's interest in him. The hope of social and individual redemption through the conciliatory agency of the *parceria* is shattered, and Espírito loses everything. As we are encouraged to speculate, his death will no doubt be followed by a further cynical betrayal, as Moacir vows to gather together Espírito's surviving compositions for 'posterity', although more probably for his personal profit.

The orphic conception of musical artistry – ambivalently bearing the promise of both redemption and fallibility – therefore underlies *Rio, Zona Norte's* hybrid combination of expressionism and naturalism, and its dreamlike quality.[10] Camus's *Black Orpheus* was released only two years later, in 1959, and while its international success – including an Oscar and the *Palme d'Or* at the Cannes Film Festival – was matched by considerable critical notoriety inside Brazil,[11] it bears some striking structural similarities to Nelson Pereira dos Santos's predecessor.

Neither film actually lays claim to a documentary realist approach to everyday life in Rio's poor neighbourhoods, and the recourse in *Black Orpheus* to colour photography, the city's dramatic landscapes and its set-piece carnival and *macumba* (popular Afro-Brazilian spirit worship) scenes are unquestionably exploited to spectacular effect. Yet while this has attracted accusations that *Black Orpheus* effectively manufactures an exoticized tourist vision of a tropical fantasy, Vinicius de Moraes's original stage-play is no less vulnerable to criticism for its consumerist, exoticizing gaze upon the internal 'other'. For Charles Perrone, the play 'celebrates beauty in the *favela* but in a mystifying fashion that conceals socio-historical contexts'.[12] Perhaps this is to miss the point, however. Regardless of the implicit perspective (foreign or local) from which the two films' respective settings in the *favela* and the suburb are viewed, both achieve a comparably vivid and intense evocation of those locations, without whose powerful sense of aura the mythical narratives that unfold in them would not be credible. Rather than offering a sociological map of the contemporary urban world, the Rio de Janeiro of both films is a city of dreams, a stage upon which the forces of creativity, love, violence and death are set in motion within the lives of ordinary people in pursuit of the extraordinary.

It makes little sense, therefore, to regard *Black Orpheus* or *Rio, Zona Norte* as failures of social realism; if anything, on the contrary, they should probably be seen as *anti*-realist in conception, if one of the priorities of the realist aesthetic is to bring us close to the palpable, material experience of the quotidian, as rendered sensorially intense in the immediate 'now' of the present. As Beatriz Jaguaribe argues,

A key element of the prevalence of the realist register is also related to the perception of realism as being closely tied to the construction of modernity. Whereas religious beliefs,

inner realms of fantasy and collective carnivalesque practices
may actually feature in realist productions, the controlling
reality principle is given by the rationalist realist code.[13]

In that sense, *Black Orpheus* also shares with *Rio, Zona Norte*
a tension between the mythic time of love and song and the
quotidian tempo of modernity; the relentless, destructive flux
of urban existence is magically suspended by the power of dream,
ritual, music or dance, as its protagonists struggle against the constraints of the real.

This is surely where the narrative dynamic and appeal of
*Black Orpheus* lie, in suggesting how the cultural world of the
Brazilian *morro*, of twentieth-century Afro-Brazilian *favelados*,
is an orphic site of convergence yet also of tension between the
realms of dream and of the everyday, the poetic and the prosaic,
the suspended ritual temporality of carnival and the ordinary
'real time' of Ash Wednesday. Camus's film might therefore
arguably be closer in spirit to Vinicius de Moraes's early thinking
about the affinities between Afro-Brazilian and Greek cultural life
than his own stage-play. In Act Two of the latter, Perrone argues,
when Orfeu searches in vain for Eurydice at a carnival ball: 'There
is no suggestion of recovery, and, consequently, no enactment of
the myth's crucial syntagm of looking back and losing her.'[14] The
film, by contrast, does retrieve that key idea in the scene of the
*macumba* session; Orfeu's singing invokes Eurydice's soul through
the spirit possession of a medium, only for Orfeu to lose her again
when he ignores her plea to have faith: 'Do you love me enough
to hear me without seeing?'

Just as important as the film's diegetic movement in suggesting
this tension and convergence between mythic time and the 'real'
time of modernity, the musical soundtrack works fundamentally
as a dialogue between the stylistic idioms and functions of samba
and bossa nova; the first being a core tradition of the country's

musical life, with its intimate relations with carnival and Afro-Brazilian religion, while bossa nova was (in 1959) the 'new wave' in songwriting and singing, which Black Orpheus itself was so instrumental in introducing to European and u.s. audiences. However, whether in the context of the film or in their own right, samba and bossa nova should not be seen as simply standing for the mythic/ritual and for the modern, respectively. Rather, bossa nova can best be heard as a contemporary reinterpretation of the samba tradition: profoundly rooted in its sense of spirituality, its cyclical, repetitive structures, its polyrhythmic approach to musical time and the interplay of language and melody, but combining these with modern concepts of melodic chromaticism, harmonic modulation and a minimalist performative attitude that together tend towards a more contemplative, reflective commentary on the experiential present, the unfolding of time in the here and now.

The opening scenes of the film establish this dialogical approach to the orphic drama and its musical expressions: amid the frenetic pulse of a samba batucada, Afro-Brazilian women carrying water up the hillside favela join others washing clothes to form an exuberant, dancing multitude blurring the boundaries between work and play; Eurydice is meanwhile seen arriving in the city, making her way across its concrete landscape, which significantly includes an icon of modernist architecture, Lúcio Costa's Ministry of Culture building, also known as the Capanema Palace, located in the city-centre street Rua da Imprensa.

If the euphoric, collective polyrhythms of carnival samba juxtapose in this way the narrative pace of urban modernity with its ludic, ritual antithesis, then the first bossa nova song to be heard, Tom Jobim and Vinicius de Moraes's 'A Felicidade' (Happiness), intervenes to transport us to a different realm of transcendent contemplation, on the hilltop above, where some children are trying to fly a kite. The song itself, in its musical and thematic tension, comments on the allegorical mini-drama unfolding before us on the screen, as the kite struggles precariously to remain afloat in the sky above the city. It shifts between the suspended limbo of its refrain, the eternity of sorrow – 'Tristeza não tem fim' (literally 'Sadness has no end') – and the realm of the present ('But happiness does') and of *tempus fugit*, the brevity of life's successive moments, epitomized by the transition between Shrove Tuesday and Ash Wednesday, between the euphoria of carnival and its aftermath.

Like the kite defying the forces of gravity and inertia, or a feather hovering in the air, the gesture of song enacts this defiance of the onward logic of real time, eternally deferring its end. Even after Death has finally caught up with Eurydice, and Orfeu carries her electrocuted body back up the hillside, he intones the words and melody of 'A Felicidade' once more, insisting that 'the sun will rise to greet us', before being stoned by the jealous 'maenads'

A scene from *Black Orpheus*.

of the *favela* and falling to his own death. The film's closing scene, back on the hilltop, re-enacts the orphic faith in the magical power of the mythic order, the rituals of song and dance, to transcend the constraints of the real, as the children joyfully perform Luis Bonfá and Antônio Maria's 'Samba de Orfeu' (Orfeu's Samba): 'I want to dance, I want to live / when the samba's over, my love, then I can die'), in an attempt to make the sun rise 'just like Orfeu'.

### RAP, FUNK AND THE RHETORIC OF REALISM SINCE THE 1990S

Ambivalence and duality are therefore central to the orphic narrative, which asserts the transcendent power of the creative imagination while simultaneously reminding us of its fallibility and frailty in the face of the real. In the four decades between *Black Orpheus* and Carlos Diegues's *Orfeu*, which encompass a 21-year military dictatorship, the profound economic crisis of the 'lost decade' of the 1980s and a democratic transition to civilian rule, the realist imperative has – not surprisingly – become the orthodoxy, both in the language of political and social critique and in their aesthetic counterparts in the artistic realms of fiction and film. An intense cycle of production of documentary and journalistic reflections on urban poverty and violence was matched from the 1990s by a new wave of literary and cinematic representations focusing particularly on the *favela*.[15] And if one assumption of these new representations was the disintegration of the old national-populist rhetoric of social harmony, then it seems to have followed from this that, musically, the realist perspective could no longer be vocalized in the traditional idioms of collective solidarity and dialogue, such as samba and bossa nova, but would require a more 'modern' and 'realistic' soundtrack.

In Diegues's *Orfeu*, Myrian Sepúlveda dos Santos observes, 'the romantic atmosphere [of *Black Orpheus*] is replaced by a realistic perspective that aims to expose the links between carnival festivities and the cultural industry'.[16] Yet samba, the quintessential music of carnival, figures very little in the film, and aside from a nodding reference to the 1959 production in the form of the bossa nova song 'Manhã de Carnaval', the dominant sounds are those of pop, MPB (an eclectic post-bossa nova style of vocal-and-guitar based songwriting epitomized by Chico Buarque and Caetano Veloso) and hip-hop.

These idioms, and the characterization of the modern, professionalized musician-protagonist Orfeu (played by Toni Garrido, vocalist of the pop reggae band Cidade Negra), have none of the symbolic and expressive meanings that were previously so essential to articulating the orphic narrative's convergence and tension between the mythic and the real. Orfeu is challenged by Eurydice to confront the violent gangsters who tyrannize the *favela* (and are associated somewhat simplistically with the film's hip-hop soundtrack), but it is hard to imagine his mundane character or his creative capacities being remotely up to the task. As Santos puts it, '*Orfeu* shows a hero who is a musician by profession. He uses his laptop to compose his music, and his success comes from this activity. The exceptional powers of music, which could even change the course of life and death as present in the legend, do not appear in the film.'[17] For all the film's apparent aspiration to a more naturalistic and sociologically 'authentic' perspective on the Rio *favela*, its unimaginative deployment of romantic pop, MPB and hip-hop has the effect of exchanging the mythic realm of *Black Orpheus*, its aura of musical enchantment, for the melodramatic register of the TV soap opera and the MTV video-clip.

One of the advisers on the production of *Orfeu* was Paulo Lins, a sociologist from the Cidade de Deus (literally, City of God) neighbourhood and the author of a novel which gave its name to Fernando Meirelles's film *City of God* (2002). In the transition from one '*favela* film' to another, in the space of just four years, the orphic model – with its theme of a redemptive struggle between

the musician's magical creativity and the forces of reality and
death – has given way to another mythical narrative, that of the
ritualistic cycle of dynastic power and violence, the endless rise
and fall of successive gangs and their leaders (a structure even
more striking in its epic scale and extent in the first, full-length,
edition of Lins's novel[18]).

If the musician, as an agent of transformation, has now
disappeared from the scene, though, music itself remains a vital
signifying element in the film's social and cultural narrative. An
interesting feature of *City of God* – and perhaps a contributing
factor of its success internationally – is a soundtrack that, while
including some familiar 'Brazilian' sounds, also challenges audiences' expectations about the musical affiliations and identities
of young, urban working-class blacks in today's Brazil. The film's
chronological span encompasses two moments – the 1970s Black
Rio soul movement and the era of post-1990s hip-hop – when the
hegemony of samba, as the symbol of an optimistic, one-nation
populist consensus rooted in the idea of an integrated *mestiço*
(mixed-race) culture, was challenged by a self-conscious and militant identification with non-local, diasporic black musical idioms.

Clearly the impulse to embrace diasporic expressions of black
identity has been, for many Afro-Brazilians, a response to the sense
that, in being appropriated by a paternalistic *mestiço* nationalism,
traditional musical forms such as samba cease to represent their
experience. As one young participant of the Black Rio soul movement complained: 'Samba? Samba isn't ours any more. Samba
schools haven't got room any more for the likes of us.'[19] On the
other hand, the musical idioms of funk and rap have supplied
Afro-Brazilians with a critical and self-assertive language for characterizing their place in Brazilian society and culture, a language
we could define as 'realist'. This rhetoric of realism is drawn from
'foreign' musical styles whose controversial, critical edge precisely
draws attention to the disjuncture between Afro-Brazilian and

Brazilian, to the social difference that divides the city from itself, the City of God from Rio de Janeiro. To take one key, rhythmic feature of this disruptive musical language, which figures prominently in the film *Cidade de Deus*, the author of a report about Black Rio in 1976 observed that, 'when James Brown's anthem-like song *soul power* is sung [by Afro-Brazilians], the expression *soul power* is repeated rhythmically by the audience in packed out sports halls in a whisper, in a murmur . . .'.[20] For Ricky Vincent, the revolutionary innovation of James Brown, and the key to funk's sense of streetwise 'realism', its gritty, earthy immediacy, was the shift of the pulse 'to the front', hitting the accent 'On the One', away from the more relaxed 'swing' of the off-beat that was typical of the r&b style (and of samba, of course) until then.[21]

But if that shift of the pulse to the front is clearly incorporated into the sound of Brazilian soul and *funk*, this is not an uncritical, unreflective assimilation. The One does not so much replace the off-beat *ginga* (lateral swing) of traditional samba as dialogue with it. It therefore introduces a certain tension between front and back, between the assertive, no-nonsense 'realism' of the funk groove and the playful, often ironic backbeat of samba, between the critical, foreign edge of the modern, diasporic *black power* sound, and something more familiar: the relaxed, playful syncopation of the Afro-Brazilian musical tradition. Just as the chronology of *Cidade de Deus* bridges and confronts two defining moments in Rio de Janeiro's modern social and cultural history, the film's soundtrack reminds us that Rio's musical identity is endlessly performed in the dialogue between tradition and innovation, the local and the diasporic, the ritual and the modern, none of which has a more privileged claim upon reality or the 'real' than any other.

# 6 RAP, RACE AND LANGUAGE: THE AESTHETICS AND POLITICS OF BLACK MUSIC-MAKING

## MPB, TROPICÁLIA AND THE CRISIS OF SONG

The late 1980s and '90s saw the emergence of a powerful musical and cultural phenomenon in Brazil. Embracing elements of soul, rap, hip-hop and *funk carioca*, a bass-heavy dance music incorporating electronic beats, this matrix of interrelated styles was associated with a new mood of social disaffection and militancy, especially, if not exclusively, among young working-class Afro-Brazilians. It quickly provoked discussion about the relationship between race, class and the notion of a 'black' identity in Brazil. This within a society whose supposed capacity for integration, for overcoming social and ethnic antagonisms, has so often been measured and celebrated in terms of its musical expressions. A 'quintessentially' Afro-Brazilian tendency towards hybridization and miscegenation is epitomized, it is suggested, by carnival and by samba, by their success in unifying a heterogeneous population within a collective social space, behind a single rhythm, moved by the same beat.

The new music, which disturbed this assumption so provocatively, broke through its commercial marginalization of the 1980s to produce some of the best-selling recordings of the end of the century, such as the rap albums *Procurados: vivos ou mortos* (Wanted: dead or alive, 1994) by Pavilhão 9 (the name of a prison block that was the scene of a massacre in 1992) and *Sobrevivendo no inferno* (Surviving in hell, 1997, 1.5 million copies sold) by the Racionais MC's (winners of Brazil's MTV music award in 1998), as well the

work of other artists strongly influenced by rap, such as Chico
Science. The phenomenon soon received serious attention in
academic literature on music and culture, notably in Hermano
Vianna's pioneering *O mundo funk carioca* (The world of Rio
funk) and in a collection of essays edited by Micael Herschmann,
*Abalando os anos 90: Funk e Hip-Hop, globalização, violência e estilo
cultural* (Rocking the 1990s: Funk and Hip-Hop, globalization,
violence and cultural style), which examined the various manifestations of the movement in urban centres across the country,
from Rio de Janeiro and São Paulo to Salvador and Fortaleza in the
northeast, as well as its relations with developments elsewhere in
Latin America and the u.s.[1]

In one contribution to this volume entitled 'The Funkification
of Rio', George Yúdice connected the rise of funk and rap in
Brazil to the collapse of what he called the 'consensual culture',
the popularized confidence in a national project of social harmonization and racial democracy symbolized since the 1930s, as
already suggested, by the unifying forces of samba and carnival.
The collapse of that consensual culture was brought to a focus
in 1992: in that year the mass street mobilization that led to the
impeachment of President Fernando Collor de Mello was quickly
followed by a massacre of between 111 and 280 prisoners by
military police in São Paulo's Carandiru jail. The beaches of
Rio's Zona Sul, meanwhile, witnessed a new form of mugging,
the *arrastão* or 'trawl' carried out en masse by poor shanty town
dwellers on local residents and tourists. This latter response to the
profound economic crisis bequeathed by the so-called 'lost decade'
of the 1980s was quickly racialized by the sensationalist media,
which simplistically identified it with the black *bailes funk* (dance
parties) of Rio's northern suburbs, and their supposed culture of
gang violence.

As Yúdice and others argued, though, the emergence of the
new, predominantly black, working class youth culture of funk

and rap signified something different: a refusal to participate in the dominant consensual culture with its mythology of cordial race and social relations. It was symptomatic of the failure of the democratic transition since the 1980s to address the deepening economic divisions left by the post-Economic Miracle years, the institutionalization and racialization of violence and the social segregation of Brazilian cities.

Given the very explicit, militantly political way in which these issues were addressed in the new idiom of Brazilian rap, it is worth considering how it relates to the tradition of songwriting that had evolved in Brazil since the 1950s, including its most explicitly 'political' version, the protest song of the mid-1960s, in terms of its core partnership between language and music. As an abbreviation of the words 'rhythm and poetry', rap draws particular attention to the self-conscious linkage between the two domains and its special resonances with a tradition so celebrated, in Brazil, for the richness of its lyrical-musical interactions. The post-bossa nova and post-protest song legacy of composition and perform-ance broadly known as MPB can be understood as an ongoing creative search to articulate a literary-intellectual lyrical discourse in the rhythms and melodies of popular tradition. It can be defined as the cultural expression of a generation (of predominantly middle-class, university-educated songwriters), shaped by the defeat of the left-populist, some would say revolutionary, move-ment of the early 1960s, but still bearing in some sense the ideal of a democratic society based on an alliance between a progressive, liberal bourgeois intelligentsia and the broader masses of the *povo* or 'people'.[2]

The extremely dynamic history of MPB songwriting from the early 1960s onwards, particularly in as far as the relationship between lyrics and music is concerned, revolved implicitly and explicitly around that politics, around the MPB generation's struggle to close up, culturally and musically, the social gap that Brazil's post-war development had widened. The political dilemma – the desire for social and cultural identification across the class and racial divide, in the absence of any social revolution that might give substance to such an identity of interests – found an aesthetic correlative in the dialectics of songwriting. How could popular song both denounce the economic and political antagonisms dividing society and at the same time articulate musically a sense of collective identity? In other words, to what extent could the *language* of political song (which confronts us with the world and with each other) be made compatible with its *melody* (which unifies and mobilizes us in the same direction) so as to produce a simultaneously enlightening and moving experience?

The political imperatives of the 1960s protest movement imposed a tension between these aesthetic functions, between language and music, which reached breaking-point at the end of the decade, at the height of the televised song festivals and the appearance of a new generation of musicians, the Tropicalistas. Up to that point, the demands of an increasingly didactic, propagandist 'message' of protest took ever more precedence, subordinating melodic intonation to rhythmic projection, the voice of spoken dialogue to the shout of ideological denunciation.

However, having come so far in stripping down the aesthetic resources of the song-form, as we saw in chapter Four, it is hard to see where the political song movement would have gone next if it had not been cut brutally short by the events of September 1968, as Vandré's 'Caminhando' was banned, and he joined the many others who were imprisoned or exiled by the new hardline shift within the military dictatorship. Perhaps this route towards the politicization of popular song – that is, subordinating all other musical functions to the rhythmic intonation of linguistic truths – had reached its logical impasse, exhausting itself on the verge of being reduced to pure propagandist chant, or cant. For some of Vandré's contemporaries who refused to conform to the ideological and cultural categories of traditional left-wing orthodoxy, it did appear as though both politics and culture had been reduced to matters of language, to partisan, propagandist pronouncements on behalf of this or that pre-determined position, rather than critical and creative activities of reinvention.

This certainly seems to characterize the spirit of Caetano Veloso's famous battle with the audience at São Paulo's International Song Festival, in the same month and year, when they greeted his performance of 'É proibido proibir' (It's forbidden to forbid), backed by the electric rock band the Mutantes, with endless booing and jeering, while he hurled back at them a virtual manifesto-tirade in defence of artistic autonomy and experimentation. What is interesting here, besides the theatrical, spectacular nature of this very political confrontation itself, are Veloso's specific comments on the audience's incomprehension of, and deafness to, the new music. These two or three phrases seem to register, along with a violent crisis in the relationship between artist and listener, a corresponding crisis in the relationship between song lyrics and music, language and melody, which would have return to first principles, perhaps, to start from scratch, if it was to rebuild a new song tradition. After shouting at the audience: 'Vocês não estão entendendo nada! . . . Para entender música é preciso ouvi-la!' (You're not understanding a thing! . . . To understand music you need to listen to it!), Veloso ended his speech bellowing at the top of his voice: 'E eu digo é proibido proibir. Fora do tom. Sem melodia!' (I tell you it's forbidden to forbid. Outside the tone. No melody!). In these last words in particular – literally 'outside of the tone' but also suggesting 'off-key', 'without any melody', Caetano appears to be talking about the unviability of song and the relationships it implies, in the form familiar to us from bossa nova onwards. The process of intonation which, according to Tatit, extends speech into song and so makes it possible to overcome the linguistic fragmentation of human existence, restoring the links between individuals and the world, has suffered a violent disruption: the shouting voice has interposed itself between speech and melody, disabling the complex interaction between the two that forms the singer/ songwriter's art.

From this moment onward within the Tropicália movement, the very term 'song' seems curiously out of place to designate the highly elaborated, set-piece studio recordings on the *Tropicália ou Panis et Circensis* album of 1968, such as 'Miserere nobis, 'Geleia Geral' and the title track itself, 'Tropicália'. Lyric and melody operate not so much as an integrated unity, but rather as disparate components among others in the multimedia *montages* typical of the group's productions. Their theatrical, spectacular gestures dispense with the role of the listener as an implied inter-locutor, familiar with the diction and voice of the performer, and instead put him in the position of a televisual spectator. This radical shift in the performer-audience relationship was symptomatic of a wider political and cultural crisis, the defeat of the left populist movement for democracy in the face of the regime's strategy of authoritarian development, and the outright rupture between the artist-intellectuals and the masses.

But in breaking altogether with the protest singers' posture of political, if didactic, engagement with their listeners, the Tropicalistas seemed intent on pursuing the impasse of the left-wing vanguard to its ultimate consquences. It is as if, in the absence of the hoped-for mobilization of the *povo*, they were opting instead for a strategy of cultural guerrilla warfare (echoing the organized left's turn to guerrilla activity following Carlos Marighella's break with the Brazilian Communist Party in 1967). As underground poet and Tropicálist collaborator Waly Salomão observed:

Not only in the lyrics and songs of the period but also in their performances, the style of intervention on the television in

that programme *Divino, Maravilhoso* [an experimental TV
show hosted by Veloso, Gil et al.] on TV Tupi, it was just like
the urban guerrilla movement, that climate of creativity of
the moment, that agonized urgency of the guerrilla fighter,
in the sense that there was no conventional army of producers
like other programmes usually have on hand.[3]

The *baianos* came already prepared for this type of dramatic
intervention, through the theatrical projects in which they partici-
pated before and after their migration from Bahia to Rio, and
through their affinities with the cinema (Veloso, remember, began
his career as a film critic). It is as if they recognized, as they came
face to face with the modernity of Brazil's southeastern cities, that
the country was becoming a kind of stage, a space in which one
was either an actor or a spectator. As Edélcio Mostaço observed:

> Tropicalism consisted above all in a *gesture*. It's true that the
> movement became best known through its musical expression,
> where the names of Caetano Veloso and Gilberto Gil shine
> out, but its origins should be sought in the theatre . . . Not
> in the narrow theatre of the big venues, but that theatre that
> was born with modernity and which transformed all human
> relations into spectacular relations, whose preferred target
> was the gaze and where corporal expression became central.[4]

The interjection of the shout between speech and song reveals
this critical moment for what it is, at the end of the decade, where
there is no longer any room for colloquial, intimate conversation,
nor for party-political dialogue, where all has become public,
gestural representation and performance in the non-place of
myths and superstars. This, perhaps, is why, in the recording
'Coração materno', Veloso appeared to revert to first principles,
to the gold standard of the singer-legend, reinterpreting the

charismatic diction of 1940s and '50s screen idol Vicente Celestino, who had begun his recording career as early as 1916. Traditional song had taken for granted a web of organic relations between the artist and the community, but military repression and the rapid expansion of the mass media were already pulverizing those old ties and imposing new relational structures in their place. In the darkest years of the military dictatorship, which lasted from 1964 until 1985, the task of attempting to rearticulate some sort of relationship between musician, listener and song would be a formidable challenge.

Caetano Veloso did indeed go back to first principles in his experimental work following his period of exile in London (1969–71), but outside the parameters of what had conventionally been thought of as political art.[5] The voice of political protest under repression and censorship, meanwhile, came to be identified during the 1970s with Chico Buarque. Chico's preferred musical idiom and rhythmic style for his coded songs of revolt and solidarity, as is well known, was samba – precisely the tradition which the regime had sought to appropriate for its ideological purposes of projecting an image of national well-being and consensus, drawing on its associations with the celebration of carnival and the idea of social mobility embodied in the figure of the mulatto *malandro*. In his interpretation of this idiom, Chico's songs aimed to reclaim its ethos of playful, euphoric celebration as the expression of a popular identity in resistance to, rather than in collusion with, the official culture of the state. Implicitly this popular identity still took for granted the same imagined alliance that had been the *raison d'être* of the CPC protest movement of the mid-1960s: between the disaffected liberal middle class for whom Chico was mainly speaking, and the wider masses of the *povo* itself.

By the beginning of the 1990s, though, as the economic consequences of the previous decade of crisis became evident, generalized disillusionment with the new post-authoritarian civilian regime set in, and the black youth of Brazil's working-class suburbs were turning increasingly to the new culture of funk and rap, the idea of a shared identity of popular, democratic interests opposed to a single, clearly defined common enemy was less and less sustainable; and with it, the symbolic appeal of a shared popular musical tradition.

Chico Buarque's own novel *Estorvo* (*Turbulence*, [1991] 1993), although not explicitly concerned with musical matters, can be read as a commentary on the bankruptcy of the ethos of *malandragem*, the tactics of cultural mediation between antagonistic poles of Brazilian society in the post-consensus era. As literary critic Roberto Schwarz observed, the reader of Buarque's narrative in the 1990s could no longer rely upon that entire framework of ideological assumptions which, in the 1960s and '70s, made it all too easy to identify with the 'oppressed' and against the 'enemy'.[6] The interpenetration of *cidade* and *morro*, middle-class Zona Sul and working-class hillside slum, segregated physically and economically yet knitted together by networks of organized crime, narco-trafficking, political corruption and institutionalized violence, had reached such a level of violent promiscuity that the protagonist who moves between these two worlds no longer displays the least trace of the *malandro*'s agility and perspicacity, which would have characterized such a marginal being in other times. This alienated, irresponsible, unconscious anti-*malandro* is therefore also essentially prosaic, anti-lyrical and anti-musical; he does not have the slightest notion of how to achieve that articulation of linguistic expression with the aleatory rhythm which moves him through the city, because he lacks the necessary awareness and creativity for those manoeuvres of language, melody and movement that constitute musical activity.

If it was not to drown in this new world of chaos, as Buarque's protagonist does, then the new musical generation of the late 1980s and '90s was obliged to articulate a different kind of dialectic between singer and listener, language and music; one based on the shared recognition of a state of conflict in which the hero, the *malandro* and the *bandido* or thug could no longer be so easily identified and categorized. As Chico Science put it in a song from his album *Da Lama ao Caos* (From Mud to Chaos, 1994), 'quem era inocente hoje virou bandido/ Pra poder comer um pedaço de pão todo fodido/Banditismo por pura maldade, banditismo por necessidade/ Banditismo por uma questão de classe' (the one who was innocent today's become a thug/ So's he can eat a piece of fucked-up bread/ Thuggery out of sheer malice, thuggery out of necessity/ Thuggery as a matter of class).

It must be significant, then, that the ascendant mode of songwriting and performance at this juncture was that of rhythmically intoned speech, and of rap itself. The dialogue between textuality and musicality could no longer be conducted in the modest, conversational tone of samba *parceiros* or partners, nor in the rhetoric of comradely solidarity or exhortation, but must be held at the top of the voice, an honestly suspicious voice of one who knows that cordiality may be nothing more than hypocrisy, and that the transition from speech to song must not pretend to smooth over the rough contradictions of a society divided by a common tongue. Instead it was obliged to uncover a new musicality of language, a new dialectic of articulation and rupture, which abandons the subtle vocalization of phrase in melody, melody in phrase, in order to emphasize rhythmically the areas of friction, the sharp edges and discontinuities between them.

It is interesting that, after two decades of experimentation and re-evaluation of the song-form, Caetano Veloso should have identified with this new mode of performance on more than one occasion, registering explicitly an analogous relationship between this form of linguistic-musical articulation and the atmosphere of violent social friction in the early 1990s. An obvious example is the 'rap' 'Haiti', from the *Tropicália II* album (1993), a blistering exposure of the mythology of cordial race and social relations against the backdrop of the the showcase tourist capital of black Brazil – Salvador. Another instance is 'O Cu do Mundo' (Arsehole of the World), from the *Circuladô* album (1991). Here, Caetano piles up a sequence of rhythmically reiterated utterances based on trochaic and dactylic assonances [vowel rhymes in accented metres: (– ·) and (– · ·), respectively] in [u] and [ ]: 'O furto, o estupro, o rapto pútrido, / O fétido seqüestro, / O adjetivo esdrúxulo em U, / Onde o cujo faz a curva / (O cu do mundo este nosso sítio)' (Mugging, rape, putrid abduction, / Foul kidnapping, / The awkward adjective in U, / Where the beast takes the bend / (Arsehole of the world this place of ours). The deliberate linguistic ugliness makes for an uncomfortable listening experience in which we are obliged to share the sense of violent agitation in the 'saddest nation of all' which, 'in the rottenest time / Is made up of potential / Lynch-mobs'.

## RAP, SOCIAL RUPTURE, RHYTHM AND VOICE

'E aí camarada é só nos escutar / Detentos do Rap com o poder de rimar' (Hey, man, you gotta hear us jus' one time / Prisoners of Rap with the power to rhyme), Detentos do Rap[7]

Veloso's 'Haiti' and 'O Cu do mundo' were the self-consciously experimental work of a middle-class, commercially and nationally celebrated artist, adopting and adapting the idiom in one or two instances for a specific effect, however. As the dominant expression of entire communities of black working-class youth, meanwhile, rap calls for a specific approach to understand its significance as a reformulation of the lyrical-musical dialectic in the new context of class and race relations in contemporary Brazil. Tricia Rose, writing on u.s. hip-hop culture, offers a suggestive point of departure that shares some striking and intriguing parallels with Luiz

Tatit's analysis of melodic continuity and linguistic segmentation in Brazilian songwriting:

> Like break-dancing and grafitti, music and vocality in rap also privilege flux, fluidity and successive ruptures. In their songs the rappers talk explicitly of flux, referring to a skill in shifting easily and powerfully through complex sounds, as well as circulating through the music. The flux and movement of the guitars and drums, in rap, are intersected sharply by scratches (a process that highlights the way in which the fluency of the basic rhythm is broken up.). The rhythmic cadence, too, is interrupted by the entry of other pieces of music. 'Stammering' in rap, which alternates with the accelerating of certain passages, always shifting along with the drumming or in response to it, is an element which constantly makes up the structure of this kind of music . . . These verbal movements highlight lyrical flux and emphasize rupture . . . Let us imagine these principles of hip-hop as a project of resistance and social affirmation: they create, sustain, accumulate, stratify, embellish and transform their narratives. But they are also prepared for rupture and even find pleasure in it, for they are in fact planning a social rupture.[8]

Similarly, discussing the political impact of rap, musicologist Simon Frith draws attention to the very obsession expressed in the genre with the by turns mobilizing and demobilizing effects of language. In other words, power comes to be defined as a 'a way with words'.

> A rap like 'Don't Believe the Hype' is significant less for its logical unfolding than for its investment of key words with force. And given the nature of these words – their obvious coding as urban black – they are being invested with urban

black force; they are at once a threat and a promise,
according to who's listening . . . [the way they are spoken]
becomes a particularly interesting (and complex) effect in a
rap, which foregrounds the problematic relationship of sung
and spoken language. Rap acts like Public Enemy imply that
such musical (or poetic) devices as rhythm and rhyme are
material ways of organizing and shaping feeling and desire;
they offer listeners new ways of performing (and thus changing) everyday life.[9]

Such strategies may indeed correspond to a new way of
conceiving the twin functions of rhythm and language and
the role of song in the context of 1990s Brazil: simultaneously
mobilizing and uniting its listeners in a common project of self-
identification and rupture from the bankrupt culture of consensus.
It is as if, in the words of Chico Science's 'Banditismo por uma
questão de classe' (Thuggery as a matter of class), the consensual
rhythms of popular culture must be inoculated with the disjunc-
tures of the social crisis in order to regenerate themselves; there
is nothing for it, then, but to 'fazer uma embolada, um samba,
um maracatu, / Tudo bem envenenado, bom pra mim e bom pra
tu / Pra a gente sair da lama e enfrentar os urubu' (dance and sing
an *embolada*, a samba, a *maracatu*, / All good and poisoned, nice
for me and nice for you / So's we can climb out the mud and face
the vultures).

But for some observers, this musical and ideological rupture
with Brazil's culture of consensus was tantamount to 'un-Brazilian
activity'. Interviewed in a national newspaper in 1998, music critic
and historian José Ramos Tinhorão referred to the dissemination
of rap in Rio de Janeiro and São Paulo as a 'process of de-national-
ization of the national musical product'.[10] Certainly the view that
rap (like soul music in the 1970s) represented an alien, imported
phenomenon with no affinity or precedent in Afro-Brazilian

musical tradition posed a problem: either Brazil's black youth had decided to adopt a borrowed model of linguistic-musical invention, that of rap, out of simple ethnic or political identification with their North American peers, and had suddenly discovered a collective talent for composing sophisticated and prolific lyrics, thus apparently contradicting the entire assumption that language was the weak element in the Afro-Brazilian contribution to the nation's heritage; or, as seems more likely, this explosion of creativity (one source estimated the number of rap groups in Greater São Paulo alone, in 1998, as around 30,000[11]) represented instead the recuperation of an inherent artistic vein under the stimulus of the North American model, the rediscovery of a linguistic-musical faculty that was already central to the black cultural tradition in Brazil.

This resource, the ability to materialize the power of words in rhythmically structured time, certainly did not spring from nowhere, but has drawn on an historically accumulated store of knowledge. From its West African antecedents, through the slave traditions of *batuque* and ring samba, the *jongo, samba de partido alto* and *samba-de-breque*, as we saw in chapter One, the matrix of Afro-Brazilian musical culture has been this capacity of musical prosody to act as the bearer of linguistic structures whose significance for black identity resides as much in their power as sonic symbols as in their discursive, semantic meaning. Rap therefore returns us to the idea of a black musical aesthetic in which bodily and linguistic expression, drum and word, rhythm and speech, are not to be counterposed but integrated in a single artistic complex.

This is not something generally recognized, either at the level of popular perceptions or much of the musical historiography, which has been so profoundly shaped by the idea of the mind-body split, and its racialized version as a paradigm in Western post-colonial ideology, the musical division-of-labour theory, in which the white European is the master of reason and language, while the essence of the black African is supposed to reside in the domains of emotion, the body and sex. As Simon Frith explains, not only is this an ideological construction, but it is also unsustainable in musicological terms:

> There is, indeed, a long history in Romanticism of defining black culture, specifically African culture, as the body, the other of the bourgeois mind. Such a contrast is derived from the Romantic opposition of nature and culture: the primitive or pre-civilized can thus be held up against the sophisticated or over-civilized – one strand of the Romantic argument was that primitive people were innocent people, uncorrupted by culture, still close to a human 'essence'. . . . And given that African musics are most obviously different from European musics in their uses of rhythm, then rhythm must be how the primitive, the sexual, is expressed . . . It is, in fact, the rhythm-focused experience of music-in-the-process-of-production that explains the appeal of African-American music and not its supposed 'direct' sensuality. The body, that is to say, is engaged with this music in a way that it is not engaged with European musics, but in musical rather than sexual terms.[12]

However, much of the commentary on Afro-Brazilian music has insisted on the assumption that the African tradition is essentially percussive and that the fundamental characteristic of the black musical aesthetic is rhythm; we can find a bald statement of this position in David Vassberg's discussion of 'African Influences on the Music of Brazil': 'Virtually all observers agree that the most salient feature of black African music is its rhythm, which is far more prominent than either melody or harmony . . . The basis of Negro music, and the principal medium of black musical

expression, is the drum.'[13] Although more sophisticated, John
Storm Roberts's version, citing Alan Merriam in *Black Music
of Two Worlds*, is essentially the same:

> It seems to be the totality of the musical concept which sees
> rhythm and percussive effect as the deep, basic organizational
> principle underlying African music. Drums and drumming,
> the use of idiophones, the forceful and dynamic vocal attack,
> and other characteristics reflect this principle; it is African
> music which is essentially rhythmic and percussive in effect,
> and the devices used simply reflect the principle.[14]

This subordination of the voice to the rhythmic imperative
has, of course, a well known and plausible explanation: that one
dimension of the material and cultural expropriation brought
about by slavery was the 'sequestration of speech', the repression
of the slaves' mother tongues and of their access to the written
language as a repository of the wisdom of the community, a
role that would be taken over by bodily, non-verbal means of
expression and communication, such as music and dance. As
Stuart Hall puts it: 'mark how, displaced from a logocentric
world – where the direct mastery of cultural modes meant the
mastery of writing . . . the people of the black diaspora have, in
opposition to all of that, found the deep form, the deep structure
of their cultural life in music.'[15] But Hall's statement should be
treated with caution, for to marginalize the black slave from the
privileges of written communication was not the equivalent of
eliminating altogether the cultural functions of language among
the slaves, especially spoken language, which has continued to
play a far from subordinate role in the musical culture of Afro-
descendants in the Americas as well as in West Africa itself.
The separation between bodily and linguistic expressions in
the cultures of the black diaspora should be discarded as at the

very least suspect and certainly little in keeping with the most up-to-date research.

In his *African Rhythm: A Northern Ewe Perspective*, Kofi Agawu plainly rebuts the assumption that 'African rhythm' simply means drumming, arguing that song and speech are the fundamental constituents of African musical art. Language and music should be considered as independent but overlapping semiotic systems, calling for a simultaneous, combined analysis:

> Ewe words, as we have seen, have a latent musicality stemming from the twin attributes of tone and rhythm. In speech or performed language, that which is latent approaches, without necessarily attaining, the condition of the patent. This interstice between language and music, although it can conceptually be smoothed over in certain contexts, is not ultimately eliminable . . . The interesting thing about the language-as-music and music-as-language metaphors is to be found in this dynamic and unstable condition, the state of language striving to become music.[16]

The similarity between this description and Luiz Tatit's analysis of the modern singer-songwriter's art, achieving the 'intonational process' that extends speech into song, is striking here.[17] Kofi Agawu again: 'If song lies at the heart of African musical expression, and since song consists of a fusion or integration or amalgamation of words (or "language" or "text") and music . . . then a productive approach to the analysis of song will include primary emphasis on the rhythms of language.'[18]

As Daphne Harrison observes, in the case of the Ashanti, there are several instruments that employ a surrogate speech with the same fluency as the linguist of the tribal court, where the tone takes the place of the word. The most famous and most often used are the *atumpan*, the legendary talking drums that declaim poetry, acclaim the chief and announce important events: 'The Yoruba counterpart to the Ashanti *atumpan* is found in the *Iyalu* of the dundun drum (an hourglass-shaped drum) ensemble. In fact, the *Iyalu* drummer is said to have wider freedom of speech through music than he would enjoy in the usual spoken discourse.'[19] The basic principle of the talking drum is simple and straightforward: rhythmic and tonal patterns of spoken language are reproduced on a drum. But, as Ashenafi Kebede explains, 'the artist is not obliged to restrict himself to a few phrases, as one might imagine. Following the ups and downs of tonal language, the good *atumpan* player can convey any situation or topic to listeners who understand the language.'[20]

But if, in West African musical practice, the rhythmic, percussive codification of linguistic structures emerges as a fundamental aesthetic principle, then we can also point to the inverse process, in which the structuring rhythmic sequences of African music are verbalized mnemonically in order to facilitate recall. After studying these techniques, Gerhard Kubik explains:

> *Verbalization of musical patterns* is, in fact, one of the most persistent musical concepts in Black Africa as a whole. This is perpetuated in Black Music of the Americas including the United States. In the Drum-and-Fife Bands of the South basic drum patterns are verbalized . . . In African traditions of the New World one can find the following kinds of mnemonics: *syllable* patterns (= patterns without any verbal meaning) which sometimes are made up of a phonetic repertory derived from African languages; *verbal patterns* either in the locally spoken dialect of a European language or made up of fragments of African words or phrases.[21]

Kubik continues: 'The phonetics of the mnemonic syllables change slightly as one goes from one language area to another . . .

But there are some recurrent traits in this system valid throughout much of the vast stretch of African land where time-line
patterns occur'[22] – that is to say, along the coast of West and
Central-western Africa, the main regions from which Brazil's
slave populations originated.

We could ask whether this characteristic that is such a striking
feature of African and Afro-American aesthetic traditions – the
reciprocal codification of rhythmic and linguistic sequences – is
also applicable to the case of Brazil. Might the African musical
complex, in which speech acts as a bearer of rhythmic structures
and the rhythmic sequence as the bearer of verbal structures,
have contributed to the construction of a black aesthetic, an
Afro-Brazilian manner of sung speech inherited from the creole
language, based on Portuguese but with a strong African content,
that was probably spoken on the Atlantic coast during the colonial
period? More than forty years ago, Melville Herskovits recom-
mended studying the possible retention of the African tonal
element as apparently displayed in the 'musical' quality of black
speech across the New World.[23]

When, at the end of the century, the black youth of Brazil
took over a musical genre whose generative principle is the vocalization of rhythmic sequences, the rhythmic articulation of linguistic
structures – in other words, rap – they were therefore not turning
their backs on the Afro-Brazilian aesthetic tradition so much
as recuperating it via another route, rediscovering it through a
parallel current within the black diaspora. This perhaps enables
us to interpret the following comment by rap artist Marcelo D2
regarding the death of *sambista* Jovelina Pérola Negra in 1998:
'No-one composed verses like her. When she sang, you understood
the connection between rap and samba. Rap is a re-reading of
samba. If you can't see that, you don't understand a thing about
rap, or about samba.'[24] But not all Brazilians would recognize
the kinship that Marcelo D2 takes for granted between these two

diasporic musical traditions; in fact, pan-American diasporic affinities such as these pose a disturbing threat to the kind of conservative thinking for which the only conceivable allegiance open to Afro-descendants should be to the Brazilian nation, as Afro-*Brazilians*, rather than as *negros*. There is a deep resistance on the part of many, too, to admitting the concept of a *black* musical identity in Brazil, as there is to any discussion of black identities at all, whether cultural or political.

## A BLACK MUSICAL AESTHETIC?

One legitimate objection to such categories might be the charge of essentialism or cultural racialism; no such category as 'black music' exists, some would say, until and unless we choose to speak of it, and in doing so we give credence to the fiction that skin colour is a meaningful marker of social and cultural identity. By taking as our premise that a field of cultural practice such as 'black music' can be identified as an integral object of study, we surely run the risk ourselves of racializing identity, of reifying the association of certain characteristics or modes of behaviour with people of a given phenotype.

Furthermore, to isolate one particular tradition and philosophy of music-making, 'black music' or *música negra*, from the heterogeneous fabric of a nation's cultural life might seem to be going against the grain. At a time when we should be embracing and celebrating the promiscuity and hybridism of contemporary global culture, its healthy, uninhibited colour-blindness, isn't any talk of 'black music' surely a backward step, a retreat into the language and politics of sectionalism, nationalism and separatism? In Brazil this argument, that merely invoking the term 'black' or *negro* itself amounts to a racializing impulse and conjures up a racial problem where none need or should exist, has a long pedigree and remains the fulcrum of debate about race and colour.[25]

As the single largest colonial importer of African slave labour, and the last nation in the Western hemisphere to abolish the institution (in 1888), Brazil faced major challenges at the end of the nineteenth century in its aspiration to join the advanced capitalist economies of the West, in particular the need to modernize its labour force and its demographic and ethnic self-image. From the 1870s the political elite eagerly embraced the eugenicist, scientific racist ideas associated with Social Darwinism, then circulating in Europe, as both diagnosis and remedy for the country's socio-economic backwardness. So, in a systematic effort to 'whiten' the nation, following Abolition preferential incentives were offered to European immigrants, while the Afro-Brazilian ex-slaves – stigmatized as degenerate – were effectively excluded from access to land and to any but the most menial urban jobs, let alone the full and effective exercize of their citizenship as free individuals.[26]

In the 1930s, these explicitly racist policies gave way to a new populist, corporatist politics of national integration and social harmony. Industrialization and social welfare reforms held out the possibility of mobility for some, but only some, in the organized urban labour sector. Meanwhile, Afro-Brazilian culture – or a selective, sanitized version of it, amenable to control and manipulation by the state – became celebrated as the mythical core of Brazilian national identity, epitomized by samba and carnival. But any attempts by black or working-class organizations to represent their own experience and interests independently of the state, or to question its rhetoric of social inclusion, were met with outright totalitarian repression – the country's first black political party, the Frente Negra Brasileira (Black Brazilian Front), was outlawed in 1937. So the apparently liberal ideology of mixture (mestiçagem), integration and racial democracy went hand in hand with repressive hostility toward those who challenged their oppression in terms of race or class.

Mirroring this *mestiço* nationalism in the political sphere were the discussions in the mid-twentieth century about Afro-Brazilian culture, including music, which were held up as models of the country's capacity to assimilate and homogenize diverse identities. Oneyda Alvarenga's pioneering study 'Black Influence on Brazilian Music' (1946) proposed a modified version of the transatlantic division-of-labour theory for Brazilian music; Alvarenga argued that Europe brought Brazil tonality, harmony, melodic structure, its instruments,

> in short, everything that forms the basis of our music, all the elements that were indispensable for its creation and that were elaborated here not in a black way [*negramente*], but in a Brazilian way [*brasileiramente*] . . . I agree with Mário de Andrade, in thinking that the task that fell to the black man, in essence, was that of colouring the material that had come from Europe.[27]

The language of 'colouring' is highly significant here; for Alvarenga, the African legacy was so deeply assimilated into the general fabric of Brazil's popular musical culture as to be barely distinguishable from it, discernible as no more than a superficial tingeing of what were essentially European structures. Implicit in this perspective was an assumption: the pre-condition for the Afro-Brazilian's admittance into the musical self-image of the nation was that black difference must be neutralized, and black cultural identity de-Africanized. The black presence in Brazil's musical life (as in its social and political life) was therefore only ever to be *felt* as a vague ancestral memory, to be recognized as a stylistic effect, but not to be heard or understood as having a living philosophy, grammar or aesthetic of its own – the latter, implicitly, could only ever be the preserve of a civilization of white, European origin.

The de-Africanization of Afro-Brazilian cultural expressions, music included, was celebrated by the leading ideologue of *mestiço*

nationalism and of Afro-Brazilian ethnic assimilation, Gilberto
Freyre, in a key passage from his 1936 study of Brazil's transition
to urban modernity, *Sobrados e Mocambos* (The Mansions and the
Shanties). Indeed, as the text makes clear, for Freyre the elaboration of national, *mestiço* cultural forms out of the 'raw material'
of African and slave traditions not only negated their alterity
but neutralized the *political* potential of black self-expression as
a source of revolt:

> What black and coloured youths did, by exploding on occasions
> into acts of hooliganism, was to give vent to energies normal
> in lusty adolescent men, which the dominant people did not
> always allow to be expressed through means less violent than
> escape to the maroon communities, the murder of white over-
> seers, or insurrection: the *batuque*, samba, capoeira, whistling,
> the cult of Ogun, the practice of the religion of Mohammed.[28]

And these cultural practices, understood by Freyre as the escape-
valve for the 'brute energies' of an immature black population,
would be attenuated, refined and appropriated, in the twentieth
century, through the process of de-Africanization:

> It is curious to observe today . . . that the descendants of
> the dancers of the razor and the knife are, as it were, being
> gradually sublimated into the dancers of the ball, that is the
> *foot*-ball . . . the steps of the samba are being rounded into
> that dance that is Bahian rather than African, danced by the
> performer Carmen Miranda to the applause of cultivated
> international audiences . . .[29]

This process, according to Freyre, was symptomatic of the black
man's longing to become assimilated, to be incorporated under
the protective wing of the dominant society: 'The point is that

even in rebellious blacks there was the almost ever-present desire, in a patriarchal, slaveowning Brazil, to be guided or protected paternally by powerful whites or masters.'[30]

During the six decades that followed the interventions of Freyre and Alvarenga, black political activism and self-organization, and their cultural counterparts, have been consistently denounced by the advocates of *mestiço* nationalism as 'divisive', as promoting the racialization of an essentially non-racialized country. An implicit assumption is that the convergence and fusion of race and nation, of Afro-Brazilian and Brazilian, of the ethnic and the popular, are such as to render redundant any separate discussion of black political or cultural identity. The latter, it is argued, implies the imposition of an alien binary racial model – either 'black' or 'white' – on a society that supposedly operates according to a different logic, that of the colour continuum, a democratic 'rainbow' of shades and identities (frequently referred to as Brazil's 'racial democracy'). Not race, but poverty or 'social' discrimination is the issue, it is claimed, as if race and class were of necessity mutually exclusive categories of oppression.

In fact the Brazilian racial system should probably be more accurately defined as one combining *both* a fluid colour continuum *and* a binary dichotomy, or rather as operating in the unresolved historical tension *between* these two taxonomies.[31] For one of the defining contradictions of Brazil's ideological and social life is precisely the co-existence (albeit conflictual) of the consensual, populist idea of racial and social integration fostered in official discourse since the 1930s with objective, statistically irrefutable evidence of colour and class discrimination – in employment, education, health, policing and so on. What this data actually shows is the inextricable interrelation between the categories of class and race, the profound racialization of working-class identity and the centrality of the black experience as tantamount to that of the class as a whole.[32]

Tens of millions of Brazilians of varying shades and physiques are therefore still identified as *negro* (a word which for three and a half centuries was synonymous with 'slave') and as such they are valued differently from their paler-skinned fellow citizens who rank 'higher' in the colour continuum. And the *mestiço* or *pardo* Brazilian is valorized only insofar as s/he possesses a lighter skin than the *negro* below her/him in the hierarchy while aspiring to the more privileged status of the *branco* higher up. In the 120 years since Abolition, the ideological legacy of 'whitening' has not 'naturally' withered away, as some believed it might. Nor has Brazil's Afro-descendant population ever ceased to be a racialized sub-category within the national society; the unfinished business left by more than three centuries of slavery has arguably deepened rather than attenuated the structural bonds linking racial and class oppression, blackness and poverty.[33]

But if the term *negro* carries the memory of that history of oppression, broadly designating the slaves and their descendants, it was also the specific appellation for the least compliant and most incalcitrant of them, and thereafter became adopted by rebels, activists and movements to denominate their identification with an entire tradition of Afro-Brazilian self-organization and struggle. As such, the term *negro* is resonant, too, with a history of resistance, consciousness and agency, and its expressive role in the anti-racist and more broadly popular movements signifies the emergence of a new, inclusive black political subject in contemporary Brazil. Recent years have seen something of a shift in Brazil from *preto* [the colour black] to *negro* as the preferred term of self-identification for Afro-Brazilians; indeed, during the last two decades (predating the Cardoso and Lula administrations' public policy initiatives on anti-racism, therefore) the increase in those self-identifying as *negro* has also been matched by a decline in the numbers opting for *branco*, 'white'.[34]

This shift probably reflects, not so much a deepening racialization of Brazilian society, as the growth of a broadly popular social consciousness (emergent from the late 1970s in an increasingly generalized, informal politics of popular self-organization and resistance) for which the black experience, anti-racism and the affirmation of black traditions of struggle and pride are central points of reference. The proliferation of cultural NGOs such as Olodum and Ilê Aiyê in Salvador, or the massive hip-hop movement of São Paulo, or youth and community initiatives like the Rio-based Afro Reggae, and their appeal both within and well beyond the ranks of darker-skinned Brazilians, are a measure of the increasingly political resonances of the term *negro* in the broader struggle against a history of oppression and denial, and for the right not only to be seen (to be visible *as* oneself) but also to be heard (to speak *for* oneself).

It is precisely in this spirit that we can insist on the formulations 'black music' and the Portuguese *música negra*, not as inert, essentialist categories, but as bearers of those notions of consciousness, agency and resistance. If we really want to de-essentialize the idea of blackness, we must first recognize that it is a contested terrain of meanings, an arena of struggle between the *objectification* of the subaltern in an aesthetic of condescension and negation, and the emergence of a new historical *subject* invested with political agency – consider the difference beween the contracted, familiar form *nego* (nigger), which can function in today's Brazil equally as a term of endearment or of abuse according to the context of power, and the defiantly unapologetic ring of the augmentative form *negão* as found, for example, in Gerônimo's 'Eu sou negão' (I'm a nigga), an iconic song for the black 'renaissance' of Salvador da Bahia from the 1970s onward.[35]

The point here, in making the case for a distinctive black musical aesthetic, is not to deny the extraordinarily rich and dynamic processes of interaction, dialogue and hybridization that have occurred between cultural traditions within and without the black diaspora – these are, after all, the very stuff of popular music history – nor to underestimate the capacity of national cultures and economies to incorporate and rebrand previously marginal art-forms as their own. Brazil is hardly a special case in this regard. The history of the blues, of jazz, soul or reggae has, like that of samba, been shaped by processes of mediation, hybridization and transculturation between African, European and other traditions; they, too, have moved from the margins to become incorporated into the mainstream of national cultures and their industries, and all have been successfully adopted by white musicians and audiences. Yet few people would surely object to the view that these are all still quintessentially black musical traditions, expressive in the most formative phases of their evolution, and in their core structures and forms, of the black experience.

On the other hand, we should also be careful not to fetishize this tendency towards musical fusion and incorporation (as some have fetishized the mantras of globalization and cultural homogenization) to the point where the contradictions, unevennesses and struggles of real social and cultural history appear to be erased, as if there were something necessarily absolute, all-absorbing about the way in which states and markets break down the distinctiveness of traditional forms, structures and practices. In the case of Brazil, we should beware of being persuaded too easily by the rhetoric of national-populism and *mestiço* nationalism, so that we fail to recognize the unresolved, contradictory nature of the interaction between the ethnic and the popular, and become deaf to the musical evidence of difference – the persistence and reinvention of traditions of music-making in the hands and voices of living human individuals who refuse, or are refused, their assimilation into a homogenous national culture.

If the projection of black agency into Brazil's historical future is a disturbing enough challenge for the defenders of *mestiço*

nationalism, then it has proved equally problematic for the
country to confront the memory of slavery and its legacy as
a living presence constitutive of modernity, rather than as some
sort of pre-historic aberration disconnected from it and from
contemporary everyday life. When one considers the enormous
formative impact of African slavery on the country's economic,
social and cultural evolution and the massive demographic presence, by anybody's standards, of the Afro-descendant population
in today's Brazil, one cannot help but be struck by the proportion-
ately low profile, the relative invisibility, that black history, political
activism and intellectual-artistic work have suffered nationally
over the last century, whether in educational curricula, official
commemorations and museums, or in the media.[36]

If music appears to be one of the exceptions to this general
picture of social and political invisibility for Afro-Brazilians, then
that ought precisely to be of special interest to us in itself. The
ease with which most Brazilians can acknowledge the African
'roots' of so much of the country's musical heritage, yet the
resistance of many to the notion of a distinctively black musical
tradition or identity as such within *today's* national culture,
exposes a central faultline in the country's dream of integrating
race and nation – the rupture between past and present, the
denial of a continuity between the historical memory and the
contemporary experience of black Brazilians. That continuity
of self across time, which is surely a core element of what we
mean by identity – remembering, re-presenting, reinventing that
commonality of being and experience that links us to earlier
generations and versions of ourselves – that sense of connectedness is something that black Brazilians have had to work hard to
bring to life in the face of a state and its official culture that, until
recently, preferred to keep a strict separation between the realm
of Afro-Brazilian history and patrimony, and the contemporary
social and political concerns of the *movimento negro*, such as the

day-to-day lived experience of racism and the role of Afro-Brazilians in the country's economy and public life.

All of which makes a compelling argument for exploring the question of a black musical aesthetic, not as a closed, bounded essentialist category, but as a dynamic, living tradition of practices and attitudes that is no more or less prone to reification than the general phenomenon of music-making itself. In this spirit, arguing both for the transformative power of creative agency, and against the essentialism of the Afro-centrists, Paul Gilroy offered in his *The Black Atlantic* a modernist defence of the living diasporic tradition as both an expression of black suffering and remembrance, and of utopian critique, the imagination of another possible world. In order 'to comprehend the reproduction of cultural traditions not in the unproblematic transmission of a fixed essence through time but in the breaks and interruptions which suggest that the invocation of tradition may itself be a distinct, though covert, response to the destabilising flux of the post-contemporary world',[37] Gilroy introduced his concept of the 'changing same'. I am not convinced, though, that this formulation – the 'changing same' – really advances our understanding of the problem of continuity and change, since it merely restates the paradox in its abstraction, leaving untouched the idea of an essence, or 'same'.

As an alternative to Gilroy's formulation, we could consider a musical analogy: that of repetition and variation, or call-and-response: the dialectical play, which runs throughout all musical practice, between the reproduction of familiar patterns of sound and their transformation. At the level of black artistic traditions and identities this model of repetition and variation corresponds to two complementary tendencies: on the one hand, the vital role of musical memory, recall and transmission in enabling individual and collective psyches to resist the traumatic, shattering effects of enslavement and the Middle Passage; and on the other, the power of musical variation, improvisation and transformation to enact and embody a utopian alternative to the suffering and oppression of the here and now, to make it possible literally to feel in one's bones the dream of moving freely and creatively in another time and space.

# CHRONOLOGY

**1889**

Abolition of slavery in Brazil as Golden Law (Lei Áurea) is passed.

**1902**

Pereira Passos takes office as Mayor of Rio de Janeiro (ends in 1906) and undertakes urban reform programme.

**1917**

'Pelo telefone' recorded, registered by Ernesto dos Santos 'Donga'.

**1933**

'Lenço no pescoço' (Wilson Batista) recorded by Sílvio Caldas.

**1937**

Estado Novo dictatorship under President Getúlio Vargas begins (ends in 1945).

**1939**

'Aquarela do Brasil' (Ary Barroso) first performed.

**1955**

First local rock-and-roll recording, Nora Ney's cover of 'Rock Around the Clock'.

**1956**

Juscelino Kubitschek presidency begins (ends 1961). *Orfeu da Conceição* stage musical by Vinicius de Moraes.

## 1957

Miguel Gustavo's 'Rock and Roll em Copacabana' recorded by Cauby Peixoto.
Film *Rio, Zona Norte* (Nelson Pereira dos Santos) released.

## 1958

'Chega de saudade' and 'Desafinado' (Antônio Carlos Jobim / Vinicius de Moraes) recorded as a single by João Gilberto.

## 1959

Film *Black Orpheus* (Marcel Camus) released.

## 1961

João Goulart 'Jango' begins presidency (deposed by military in 1964) and launches 'Grassroots Reforms' programme.
CPCs (Popular Culture Centres) launched by Carlos Lyra, Leon Hirzsman and others.

## 1962

'Garota de Ipanema' (Antônio Carlos Jobim / Vinicius de Moraes) first perfomed.
'Influência do Jazz' (Carlos Lyra) released.
Bossa Nova concert in New York's Carnegie Hall.

## 1963

Baden Powell and Vinicius de Moraes begin composing Afro-sambas such as 'Berimbau'.
Nara Leão performs in musical *Pobre menina rica* by Carlos Lyra and Vinicius de Moraes.

## 1964

Coup deposes President João Goulart and ushers in 21-year period of military dictatorship.
Caetano Veloso, Gilberto Gil, Maria Bethânia et al (so-called *Baianos* who went on to found Tropicália) arrive in Rio de Janeiro from Salvador da Bahia.
Maria Bethânia replaces Nara Leão in protest musical *Opinião* by Oduvaldo Viana Filho.

## 1965

TV Record begins weekly broadcasts of *Jovem Guarda* rock programme and Bossa Nova programme *O Fino (da Bossa)*.

## 1966

Rio de Janeiro's Maracanãzinho arena begins staging International Song Festival. 'Disparada' by Geraldo Vandré and Théo de Barros shares first prize with Chico Buarque's 'A Banda' in TV Record's 2nd Festival of Brazilian Popular Music.

## 1968

É proibido proibir' performed by Caetano Veloso and Mutantes, booed by audience at TV Globo Song Festival in São Paulo.
*Tropicália, ou Panis et Circensis* album released.
Geraldo Vandré's 'Pra não dizer que não falei das flores (Caminhando)' loses third International Song Festival but is acclaimed by audience.
September street protests followed by Institutional Act No. 5, suspending *habeas corpus* and ushering in hard-line radicalization of military dictatorship.

## 1973

*João Gilberto*, Gilberto's 'white album', released.

## 1985

Democratic transition officially ends dictatorship, amidst rampant inflation and social crisis.

## 1994

Antônio Carlos 'Tom' Jobim dies.
Pavilhão 9's *Procurados: vivos ou mortos* and Chico Science's *Da lama ao caos* released.

## 1997

Racionais MCs' *Sobrevivendo no inferno* released.

## 1998

Film *Orfeu* (Carlos Diegues) released.

## 2002

Film *City of God* (Fernando Meirelles / Kátia Lund) released.

# REFERENCES

**1 BRAZILIAN JIVE TALK: MUSIC, LANGUAGE, COMMUNITY**

1 Graciliano Ramos, *Memórias do Cárcere*, 2 vols (Lisbon, n.d.), vol. 1, p. 113. My translation. All translations from the Portuguese are the author's.

2 Robert Jourdain, *Music, the Brain, and Ecstasy: How Music Captures our Imagination* (New York, 1997), pp. 296–7.

3 Leonard B. Meyer, *Emotion and Meaning in Music* (Chicago, 1956), p. 265.

4 Susanne K. Langer, *Philosophy in a New Key* (New York, 1951), p. 155, cited ibid., p. 265.

5 John Shepherd and Peter Wicke, *Music and Cultural Theory* (Cambridge, 1997), p. 103.

6 Ibid., p. 129.

7 Ibid.

8 Paul Gilroy, *The Black Atlantic: Modernity and Double Consciousness* (London and New York, 1993), p. 77.

9 For an introduction to these diverse traditions see Chris McGowan and Ricardo Pessanha, *The Brazilian sound: Samba, Bossa Nova and the Popular Music of Brazil* (Philadelphia, PA, 1998) and John P. Murphy, *Music in Brazil: Experiencing Music, Expressing Culture* (New York and Oxford, 2006)

10 Kofi Agawu, *African Rhythm: A Northern Ewe Perspective* (Cambridge, 1995), p. 2.

11 Luiz Tatit, *O Cancionista: composição de canções no Brasil* (São Paulo, 1996).

12 Anthony Storr, *Music and the Mind* (London, 1993), p. 37.

13 Jourdain, *Music, the Brain and Ecstasy*, p. 281.

14 Tatit, *O Cancionista*, and Luiz Tatit, 'Analysing Popular Songs', in *Popular Music Studies*, ed. D. Hesmondhalgh and K. Negus (London and New York, 2002), pp. 33–50.

15 Tatit, *O Cancionista*, p. 16.

16 Thrasybulos Georgiades, *Music and Language* (Cambridge, 1982), p. 6.

17 Kazadi wa Mukuna, *Contribuição bantu na música popular brasileira* (São

Paulo, 1976), p. 77.

18 Edison Carneiro, *Samba de Umbigada* (Rio de Janeiro, 1961), p. 33.

19 Nei Lopes, 'Sambangola: presença bantu na música do povo brasileiro, *Boletim do Centro de Memória unicamp*, iii/6 (July–December 1991), p. 22.

20 Gerhard Kubik, *Angolan Traits in Black Music, Games and Dances of Brazil: A Study of African Cultural Extensions Overseas* (Lisbon, 1979), p. 20.

21 Ibid., p. 18.

22 Marília Trindade Barboza da Silva, 'Negro em roda de samba: herança africana na Música Popular Brasileira', *Revista Tempo Brasileiro*, 92–3 (1988), special issue: 'O Negro e a Abolição', pp. 107–8.

23 Cited in Lopes, 'Sambangola', p. 23.

24 Maria de Lourdes Borges Ribeiro, *O Jongo* (Rio de Janeiro, 1984), p. 11.

25 Mário de Andrade, 'O Samba rural paulista', *Aspectos da Música Brasileira* (São Paulo, 1965), pp. 149–50.

26 João José Reis, 'Batuque: African Drumming and Dance between Repression and Concession, Bahia, 1808–1855', *Bulletin of Latin American Research*, xxiv/2 (2005), pp. 201–14.

27 Samuel A. Floyd Jr, The *Power of Black Music: Interpreting its History from Africa to the United States* (New York, 1995), pp. 6, 21.

28 Muniz Sodré, *O Terreiro e a Cidade: a forma social negro-brasileira* (Petrópolis, 1988), p. 96.

29 Ibid., pp. 50–51.

30 Ibid., pp. 51–3.

31 Jeffrey Needell, 'Rio de Janeiro at the Turn of the Century: Modernization and the Parisian Ideal', *Journal of Interamerican Studies and World Affairs*, xxv/1 (1983), pp. 83–103.

32 Roberto Moura, *Tia Ciata e a Pequena África no Rio de Janeiro* (Rio de Janeiro, 1995), pp. 54–5.

33 Ibid., p. 58.

34 Carlos Sandroni, *Feitiço Decente: transformações do samba no Rio de Janeiro (1917–1933)* (Rio de Janeiro, 2001), pp. 39–61. See also Daniella Thompson, 'Praça Onze in Popular Song', at http://daniellathompson.com, accessed 20 June 2012.

35 Sodré, *O Terreiro e a Cidade*, p. 137.

36 Ibid., p. 76.

37 Mukuna, *Contribuição bantu na música popular brasileira*, p. 12. See also Kubik, *Angolan Traits in Black Music*, pp. 14–18.

38 Sandroni, *Feitiço Decente*, pp. 118–30. See also Flávio Silva's pioneering study

of the recording, 'Pelo Telefone e a história do samba', Cultura, VIII/8 (1978), pp. 64–73.

39 Cláudia Neiva de Matos, Acertei no milhar: samba e malandragem no tempo de Getúlio (Rio de Janeiro, 1982); Lisa Shaw, The Social History of the Brazilian Samba (Aldershot and Brookfield, VT, 1999)

40 Cláudia Neiva de Matos, 'Dicções malandras do samba', in Ao encontro da palavra cantada poesia, música e voz, ed. C. Neiva de Matos, E. Travassos and F. Teixeira de Medeiros (Rio de Janeiro, 2001), p. 69.

41 Júlio Tavares, 'Educação através do corpo; a representação do corpo em populações afro-americanas', Revista do Patrimônio Histórico e Artístico Nacional, XXV (1997), pp. 216–22.

42 Muniz Sodré, 'Corporalidade e Liturgia Negra' in Negro brasileiro negro, ed. J. Rufino (Rio de Janeiro, 1997).

43 Muniz Sodré, Samba, o dono do corpo (Rio de Janeiro, 1998), pp. 11, 31–2.

44 Ralph Ellison, Invisible Man (London, 2001), p. 8.

45 Melville J. Herskovits, The Myth of the Negro Past (Boston, MA, 1968), p. 71.

46 Samuel A. Floyd, (New York, 1995), p. 74.

47 Henry Louis Gates Jr, The Signifying Monkey: A Theory of African-American Literary Criticism (New York and Oxford, 1988), p. 6.

48 Matos, 'Dicções malandras do samba', p. 68.

49 Ibid., pp. 71–2.

50 Ramos, Memórias do Cárcere, I, p. 113.

51 Translated from Carlos Drummond de Andrade, 19 livros de poesias (Rio de Janeiro, 1983).

52 The acronym stands, somewhat confusingly, for Música Popular Brasileira.

53 Tatit, O Cancionista, p. 17.

54 Friedrich Nietzsche, Basic Writings of Nietzsche (New York, 1968), p. 750.

55 Friedrich Nietzsche, The Gay Science (New York, 1974), p. 373.

56 José Miguel Wisnik, 'The Gay Science: Literature and Popular Music in Brazil', Journal of Latin American Cultural Studies: Travesia, V/2 (1996), pp. 191–202.

57 For an analysis of the phenomenon of MPB and the concept of a Brazilian musical 'tradition' or mainstream, see Sean Stroud, The Defence of Tradition in Brazilian Popular Music: Politics, Culture and the Creation of Musica Popular Brasileira (Aldershot, 2008).

58 Istvan Mészaros, Marx's Theory of Alienation (London, 1975).

59 Victor Zuckerkandl, Man the Musician, Sound and Symbol (New Jersey, 1973), p. 75.

60 João Guimarães Rosa, The Jaguar and other stories, trans. David Treece (Oxford, 2001), pp. 168–72.

## 2 THE BOSSA NOVA REVOLUTION

1 For an appreciation of Tom Jobim, see Suzel Reily, 'Tom Jobim and the Bossa Nova Era', *Popular Music*, xv/1 (1996), pp. 1–16.

2 Ruy Castro, *Chega de saudade: a história e as histórias da Bossa Nova* (São Paulo, 1990), p. 419.

3 Marcos Valle, *Nova Bossa Nova* (Farout Records, 1997); Bebel Gilberto, *Tanto Tempo* (Ziriguiboom/Crammed Discs, 2000); D. J. Patife, *Cool Steps: Drum 'N' Bass Grooves* (Trama, 2002).

4 Theodor W. Adorno, 'On the Fetish Character in Music and the Regression of Listening' in *The Culture Industry: Selected Essays on Mass Culture* (London, 1991), p. 27.

5 Chris McGowan and Ricardo Pessanha, *The Billboard Book of Brazilian Music: Samba, Bossa Nova and the Popular Sounds of Brazil* (New York, 1991), pp. 67–8. See also Jeroen Gevers, 'Reinterpreting Bossa Nova: Instances of Translation of Bossa Nova in the United States, 1962–1974', MA Dissertation (Utrecht University, 2010).

6 McGowan and Pessanha, *The Billboard Book of Brazilian Music*, pp. 68–71.

7 Castro, *Chega de saudade*, pp. 310–11.

8 Mary Yelanjian, 'Rhythms of Consumption', *Cultural Studies*, v/1 (1991), pp. 92, 94.

9 Castro, *Chega de saudade*, p. 337.

10 Ibid., p. 254.

11 Luiz Tatit, *O Cancionista: composição de canções no Brasil* (São Paulo, 1996), p. 11.

12 José Miguel Wisnik, 'O minuto e o milênio ou Por favor, professor, uma década de cada vez', in *Anos 70: 1 - Música Popular*, ed. M. Autran, A. M. Bahiana and J. M. Wisnik (Rio de Janeiro, 1980), p. 11.

13 Tatit, *O Cancionista*, p. 9.

14 For a detailed account of these processes, see Robert Jourdain, *Music, the Brain and Ecstasy: How Music Captures our Imagination* (New York, 1997).

15 José Miguel Wisnik, *O Som e o Sentido: uma outra história das músicas* (São Paulo, 1989), pp. 20–23.

16 Castro, *Chega de saudade*, p. 168.

17 Ibid., pp. 168, 230, 280.

18 Ibid., p. 87.

19 Portuguese original: '*Brasil/ Meu Brasil brasileiro/. . ./ O Brasil, samba que dá/ Bamboleio, que faz gingar/ Brasil do meu amor/ Terra de Nosso Senhor/ Brasil, Brasil/ Pra mim, pra mim*'.

20 Castro, *Chega de saudade*, pp. 131–32 & 240.

21 Portuguese original: '*Só Deus que está no céu/ sabe dizer da minha angústia/ das horas que passei/ do desespero sem você/ foi bom nada lhe contarem/ bem bom não acreditarem/ pois deus que ouviu os meus ais/ também achou demais.*'

22 Castro, *Chega de saudade*, pp. 137–8.

23 Ibid., pp. 136–7.

24 Ibid., pp. 62–3.

25 Ibid., p. 147.

26 My thanks to Mercia Pinto for this observation.

27 In Almir Chediak, ed., *Bossa Nova Songbook*, 1 (Rio de Janeiro, 1990), p. 24.

28 J.E.H. de Mello, *Música popular brasileira cantada e contada por Tom, Baden, Caetano e outros* (São Paulo, 1976), p. 131.

29 Ibid., p. 76.

30 I base this broad characterization of the modal and tonal systems on the formulation elaborated by Wisnik in *O Som e o Sentido*.

31 Leonard B. Meyer, *Emotion and Meaning in Music* (Chicago, 1956), p. 220.

32 Walter Garcia, *Bim bom: a contradição sem conflitos de João Gilberto* (São Paulo, 1999).

33 I have borrowed the term 'metric dissonance' from Irna Priore's 'Authenticity and Performance Practice: Bossa Nova and João Gilberto', *Lied und populäre Kultur/ Song and Popular Culture*, LIII (2008), pp. 109–30.

34 João Gilberto, *João Gilberto: Live at Montreux* Elektra 9 60760 (1987).

35 João Gilberto, *João Gilberto* (1973). PolyGram/ Verve 837 589–2 (1988).

36 Christopher Dunn, *Brutality Garden: Tropicália and the emergence of a Brazilian counterculture* (Chapel Hill, NC, London, 2001).

37 Victor Zuckerkandl, *Sound and Symbol: Music and the External World* (Princeton, NJ, 1956), pp. 227–8, cited in J. Shepherd and P. Wicke, *Music and Cultural Theory* (Cambridge, 1997), pp. 134–5.

### 3 THREE MASTERS, THREE MASTERPIECES: JOBIM, MORAES, GILBERTO

1 Almir Chediak, ed., *Songbook: Bossa Nova*, 5 vols (Rio de Janeiro, n.d).

2 Released in 1988 by EMI on a single CD entitled *The Legendary João Gilberto: The Original Bossa Nova Recordings (1958–1961)*, World Pacific 93891, 1990; João Gilberto, *João Gilberto* (1973), PolyGram/ Verve 837 589–2, 1988.

3 Irna Priore, 'Authenticity and Performance Practice: Bossa nova and João Gilberto', *Lied und populäre Kultur / Song and Popular Culture*, LIII (2008),

pp. 109–30.

4 'Entrevista: Carlos Lyra', in *Songbook: Bossa Nova*, ed. Almir Chediak, vol. II (Rio de Janeiro, n.d.), p. 20.

5 See the volume of essays dedicated to João Gilberto on the eightieth anniversary of his birth, Walter Garcia, ed., *João Gilberto* (São Paulo, 2012).

6 See Christopher Dunn's interview with Sonny Carr ibid.

7 See Arthur Nestrovski's formulation of this idea in his essay 'O samba mais bonito do mundo', in *Três canções de Tom Jobim*, ed. Lorenzo Mammi, Arthur Nestrovski and Luiz Tatit (São Paulo, 2004), p. 41.

8 *Coisa mais linda: história e casos da bossa nova*, dir. Paulo Thiago, Sony Pictures Home Entertainment, 42748, 2005.

## 4 GUNS AND ROSES: BRAZIL'S MUSIC OF POPULAR PROTEST, 1958–68

1 Mike Gonzalez and David Treece, *The Gathering of Voices: The Twentieth-century Poetry of Latin America* (London, 1992), pp. 227–53.

2 J. D. Straubhaar, 'Mass Communication and the Elites', in *Modern Brazil: Elites and Masses in Historical Perspective*, ed. M. L. Coniff and F. D. McCann (Lincoln, NE, and London, 1991), pp. 225–45.

3 José Ramos Tinhorão, *Música Popular do Gramofone ao Rádio e TV* (São Paulo, 1981), p. 176. For a full account of the song festivals, see Sean Stroud, '"Música é para o povo cantar": Culture, Politics and the Brazilian Song Festivals, 1965–72', *Latin American Music Review*, XXI/2 (Fall/Winter 2000), pp. 87–117.

4 Tinhorão, *Música Popular*, pp. 181–2.

5 José Eduardo Homem de Mello, *Música popular brasileira cantada e contada por Tom, Baden, Caetano e outros* (São Paulo,1976), pp. 334; Geraldo Vandré, sleevenotes to *Geraldo Vandré: História da Música Popular Brasileira* (Abril: HMPB-67-A, 1979), p. 10.

6 Walnice Nogueira Galvão, 'MMBP: uma análise ideológica', in *Saco de gatos: ensaios críticos* (São Paulo, 1976), pp. 93–6).

7 Michael Chanan, *Musica Practica: The Social Practice of Western Music from Gregorian Chant to Postmodernism* (London, 1994), pp. 37–9.

8 Ibid., p. 51.

9 Ruy Castro, *Chega de saudade: a história e as histórias da Bossa Nova* (São Paulo, 1990), p. 258.

10 Mello, *Música popular brasileira*, p. 112.

11 Castro, *Chega de saudade*, p. 344.

12  Mello, *Música popular brasileira*, p. 96.
13  A. Pavão, *Rock brasileiro 1955–65: trajetória, personagens, discografia* (São Paulo, 1989), pp. 13–16.
14  Ibid., p. 44.
15  Ibid., p. 27.
16  Ibid., p. 19.
17  Ibid., pp. 22–7.
18  Mello, *Música popular brasileira*, pp. 104–5.
19  C. E. Martins, 'Anteprojeto do Manifesto do CPC', *Arte em Revista: Anos 60*, 1/1 (January–March 1979), p. 73.
20  Ibid., p. 69.
21  Ibid., p. 71.
22  Ibid., p. 79.
23  Ibid., p. 75.
24  Ibid.
25  Mello, *Música popular brasileira*, p. 116.
26  Castro, *Chega de saudade*, p. 261.
27  Mello, *Música popular brasileira*, p. 111.
28  *Bossa Nova Songbook III* (Rio de Janeiro, 1990–91), pp. 24–5.
29  *Bossa Nova Songbook V* (Rio de Janeiro, 1990–91), p. 20.
30  Tárik de Souza, sleevenotes to *Sérgio Ricardo, Um Sr Talento*. Elenco, 1967. 512 055–2.
31  Castro, *Chega de saudade*, pp. 348–9.
32  Anon., 'Debate: caminhos da MPB' (1965), *Arte em revista*, 1 (January–March 1979), p. 40.
33  Anon., 'Baianos', *Violão e Guitarra Especial* (São Paulo, n.d.).
34  Mello, *Música popular brasileira*, p. 122.
35  Pavão, *Rock brasileiro 1955–65*, p. 34.
36  Ibid., pp. 33–6.
37  Anon., 'Jovem Guarda', *Vigu Especial*, V/56 (1983), pp. 10–11.
38  Anon., 'Os anos 60 – retrospectiva', *Violão e Guitarra Especial*, IV/37 (1981), p. 9.
39  Ibid.
40  Roberto Schwarz, 'Culture and Politics in Brazil, 1964–68', in *Misplaced Ideas: Essays on Brazilian Culture* (London, 1992), p. 127.
41  Ibid., p. 127.
42  Mello, *Música popular brasileira*, p. 115.
43  Ibid., p. 128.
44  Ibid., p. 129.

45  Ibid., p. 118.
46  A. Mauro, 'Festivais: a época de ouro da MBP', *Vigu Especial*, v/54 (1983), p. 5.
47  Mello, *Música popular brasileira*, pp. 119–20.
48  Anon., 'Os anos 60 – retrospectiva', p. 15.
49  For a more detailed account of the televised song festivals, see Stroud, '"Música é para o povo cantar": Culture, Politics and the Brazilian Song Festivals, 1965–72', *Latin American Music Review*, xxi/2 (Fall/Winter 2000), pp. 87–117. See also Sean Stroud, *The Defence of Tradition in Brazilian Popular Music: Politics, Culture and the Creation of Musica Popular Brasileira* (Aldershot, 2008).
50  Mauro, 'Festivais: a época de ouro da MBP', p. 8.
51  V. Krausche, *Música popular brasileira: da cultura de roda à música de massa* (São Paulo, 1983), p. 81).
52  Anon., 'Os anos 60 – retrospectiva', pp. 13–15.
53  See Christopher Dunn, *Brutality Garden: Tropicália and the mergence of a Brazilian counterculture* (Chapel Hill, NC, and London, 2001), for a full account of the Tropicália movement.
54  Heloísa Buarque de Hollanda, *Impressões de viagem: CPC, Vanguarda e Desbunde: 1960/1970* (São Paulo, 1981), p. 33.
55  Sue Branford and Bernardo Kucinski, *Brazil: Carnival of the Oppressed: Lula and the Brazilian Workers' Party* (London, 1995), p. 8.

## 5 ORPHEUS IN BABYLON: MUSIC IN THE FILMS OF RIO DE JANEIRO

1  See Lisa Shaw and Stephanie Dennison, *Popular Cinema in Brazil* (Manchester, 2004).
2  Charles Perrone, 'Don't Look Back: Myths, Conceptions, and Receptions of *Black Orpheus*', *Studies in Latin American Popular Culture*, xvii (1988), pp. 155–77.
3  Perrone, 'Don't Look Back'; Charles A. Perrone, 'Myth, Melopeia, and Mimesis: *Black Orpheus*, *Orfeu*, and Internationalization in Brazilian Popular Music' in *Brazilian Popular Music and Globalization*, ed. C. A. Perrone and C. J. Dunn (Gainesville, fl, 2001), pp. 46–71; Myrian Sepúlveda dos Santos, 'The Brazilian Remake of the Orpheus Legend: Film Theory and the Aesthetic Dimension', *Theory, Culture and Society*, xx/4 (2003), pp. 49–69; Jonathan Grasse, 'Conflation and Conflict in Brazilian Popular Music: Forty Years between "Filming" Bossa Nova in *Orfeu Negro* and Rap in *Orfeu*', *Popular Music*, xxiii/3 (2004.), pp. 291–310.

4  Micael Herschmann, ed., *Abalando os anos 90: Funk e Hip-Hop, globalização, violência e estilo cultural* (Rio de Janeiro, 1997).

5  José Miguel Wisnik, 'A gaia ciência: literatura e música popular', *Revista de Occidente*, CLXXIV (1995), pp. 53–72.

6  Author's translation from the Portuguese: Carlos Drummond de Andrade, *Obra Completa* (Rio de Janeiro, 1967), p. 105.

7  Zuenir Ventura, *Cidade Partida* (São Paulo, 1994).

8  Luís Alberto Rocha Melo, 'Rio Zona Norte de Nelson Pereira dos Santos, Brasil, 1957', *Contracampo Revista de Cinema*, 80 (n.d.), at www.contracampo. com.br, accessed 19 February 2011.

9  Irineu Guerrini Jr, *A música no cinema brasileiro: os inovadores anos sessenta* (São Paulo, 2009), pp. 26–8, 146–7.

10  For Luís Alberto Rocha Melo Rio, Zona Norte is a film essentially defined by the concept of 'enchantment' (Melo, 'Rio Zona Norte de Nelson Pereira dos Santos').

11  Perrone, 'Don't Look Back'; Santos, 'The Brazilian Remake of the Orpheus Legend'.

12  Perrone, 'Don't Look Back', p. 5.

13  Beatriz Jaguaribe, 'Favelas and the Aesthetics of Realism: Representations in Film and Literature', *Journal of Latin American Cultural Studies*, XIII/3 (2004), p. 330.

14  Perrone, 'Don't Look Back', p. 5.

15  Jaguaribe, 'Favelas and the Aesthetics of Realism'.

16  Santos, 'The Brazilian Remake of the Orpheus Legend', p. 50.

17  Ibid., p. 63.

18  Paulo Lins, *Cidade de Deus* (São Paulo, 1997).

19  Anon., sleeve notes, *Black Rio* STRUTCD 015 (2002).

20  Lena Frias, 'Black Rio: o orgulho (importado) de ser negro no Brasil', *Jornal do Brasil*, 17/7/76, Caderno B, p. 1.

21  Ricky Vincent, *Funk: The Music, the People, and the Rhythm of the One* (New York, 1996), p. 8.

## 6 RAP, RACE AND LANGUAGE: THE AESTHETICS AND POLITICS OF BLACK MUSIC-MAKING

1  Hermano Vianna, *O mundo funk carioca* (Rio de Janeiro, 1988); Micael Herschmann, ed., *Abalando os anos 90: Funk e Hip-Hop, globalização, violência e estilo cultural* (Rio de Janeiro, 1997).

2  See Sean Stroud, *The Defence of Tradition in Brazilian Popular Music: Politics,*

*Culture and the Creation of Musica Popular Brasileira* (Aldershot, 2008), especially the Conclusion.

3 Waly Salomão, 'A praia da Tropicália' in *Tropicália, 20 anos*, ed. José Saffioti Filho et al. (São Paulo, 1987), p. 34.

4 Edélcio Mostaço, 'Do corporal na arte', in *Tropicália, 20 anos*, ed. Filho et al., p. 70.

5 See Lorraine Leu, *Brazilian Popular Music: Caetano Veloso and the Regeneration of Tradition* (Aldershot and Burlington, VT, 2006).

6 Roberto Schwarz, 'Chico Buarque's New Novel', *Misplaced Ideas: Essays on Brazilian Culture* (London, 1992), pp. 197–201.

7 Detentos do Rap, 'Oração ao Pai' *Apologia ao crime*. fiELDZZ. 74321603632 (1998).

8 Tricia Rose, 'Um estilo que ninguém segura: política, estilo e a cidade pós-industrial no hip-hop', in *Abalando os anos 90: Funk e Hip-Hop, globalização, violência e estilo cultural*, ed. Micael Herschmann (Rio de Janeiro, 1997), pp. 207–8.

9 Simon Frith, *Performing Rites: On the Value of Popular Music* (Oxford, 1996), p. 169.

10 Cited in Cristina Magaldi, 'Adopting Imports: New Images and Alliances in Brazilian Popular Music of the 1990s', *Popular Music*, XVIII/3 (October 1999), p. 327, footnote 4.

11 Marina Amaral, 'Mais de 50.000 manos', *Caros Amigos Especial*, III (September 1998), pp. 4–8.

12 Frith, *Performing Rites*, pp. 127 and 141.

13 David E.Vassberg, 'African Influences on the Music of Brazil', *Luso-Brazilian Review*, XIII/1 (Summer 1976), pp. 37 and 40.

14 John Storm Roberts, *Black Music of Two Worlds* (New York, 1972), p. 11.

15 Stuart Hall, 'What is this "Black" in Black Popular Culture?' in *Black Popular Culture*, ed. Gina Dent (Seattle, 1992), p. 27.

16 Kofi Agawu, *African Rhythm: A Northern Ewe Perspective* (Cambridge, 1995), pp. 180–81.

17 Luiz Tatit, *O Cancionista: composição de canções no Brasil* (São Paulo, 1996).

18 Agawu, *African Rhythm*, p. 2.

19 Daphne D. Harrison, 'Aesthetic and Social Apects of Music in African Ritual Settings' in *More than Drumming: Essays on Afro-Latin American Music and Musicians*, ed. Irene V. Jackson (Westport, CT, 1985), pp. 51–2.

20 Ashenafi Kebede, *Roots of Black Music: The Vocal, Instrumental and Dance Heritage of Africa and Black America* (Trenton, NJ, 1995), p. 64.

21 Gerhard Kubik, 'Oral Notation of some West and Central African Time-line Patterns', *Review of Ethnology*, III/2 (1972), pp. 20–21.

22  Ibid., pp. 14–15.

23  Melville J. Herskovits, *The Myth of the Negro Past* (Boston, 1968).

24  Renato Lemos, 'O espalha-brasa', *Suplemento Domingo, Jornal do Brasil*, 8 November 1998, p. 14.

25  I italicize the Portuguese *negro* to distinguish it from the English 'Negro', with its somewhat different history and connotations; Michael George Hanchard, *Orpheus and Power: The 'Movimento Negro' of Rio de Janeiro and São Paulo, Brazil, 1945–1988* (Princeton, NJ, 1998), pp. 64–7.

26  Thomas Skidmore, *Black into White: Race and Nationality in Brazilian Thought* (Durham, NC, 1993), chaps 2–4.

27  Oneyda Alvarenga, A influência negra na música brasileira', *Boletín Latinoamericano de Música*, VI (1946), p. 370.

28  Gilberto Freyre, *Sobrados e Mocambos: Decadência do Patriarcado Rural e Desenvolvimento do Urbano* (Rio de Janeiro, 1961), II, p. 522.

29  Ibid., p. 522.

30  Ibid., p. 523.

31  As proposed in an important essay by Peter Fry, predating his more recent interventions in the campaign against the affirmative action policies of the Lula administration: 'Politics, Nationality, and the Meanings of "Race" in Brazil', *Dædalus*, CXXIX/2 (Spring 2000), pp. 97.

32  Lilia Moritz Schwarcz, *Not Black, Not White: Just the Opposite. Culture, Race and National Identity in Brazil*, Working Paper Number CBS–47-03 (Oxford, 2004), pp. 36–40.

33  Ibid., pp. 43–4.

34  Phydia de Athayde, 'Somos, sim, racistas', *Carta Capital*, 24 August 2009.

35  Mércia Flannery, 'Language, Stigma and Identity: An Analysis of the Narrative Discourse of Racial Discrimination', *Luso-Brazilian Review*, XLV/2 (2008), pp. 154–76; see Osmundo de Araújo Pinho, '"Fogo na Babilônia": Reggae, Black Counterculture, and Globalization in Brazil', in *Brazilian Popular Music and Globalization*, ed. C. Perrone and C. Dunn, (Gainsville, FL, 2001), pp. 192–206.

36  Save for some recent exceptions, such as São Paulo's extraordinary museum of Afro-Brazilian culture, the Museu Afro Brasil, opened in 2004 on the initiative of curator Emanoel Araújo.

37  Paul Gilroy, *The Black Atlantic: Modernity and Double Consciousness* (London and New York, 1993), p. 101.

# GLOSSARY OF TERMS

| | |
|---|---|
| *axé* | in Yoruba religious culture, the vital transformative force or energy; *Axé Music* – Afro-pop from northeastern state capital Salvador da Bahia, commercially marketed in the 1990s. |
| *baiano* | someone from the northeastern state of Bahia, including the freed slaves who migrated to Rio de Janeiro from the late nineteenth century, and the musicians of the Tropicália movement who moved south in the early 1960s. |
| *baião* | a lively, urban, accordion-based, two-step dance rhythm popularised at national level in the 1940s by northeastern songwriter and performer Luis Gonzaga. |
| *bateria* | percussion ensemble (as in samba bands); drum-set. |
| *batida* | 'beat' or pulse in general; right-hand guitar plucking technique developed by João Gilberto to combine functions of rhythm and harmony in bossa nova. |
| *batucada* | multi-layered, polyrhythmic drumming associated with samba and Afro-Brazilian tradition. |
| *batuque* | a central manifestation of slave culture, involving participants in drumming, dancing, singing and religious celebration. |
| *brasileirinho* | a rhythmic pattern ubiquitous in Brazilian popular music, consisting of a cell of 8 pulses divided into 5 stresses – 1+2+1:2+2 ('we are the champions!'). |
| *candomblé* | the matrix of Afro-Brazilian religions based on Yoruba, Fon and Bantu traditions, together with other influences, and centred on identification with a pantheon of deified ancestral spirits. |
| *capoeira* | a combat game, thought to have been derived from Bantu practices but developed under slavery, possibly as a form of training or preparation for rebellion, and involving pairs |

of combatants in dance-like movements of great agility and skill.

*chromatic/*
*chromaticism* characterizing melodies that use all twelve available tones within the octave range, not just those of the diatonic scale (doh-re-mi), allowing for unusual, often dissonant or 'bluesy' sequences and an enriched and more complex harmonic palette.

*CPCS* Popular Culture Centres, organized by the Communist Party-led National Students Union in the early 1960s to coordinate cultural initiatives (in drama, cinema, poetry, music, etc.) committed to socialist education and agitation.

*escolas de* neighbourhood-based carnival associations that began to be
*samba* founded from the late 1920s and which make year-long prepara tions for competitive parades in the carnivals of Rio de Janeiro and other major cities

*favela* a popularized term for poorer communities or 'shanty towns' on the periphery of major cities, often in improvised and precarious conditions, but many of them longer-standing and more permanently established; Favela was one of the first hillside communities to appear in Rio de Janeiro at the turn of the twentieth century (see *morro*, below).

*funk* Brazilian offspring of Miami bass, with r&b-like vocals and bass-heavy electronic beats, played at large dance-parties in working-class neighbourhoods of major cities from the late 1980s, with specific local variants (for example, *funk carioca* from Rio de Janeiro).

*getulismo* a brand of national-populism identified with the presidential administrations (1930–45 and 1951–4) and political legacy of Getúlio Vargas.

*iê-iê-iê* (from English 'yeah, yeah, yeah') – Brazilian rock'n'roll in the 1960s (see *Jovem Guarda*).

*interval* a gap between two notes of different pitch, defined according to the relative number of steps in the scale (for example, third, fifth, octave).

*jongo* a cultural event associated with Afro-Brazilian communities in the Southeast, and including dance, drumming, singing and improvisational poetic riddling; closely related to *batuque* and an important precursor of modern urban samba.

| | |
|---|---|
| *Jovem Guarda*<br>(literally<br>'Young Guard') | a youth movement dating from the late 1950s and identified with rock'n'roll (*iê-iê-iê*); it gave its name to a television programme broadcast on TV Record, from 1965 to 1968, as a vehicle for bands and vocalists such as Roberto Carlos. |
| *lundu* | dance and song-form dating from the eighteenth century, probably descended from slave practices such as *batuque*, and one of the precursors of modern samba. |
| *macumba* | referring in the nineteenth century specifically to Bantu religious practices, since the 20th century *macumba* has been used, sometimes pejoratively, to designate all contemporary forms of spirit worship or 'black witchcraft' of African origin, embracing variants such as *umbanda* and *quimbanda*. |
| *malandro/*<br>*malandragem* | as an urban folk legend and social type dating from the nineteenth century, closely associated with samba and *capoeira*, the *malandro* is the sauntering, sharp-dressing, work-shy, smooth-talking, womanizing hustler inhabiting a marginal world of recreation, petty criminality, defiance of authority and of respectable values; adjectivally, *malandro* refers to behaviour that is wilfully, mischievously resistant to discipline and moral consistency, while the practice of *malandragem* ('jive') informs the ethos of samba with its ambivalent playfulness, witty loquacity and agile syncopation. |
| *mestiço* | mixed-race. |
| *modal* | describing a tendency to work musically within the structures of certain melodic scales, that is, the systems of intervals organizing the vertical range of pitch we hear as 'up and down', and the distinct character, mood and sense of 'home' location that each of these scales produces (cf *tonal*). |
| *modinha* | sedate, sentimental love-song dating from the eighteenth century. |
| *morro*<br>(literally<br>'hillside') | in Rio de Janeiro, particularly, the *morro* has become synonymous with *favela* as the location for poorer, peripheral communities and the mythical site of traditional urban Afro-Brazilian culture, including samba; it is counterposed to 'downtown' Rio, referred to as the *cidade* or *asfalto*. |
| MPB | an acronym standing for Música Popular Brasileira, MPB is sometimes used to refer to the entire, 'authentically' national tradition of music-making in Brazil, but it also designates the eclectic post-bossa nova style of vocal-and-guitar based |

|  | songwriting and performance epitomized by Chico Buarque, Milton Nascimento and Caetano Veloso. |
| --- | --- |
| *polyrhythm* | an approach to musical time that holds two or more distinct 'beats' or patterns of regular pulses together, simultaneously. |
| *root* | fundamental note, often but not always heard as the lowest, upon which is built a chord, a harmonic structure of simultaneously sounded tones. |
| *samba-canção* | a romantic, sentimental version of the samba song-form, slower and more melodically developed than other variants, reaching its height in the 1950s. |
| *samba-exaltação* | spectacular hymn of patriotic celebration emerging from the nationalist agenda of the Estado Novo period (1937–45). |
| *samba de partido alto* | ('broken high samba') reverentially regarded as the roots tradition of urban samba, involving elements of improvisation and challenge-singing. |
| *samba de roda* | traditional circle dance associated with the northeastern state of Bahia but broadly descended from the *batuque* of slave culture, and an important forerunner of modern urban samba. |
| *sambista* | composer and/or performer of sambas. |
| *terreiro* | consecrated ground, indoors or outdoors, that could constitute the temple of *candomblé* religion or the sacred space for the performance of *batuque, jongo* or *samba de roda*. |
| *tonal* | describing an approach to musical structure based on the harmonic relationships between pitches, organized hierarchically, starting with the 'tonic' centre or 'key' and moving away and back again, via the principles of dissonance and resolution, through progressions of related chords and even modulations into new keys (cf *modal*). |
| *Zona Norte/ Zona Sul* | north side/south side of Rio de Janeiro city; while the predominantly working-class north side expanded following the redevelopment of the Centre at the turn of the twentieth century, the beachside neighbourhoods of the south side, including Copacabana and Ipanema, have been reserved mainly for the city's middle-class residents. |

# SELECT BIBLIOGRAPHY

Avelar, Idelber, and Christopher Dunn, eds, *Brazilian Popular Music and Citizenship* (Durham, NC, and London, 2011)

Browning, Barbara, *Samba: Resistance in Motion* (Bloomington, IN, 1995)

Castro, Ruy, *Bossa Nova: The Story of the Brazilian Music That Seduced the World* (Atlanta, GA, 2000)

Crook, Larry, *Brazilian Music: Northeastern Traditions and the Heartbeat of a Modern Nation* (Santa Barbara, 2005)

Dunn, Christopher, *Brutality Garden: Tropicália and the Emergence of a Brazilian Counterculture* (Chapel Hill, NC, and London, 2001)

Fryer, Peter, *Rhythms of Resistance: African Musical Heritage in Brazil* (London, 2000)

Leu, Lorraine, *Brazilian Popular Music: Caetano Veloso and the Regeneration of Tradition* (Aldershot and Burlington, VT, 2006)

McCann, Bryan, *Hello, Hello Brazil: Popular Music in the Making of Modern Brazil* (Durham, NC, 2004)

McGowan, Chris and Ricardo Pessanha, *The Brazilian Sound: Samba, Bossa Nova and the Popular Music of Brazil* (Philadelphia, 1998)

Murphy, John P., *Music in Brazil: Experiencing Music, Expressing Culture* (with CD) (New York and Oxford, 2006)

Perrone, Charles A., *Masters of Contemporary Brazilian Song: MPB, 1965–1985* (Austin, TX, 1988)

—, and Christopher Dunn, eds, *Brazilian Popular Music and Globalization* (Gainesville, FL, 2001)

Shaw, Lisa, *The Social History of the Brazilian Samba* (Aldershot and Brookfield, 1999)

Stroud, Sean, *The Defence of Tradition in Brazilian Popular Music: Politics, Culture and the Creation of Musica Popular Brasileira* (Aldershot, 2008)

Vianna, Hermano, *The Mystery of Samba: Popular Music and National Identity in Brazil* (Chapel Hill, NC, 1999)

# DISCOGRAPHY AND FILMOGRAPHY

## DISCOGRAPHY

*Baden Powell e a Bossa Nova.* Abril: Nova Historia da Musica Popular Brasileira.
HMPB–61-A (1979)

*Beginner's Guide To Brazilian Music* (3CD). Nascente. B0009EMOPK (2006)

*Black Orpheus (Orfeu Negro): The Original Sound Track From The Film.* Verve.
B000004726 (1990)

*Geraldo Vandré, Pra não dizer que não falei das flores.* RGE. 303. 6106-A (1988)

*João Gilberto* (1973), PolyGram / Verve 837 589–2 (1988)

*João Gilberto: Live at Montreux* Elektra 9 60760 (1987)

*The Legendary João Gilberto: The Original Bossa Nova Recordings.* World Pacific. CDP
7 738912 (1990)

*A música de Edu Lobo por Edu Lobo.* Elenco. 848 967–2 (1967)

*Nara.* Elenco. EMLP–6309-A (1963)

*Sérgio Ricardo, Um senhor talento.* Elenco. 512 055–2 (1967)

## FILMOGRAPHY

*Cidade de Deus (City of God).* Dir. Fernando Meirelles, Kátia Lund. O2 Filmes,
VideoFilmes, Globo Filmes (2002)

*Orfeu Negro (Black Orpheus).* Dir. Marcel Camus. Dispat Film, Gemma
Cinematográfica, Tupan Filmes (1959)

*Orfeu.* Dir. Carlos Diegues. Mima Fleurent, Rio Vermelho Filmes, Globo Filmes
(1998)

*Rio, Zona Norte.* Dir. Nelson Pereira dos Santos. Nelson Pereira dos Santos
Produções Cinematográficas, Santos (1957)

# ACKNOWLEDGEMENTS AND
# PHOTO ACKNOWLEDGEMENTS

The chapters in this book draw in part on material in the following publications: 'Between Bossa Nova and the Mambo Kings: The Internationalisation of Latin American Popular Music', *Journal of Latin American Cultural Studies*, 1/2 (November 1992). 'Melody, Text and Luiz Tatit's *O Cancionista*: New Directions in Brazilian Popular Music Studies', *Journal of Latin American Cultural Studies*, v/2 (1996), pp. 203–16. 'Guns and Roses: Bossa Nova and Brazil's music of popular protest, 1958–68', *Popular Music*, xvi/1 (January 1997), pp. 1–29. 'Tropicália: A canção popular e a cultura de massas', *Studies in Latin American Popular Culture*, xix (2000), pp. 51–5. 'Rhythm and Poetry: Politics, Aesthetics and Popular Music in Brazil since 1960', in *Cultural Politics in Latin America*, ed. A. Brooksbank Jones and R. Munck (London, 2000), pp. 29–42. 'Mapping mpb in the 1990s: Music and Politics in Brazil at the End of the Twentieth Century', in *I Sing the Difference: Identity and Commitment in Latin American Song: a Symposium in Honour of Robert Pring-Mill*, ed. J. Fairley and D. Horn (Liverpool, 2002), pp. 99–105. 'Linguagem, música e estética negra', *Revista Ethnos Brasil*, ii/3 (March 2003), pp. 51–66. 'Suspended Animation: Movement and Time in Bossa Nova', *Journal of Romance Studies* vii/2 (August 2007), pp. 75–97. 'Conversa de malandro *or Brazilian Jive Talk*', Music, Language, Community, Institute for the Study of the Americas Lecture series Paper no. 8 (London, 2008). Chapter Five was originally published in its entirety as 'Orpheus in Babylon: Music, Myth and Realism in the Films of Rio de Janeiro', in *Screening Songs in Hispanic and Lusophone Culture*, ed. L. Shaw and R. Stone (Manchester, 2012).

The author and publishers wish to express their thanks to the below sources of illustrative material and / or permission to reproduce it:
Author's collection pp: 35, 43, 58, 74, 129, 134, 155: Agência Estado: pp. 57, 66, 68, 81, 91, 119, 140, 146: Instituto Moreira Salles, Rio de Janeiro: pp 31, 36.

# COPYRIGHT ACKNOWLEDGEMENTS

# INDEX

Numerals in italics refer to illustrations

Adorno, Theodor, 'On the Fetish Character in Music and the Regression of Listening' 59–60
African cultural traditions 14, 15, 19–27, 40, 46, 85, 144, 164, 191–5, 198–9, 204
Agawu, Kofi 193
'Águas de Março' 56, 80, 99, 100, 109–11
Alvarenga, Oneyda 198
'Aquarela do Brasil' 72
'Avarandado' 109
*axé* 26, 27, 219

Babilônia, Morro da 162–3
Baden Powell 19, 93, *140*, 141, 143, 146, 155
Bahia 27, 28, *36*, 109, 133, 141, 142, 152, 183, 202, 219
*bateria* 33, 89, 219
*batida* 74, 89, 100, 219
Batista, Wilson, 'Lenço no pescoço' *36*, 37
*batuque* 20, 21, 22, 25, 39, 164, 190, 199
*berimbau* 38, 117, 141, 143
Bethânia, Maria 133–5, 151, 152
*Black Orpheus* (*Orfeu Negro*) 62, 159, 160, 163, 166, 168–73, *172*
Bôscoli, Ronaldo 70, 72, 75, 82, 123, 124, 125

bossa nova 14, 15, 46, 47, 49, 50, 56–112, 113, 114, 117, 118, 119, 120–21, 123–5, 128, *129*, 130–33, 135, 136–9, 141, 144, 147, 148, 149, 153, 165, 166, 170, 171, 173, 174, 181
*brasileirinho* 33, 89, 219
Buarque, Chico 97, 120, 148, 151, 174, 184–6

'Caminhando' ('Pra não dizer que não falei das flores') 113, 118–19, 153–6
Camus, Marcel 159, 163, 168, 170
*candomblé* 27, 28, 30, 141, 147, 219
*capoeira* 28, 34, *36*, 38, 118, 141, 142, 199, 219
Carlos, Roberto 124
carnival 14, 28, 30, 32, 33, 42, 48, 106, 113, 115, 126, 149, 161, 167, 169, 170, 171, 172, 173, 174, 177, 178, 184, 197
'Chega de saudade' 75–7, 124
'Chegança' 143–5
chromaticism 59, 69, 75, 79, 87, 91, 131, 145, 171, 220
*Cidade de Deus* (*City of God*) 174–6
Cidade Nova 28, 30, 34

Cinema Novo 114, 165
'Corcovado' 81–2
CPC (Centro Popular de Cultura) 123,
    126–8, 129, 130, 133, 143, 150, 153,
    154, 157, 184
'O Cu do Mundo' 187

'Desafinado' 56, 62, 63, 68–70, 73,
    88–90
diaspora, African or black 13, 15, 27,
    192, 195, 203
Diegues, Carlos 159, 173
'Disparada' 149–50
Donga (Ernesto dos Santos) 30, 35
Drummond de Andrade, Carlos 45–6,
    162–3

'É preciso perdoar' 90–94, 99, 100, 109
Economic Miracle 114, 115, 152, 158
embolada 14, 189
escola de samba (samba school) 33, 42,
    131–2, 147, 149, 167, 175, 220
Exu 40–41

'A Fábrica' 130,31
'A Felicidade' 105–8
'Feio não é bonito' 131–32
festivals, televised song 116–18, 136, 145,
    147–54
'Fica mal com Deus' 148–9
frevo 14, 147
Freyre, Gilberto 198–200
Frith, Simon 188–9, 190
funk carioca 160, 175, 176, 177–8, 185

Galvão, Walnice Nogueira 120, 158
'Garota de Ipanema' ('The Girl from
    Ipanema') 56, 60, 63, 89, 100,
    101–5

Getz, Stan 61, 62, 63, 102, 125
Gil, Gilberto 48, 99, 109, 120, 130, 133,
    150, 151, 152, 153, 183
Gilberto, João 56, 61, 63, 68, 72, 73, 74,
    75, 89, 90, 91, 97–101, 102, 108, 109,
    111, 112, 113, 125, 134
Gilroy, Paul The Black Atlantic 13, 205
ginga 38, 176
Globo TV network 115–16, 118, 151
Guimarães Rosa, João, 'Soroco') 52–5

'Insensatez' 56, 60, 79, 100

jive 34, 35, 41
João Gilberto ('white album') 97–112
Jobim, Antônio Carlos (Tom) 56, 57, 57,
    60, 61, 63, 68, 72, 75, 77, 79–81, 81,
    86, 97, 989, 99, 101, 105, 108, 109,
    110, 113, 154, 171
jongo 22, 23, 25, 190, 220

Kéti, Zé 129, 133, 167, 168
Kubik, Gerhard 194–5
Kubitschek, Juscelino 70, 83, 114, 165

language and music 8, 9, 12–18, 19,
    40–41, 42, 45, 46, 51–3, 193–5
Leão, Nara 132–3, 134
Lins, Paulo 174, 175
Lobo, Edu 120, 143–5, 145, 146, 147, 151,
    155
lundu 20, 221
Lyra, Carlos 74, 75, 79, 83, 98, 123, 124,
    125, 128–32, 138, 143, 145, 147, 155,
    165, 16

macumba 30, 110, 169, 170, 221
malandro 28, 35, 36–43, 47, 184, 185, 186,
    221

Matos, Cláudia 38, 41
Maysa 72
melody 6, 9, 11, 15, 16, 17, 19, 24, 32, 50,
   53, 59, 60, 63– 5, 67, 68, 69, 73, 75,
   78–80, 84, 86–88, 90, 92, 100, 102–6,
   109–11, 131, 142, 171, 180–82, 186
Menescal, Roberto 72, 74, 75, 82, 123
Miranda, Carmen 153, 164, 199
modal figures and system 46, 85–6, 89,
   91, 93, 94, 99, 101, 102, 109, 221
modinha 14, 15, 98, 221
Moraes, Vinicius de 19, 56, 66, 75, 79,
   93, 97, 98, 101, 105, 109, 113, 132, 141,
   145, 159, 165, 166, 169, 170, 171
morro 28, 130, 132, 162, 164, 170, 185, 221
MPB (música popular brasileira) 14, 15,
   46, 47, 49, 50, 158, 174, 177, 179, 221

negro (Brazilian Portuguese term) 19,
   196, 201–2

Orfeu 159, 173–4
Orfeu da Conceição 159, 169, 170
Orpheus myth 159, 160–61

Pavilhão 9 177
'Pelo Telefone' 30–34
Pereira Passos 28
Perrone, Charles 169, 170
Pobre Menina Rica (Poor Little Rich Girl)
   132, 165–6
Praça Onze (de Junho) 28, 31

Racionais MC's 177
Ramos, Graciliano 89, 44
rap 14, 173, 175, 177–9, 185–90, 195
repetition, musical principle of 25, 46,
   60, 79, 84, 86, 94, 100–1, 107, 110,
   171, 205

rhythmic assymetry 88–90
Ricardo, Sérgio 112, 123, 130, 138, 148,
   152, 155, 165
Rio, Zona Norte 166–8, 169, 170
roda (ring) 24–6, 110
Rose, Tricia 187–88

samba 7, 14, 19, 20, 21, 22, 24, 27, 28, 30,
   31, 33, 35, 35, 36, 41, 42. 43, 43, 47, 59,
   60, 72, 74, 88, 89, 98, 99, 124, 129,
   129, 130, 131, 132, 133, 138, 141, 142,
   147, 149, 164, 166, 167, 168, 170, 171,
   173, 174, 175, 176, 177, 178, 184, 186,
   189, 190, 195, 197, 199, 203
'Samba de uma nota só' 77–8
samba de partido alto 14, 22, 49, 168, 190,
   222
samba de roda 25, 117, 141, 144, 222
samba-canção 14, 37, 72, 98, 222
samba-de-breque 41, 190
samba-exaltação 72, 131, 222
samba-rock 14
Santos, Nelson Pereira dos
Science, Chico 178, 186, 189
'Se gostares de batuque' 164
Shepherd, John, and Peter Wicke 11, 12
slavery, legacy of 19–20, 25, 26, 28, 38–40,
   50–51, 59, 144, 1192, 195, 197, 199–
   200, 201, 204–5
Sodré, Muniz 26, 29, 30, 38
speech and song 15, 16–17, 39, 41, 42, 51,
   60, 64, 181, 182, 183, 186, 190,
   192–95
'suspended animation', concept of 47,
   67, 84–5, 90, 94–5, 99, 102
syncopation 34, 39, 69, 89, 105, 176

Tatit, Luiz 15, 16–18, 47, 64, 65, 181, 188,
   193

*terreiro* 26, 27, 30, 222
Tia Ciata 30
tonal system 46, 67, 85–7
Tropicália 49, 95, 152, 158, 177, 182, 219

*umbanda* 30, 40

Vandré, Geraldo 113, 118, *119*, 119, 120,
    128–30, 138–9, 148–54, *155*, 180
Vargas, Getúlio 42, 43, 45, 46, 71, 83,
    163, 164, 165, 220
Veloso, Caetano 48, 60, 99, 109, 120,
    133, 139, 151, 152, 153, 174, 181, 183,
    184, 186, 187

West Africa 19, 22, 33, 40, 89, 90, 141,
    190, 192, 194, 195
Wisnik, José Miguel 47, 48, 50, 64, 65,
    66, 161
Workers' Party (PT) 156–57

*Yoruba* culture and language 27, 30, 40,
    41, 143, 145, 194

*Zona Sul* (South Side) 59, 71, 72, 83, 178,
    185
Zuckerkandl, Victor 51, 95